BORN IN THE BERKSHIRES

BORN IN THE
BERKSHIRES

Dennis G. Pregent

Born in the Berkshires
Copyright © 2021 Dennis G. Pregent

Printed in the United States of America
ISBN 978-1-946425-96-6

Book design: CSinclaire Write-Design
Editor: Jane Hobson Snyder

www.writewaypublishing.com

CONTENTS

ACKNOWLEDGMENTS

I would like to acknowledge my ever-patient wife of fifty-six years, Carol Pregent, who is my sounding board and confidante. Her encouragement and ability to listen to my incessant chatter about this book are greatly appreciated.

I am indebted to Maggy Button and Justyna Carlson for sharing their detailed knowledge of the Berkshires, its people, and its many places. Maggy provided names of people who were the genesis of this book. Justyna and her husband Gene were always available to answer questions about the area and fact-check my efforts. Justyna proofread the entire manuscript for regional accuracy and helped me understand the difference between Hoosac (a bank or tunnel), Hoosic (a river), and Hoosick (a nearby New York town).

Above all, I want to thank the participants themselves for trusting me with their stories, providing instrumental help, introductions, support, and great kindnesses. Their family members, colleagues, and friends were always ready to spend time with me to relate short accounts of notable or amusing events.

Jane Hobson Snyder, the developmental editor, once again has provided solid and responsive support and was the person I leaned on when things became too technical, complicated, or slightly overwhelming. Her sustained and crucial help was a godsend in shaping the manuscript.

The Garner, North Carolina, writing group to which I belong, Senior Writers and Guests (SWAG), has always been reassuring and affirming of my writing efforts.

Thank you to those family members who have been supportive and interested in my writing, including Chris who was key in creating the book's cover, and Grace for her continued encouragement.

A special thanks to Dr. Jim Clark and Dr. Tobe Berkovitz as well as to Jay Newton-Small for providing their endorsements.

Tributes from these esteemed and accomplished individuals are greatly appreciated.

And finally, Lee Heinrich, Senior Editor of Write Way Publishing, has always been there to explain the intricacies of pulling together the disparate components that constitute a well-crafted book.

To all others I may have missed: Thank you for your help.

FOREWORD

Born in the Berkshires began as a retirement project of a proud son of North Adams and Adams in northwestern Massachusetts. Dennis Pregent left there for tours as a Marine during the Vietnam era, returned home for college, and now lives in North Carolina. From that southern perspective he has identified, researched, and profiled thirty-five men and women whose working lives have been personally meaningful to them and their picturesque native region.

He presents, for example, former Governor Jane Swift and Martha Coakley, a recent state attorney general. Meet the artistic barber Gus Jammalo and a family of mechanics that includes Stanley L. Brown who proudly says, "I still have all ten fingers." Each fascinating profile does what Studs Terkel did in his 1974 classic entitled *Working: People Talk About What They Do All Day and How They Feel About What They Do.*

Again and again in it, as in this book about making life better, heartening local success stories whet our appetites for more. Here is Jeff Levanos, the third-generation Greek owner of Jack's Hot Dog Stand in North Adams: "He cooks by ear. The two grills have no thermostats and lack precise controls making it difficult to tell how hot they are. Jeff determines the temperature from the sound of the sizzle . . . ." And you can get a hot dog for $1.45!

— Dr. Jim Clark, Professor Emeritus
North Carolina State University

INTRODUCTION

You are about to meet some most interesting people who were *Born in the Berkshires*.

You will read about the long-time barber who has given 120,000 haircuts; an owner of a renowned local eatery who has cooked over two million hot dogs; the first woman to serve as governor and the first woman to serve as attorney general of Massachusetts; directors of a century-old funeral business; one of the few fifty-year managers in McDonald's history; a scoutmaster with eighty-five confirmed Eagle scouts; and the family that ran a local garage from Prohibition until quite recently (almost one hundred years).

This is only the beginning. *Born in the Berkshires* spends time with decades-long football and baseball coaches, a nationally acclaimed artist, a golf-course owner, several beloved educators, a matriarch, a genealogist, a crime novelist, the *de facto* town historian, two longtime mayors, and one journalist who became a priest.

For a century, Brown's Garage was known for helping travelers along the Mohawk Trail.

Their stories depict the bedrock of the northern Berkshires, all from the towns of Adams and Williamstown and the City of North Adams. It's amazing the outsize role these three communities totaling fewer than thirty thousand citizens have played in a state with over seven million people.

As the land of my youth, the Berkshires loom large in my mind's eye. My earliest years were spent in the Greylock section of North Adams. Then my family moved to Adams, so I attended parochial and public schools in both towns. As a youth I hiked, fished, and hunted from the wooded areas of Mount Greylock all the way through the beautiful river valleys of the Mohawk Trail, always enthralled with the area's natural beauty.

After serving six and a half years in the Marine Corps, I returned to the area with my wife, Carol, and bought a home in Greylock. I attended North Adams State College, graduating in 1975, and subsequently obtained my master's degree in business from the University of Massachusetts.

Making this book has been personally rewarding. As I talked with people and began to collect names of influential local citizens, glimmers of stories began to enthrall me. I was fascinated to learn that North Adams has produced two women who had served in the highest political posts in Massachusetts—Governor and Attorney General—and that Williamstown had a world-class resident botanist, not to mention a Superior Court Judge with over 600 trials under his belt. The town of Adams brought forth a courageous missionary in her seventies, even now serving in Africa; an Air Force aeromedical nurse, who helped save the lives of those wounded in Iraq and Afghanistan; and an equestrian who raises rare Austrian horses not far from the center of town.

Hearing these captivating stories, I decided to write about some of the area's notable and vibrant citizens. Initially, I thought the group would include only baby boomers who were born and currently reside in the Berkshires. As I became engrossed in their lives, my parameters broadened, and the book now has several people born outside the boomer era, some who no longer live in the Berkshires, and some who moved to the area as young children.

It's taken twelve months and hundreds of hours of interviewing, recording, and writing to capture the stories of the participants, their family, and friends.

The people in the book are cornerstones of their communities. They are devoted, steadfast, distinguished, upstanding citizens who have really shaped the Berkshires. In different measures, they are all part of the fabric of the local communities and provide a wonderful snapshot of local citizenry.

The reader should be aware that these stories are meant to be representative of the people currently in the communities of Adams, North Adams, and Williamstown. There are innumerable people not included in this snapshot in time—active, caring,

Stanley and Maralyn Brown show off their 1925 Model T at the 2014 North Adams Fall Foliage Parade, celebrating the 100th Anniversary of the Mohawk Trail.

and involved citizens—who came before them and will follow after. Entire bookshelves could be filled.

The subjects of *Born in the Berkshires* came from many sources: a local editor, friends, family, and from the participants themselves. In all cases, I used my own judgment on which stories to be included, how to keep readers interested, and where to find the best balance of citizenry.

Coach John Allen, left, confers with team captain John Barrett, circa 1965.

Individual stories range from 2500 to 4000 words, representing multiple interviews and hours of online research and perusing old newspaper articles. Interviewing, typing notes, and crafting each chapter took about twenty hours per person.

As expected in small communities, wonderful, abundant interconnections appear. Gus Jammalo, the barber, painted a picture of the school at which former mayor John Barrett taught; John Allen coached Judge Agostini and State Representative Barrett and worked with Jane Swift's husband Chuck; Jane Allen and George Haddad consulted each other as selectmen of their respective towns.

Dick Alcombright supported Mary Lou Accetta and Sherry Wein in Brooklyn Street Neighbors. Alan Horbal has worked with Justyna Carlson at the Historical Society. Mike Deep has played basketball and golf with Don Dagnoli and Nick Flynn. Everyone seems to have enjoyed breakfast at Al Caproni's local McDonald's. Maggy Button, in her role as local editor, pretty much knows everyone.

I hope you will enjoy reading about the people in the book as much as I did spending time with each of them. While these stories are but a glimpse of its citizenry, they are encouraging and heart-warming. The Berkshires is truly defined by its people, and what good people they are.

— DGP

MARY LOU ACCETTA & SHERRY WEIN

Brooklyn Street Neighbors

Mary Lou Accetta, with the support of her friend Sherry Wein, is creating a neighborhood community in a time-worn section of North Adams. It's a place that recalls days gone by, where neighbors look out for each other and share communal gatherings and celebrations. As one admirer phrased it, "Mary Lou doesn't give up on people."

Brooklyn Street is not very long: its lower portion connects to Houghton, a tributary block off of River Street. Then it runs a half-mile uphill, dog-legs left, and reconnects to Houghton. It's a challenged area of older, worn, mostly two-story homes built in the last century. Frequently, two or three houses in distressed condition are listed for sale.

The houses are situated near an area of town being revitalized. Nearby is the sprawling and highly acclaimed Massachusetts Museum of Contemporary Art (MASS MoCA); close by is the newly established Porches Inn, which offers luxury accommodations to tourists.

It is here, in a formerly poor section of North Adams, that the Brooklyn Street Neighbors, an "intentional inclusive community," is being lovingly created. This community of privately-owned homes encourages people of diverse ages, abilities, incomes, and backgrounds to live in the area and support each other.

1

The idea began with several members and has been spearheaded by Mary Lou Accetta.

Mary Lou, an only child, was born on May 10, 1953, at the small, local North Adams Hospital established in the late 1800s. Her parents, Louis and Natalie Connie (Constance) Accetta, lived at 107 Brooklyn Street, where Mary Lou and her son Mel reside today.

Her dad served in the U.S. Navy in the South Pacific during World War II. When he returned from the war, Louie was employed at the Wall Streeter Shoe Company, dyeing leather for fine dress shoes. After developing a chemical allergy, he reluctantly left and worked for years as a custodian at what is now the Massachusetts College of Liberal Arts. On occasion, he supplemented the family's income by bartending. Mary Lou's mom, Connie, worked at Molly's Bakery, helping in sales and occasionally using her culinary skills.

Both sets of grandparents emigrated from northern and southern parts of Italy. Mary Lou knows little about her paternal grandparents, Louis and Filomena Accetta. They had three children, two boys and a girl. The mom abandoned the family when Louie (Mary Lou's father) was eleven years old; he never saw her again. Much later in life, Louie received a letter from his mom, who was in Springfield, asking to meet with him and his sister. Having been grievously hurt as a child by her behavior, he tore up the letter and never did meet with her.

Mary Lou's maternal grandparents, Anthony and Mary Grillone, had six children: one girl (Mary Lou's mom) and five boys. Anthony, who worked for years at Strong-Hewatt Mills, struggled with alcoholism, and Mary was a stay-at-home mom.

Mary Lou attended Freeman Elementary School until it closed and finished grammar school at Johnson Elementary. She attended Drury High School where she participated in Spanish Club, school plays, Future Teachers of America, and was a member of the Pro Merito Society, graduating in 1971.

Mary Lou then attended North Adams State College (now known as Massachusetts College of Liberal Arts—MCLA) for one year and graduated from Westfield State in 1975 with a bachelor's degree in elementary/special education. In 1979, she received her master's degree in special education from Westfield State College. She also attended Syracuse University and completed most of her post-graduate work in special education administration.

At the early age of thirteen, Mary Lou, while working at the Mary Jezyk Sunshine Camp in North Adams, had become involved with young people that had developmental and physical challenges. This experience gently nudged her toward a career in special education. She remembers, "The kids became my friends," and "I enjoyed just being *people* together." With this comfort and affinity, in high school she often acted as a substitute teacher in a class for challenged learners.

After college, Mary Lou worked as a social worker for cerebral palsy and taught in Amherst public schools. During this time period, she worked as a coach for three children with autism and also as a research assistant. For the next ten years, she lived in Syracuse, New York, and at one point was hired as the principal of Jowonio School, a nationally recognized model of inclusive education.

It was in Syracuse that Mary Lou came into contact with Mel, a nonverbal five-year-old child with autism, who was living at a state institution. She began working with him, and as their time together increased, she felt him "speaking to her through his eyes." She was touched by his care and concern for others.

Mary Lou was single and in the midst of completing her Ph.D.; she had no intention of adopting a child. Over the next six months, she and Mel grew closer, and she began searching for a foster home for him. The institution he was in presented a difficult situation, at times too violent for Mel's peaceful nature. It was understaffed and had few ambulatory patients, many of whom were in poor medical health. The search for a foster home proved to be fruitless, and as Mary Lou's appreciation of Mel's resilience grew, she fell in love with him. Initially, Mel came to live with Mary Lou as a foster child when he was seven years old. Finally, after a number of court appeals, she officially adopted Mel in 1986 when he was eleven years old.

A close hometown friend, Mary, a special education teacher who was also attending Syracuse University, moved in to help Mary Lou and Mel begin their lives together. Mary's help was so very important to Mary Lou and Mel. They quickly became a close-knit family of three. (Today, Mary lives with her aging mom, next door to Mary Lou and Mel. Ironically, both are living in their childhood homes.)

COURTESY MARY LOU ACCETTA

Mary Lou and Mel share a happy moment.

In 1987, Mary Lou and Mel moved to North Adams, where she taught at Johnson Elementary school for several years. Her next professional move was to the position of Director of Inclusive Education for the City of North Adams. Simultaneously, she taught at Massachusetts College of Liberal Arts and still serves as an adjunct professor.

She then worked at McCann Technical School from 2002 to 2019 as the Director of Student Services and was in charge of all special needs programs, including federal programs for the reading disabled and the nursing services department. During this time period, she also served on the North Adams School Committee for ten years.

In 1994, Mary Lou's father passed away, and she and Mel moved into the home on 107 Brooklyn Street. Subsequently, she rehabbed and added on to the home and now lives in the addition. Mel and Eric, his shared living provider and close friend, live in the main part of the house. Mary Lou says Eric is like a brother to Mel. He understands and accepts him just as he is, while continually helping him to lead his best life.

SHERRY'S STORY

This story would not be complete without including Sherry Wein, Mary Lou's close friend and helpmate in developing the Brooklyn Street Neighborhood. Sherry, a North Adams native, the oldest of four children, was the child of Eugene and Jacqueline Wein. Wein was a well-known local name. Eugene owned the Wein Shoe Store on Eagle Street and was a devoted, longtime Drury High School basketball fan. In 2002, the high school named its annual holiday basketball tournament after him.

Sherry's paternal grandparents were Harry and Anna Wein. Harry emigrated from Poland via Ellis Island and followed his older brother to North Adams, where he set up his cobbler shop. Sherry's maternal grandparents were Nathan and Bessie Winer. Nathan emigrated from Ukraine at eighteen years old and established a very successful egg business. Bessie was born in Springfield, MA, and helped in the business.

Sherry attended Greylock School from kindergarten through the sixth grade, then Brayton School for seventh and eighth grades, graduating from Drury in 1966. She received a bachelor's degree in elementary education from Long Island University in 1971.

Sherry and Robert Wray lived for a time in San Francisco, where their son Aaron was born in 1984. By the age of three, he was still unable to speak and at four years old was diagnosed with autism.

Sherry's mom had read a complimentary newspaper article about

Sherry Wein and her now-adult son Aaron.

Mary Lou and Mel and arranged for the two women to meet. Within a year, Sherry, Robert, and Aaron had moved to Brooklyn Street, nestled in what was the beginning of their intentional community. Aaron enrolled in school and Sherry began her teaching career.

INTENTIONAL COMMUNITY

The goal of Brooklyn Street Neighbors, referred to as BSN, has been to create a "neighborhood where children can play safely, neighbors can count on each other, and families can live separately but share many resources that promote healthy and sustainable living, including a common space for community events." Mary Lou and Sherry have worked together on the Brooklyn Street initiative for almost twenty years. They were joined early on by their friends Mary Anne and Peter Belouin and their son Stephen. Sadly, Brooklyn Street lost a "gentle giant" and Mel's best friend when Stephen passed away in 2007.

What they describe as an *intentional community* is one in which members purchase property close to each other, living in their own houses but as an extended family with common values and a desire to share aspects of their lives. It resembles what they call a new "old-fashioned" neighborhood with the benefit of looking out, caring, and sharing with each other. This community includes people with disabilities, families, and friends. All are welcomed and can avail themselves of the community's core values. Realtors advise potential buyers that the neighborhood is building a community welcoming to all.

Houses on Brooklyn Street are clustered together for mutual support.

Mary Lou and Sherry are hoping this environment will live on after they are gone and support and care for their sons; part of the community's sixteen Core Values is to establish a community that will outlive its founders. Sherry and Mary Lou want challenged people to be part of the world. They hope BSN will provide a place where they themselves can age in place and remain part of the community as long as they can, sharing resources, friendships, and the trials they may have with their kids.

"It's hard on your own, but helps to have each other," says Sherry.

They and a core group of parents are avid promoters of Brooklyn Street Neighbors, bringing welcome baskets to new residents and inviting realtors to meetings so they will understand how the neighborhood is being revitalized. Early on, they received help from the former mayor, Dick Alcombright, who was glad to assist in reconceptualizing an old, established neighborhood. Repairing houses and attracting residents received his ardent support.

Habitat for Humanity has adopted the street and helps the residents retrofit houses for the disabled or those struggling financially. The community has a representative on Habitat's board, and several neighbors act as liaisons and donate time to improvement projects. Just recently, Habitat completed a bathroom renovation for a cash-strapped family. It's a close relationship, and Habitat even keeps some of their tools in the garage at 108 Brooklyn Street.

At one point, the home at 108 Brooklyn was envisioned for use as a common gathering place. Four community members secured the house out of foreclosure, wanting to ensure there would be a central retreat for all. Brooklyn neighbors use the house to watch movies, play board games, host pancake breakfasts, have potluck suppers, share a small library, celebrate birthdays, and plan community forays. The BSN also sponsors a yearly block party. Mary Lou and Sherry jokingly talk about "illegally" trying to block off the street for the celebration that includes food, drinks, music, and games for the children.

With the recent COVID-19 pandemic, inside gatherings have been limited, although the group travels weekly to the Fish Pond, a local lake, for an afternoon or evening of social distancing and bring-your-own dinners or lunch.

In support of the Brooklyn Street community, the Nonotuck Resource Associates, an organization whose focus is on supporting people with disabilities and promoting shared living situations, purchased 108 Brooklyn Street. It remains available and continues to be put to good use by the community.

Nonotuck's largesse was a financial relief for the community members. Even more importantly, Nonotuck has helped to develop and support BSN's vision. Mary Lou and Sherry both acclaim the agency and its leadership's undaunted support.

As word of the community spread, others moved there. A college professor purchased a house, gutted and rehabbed it, moving in with her son diagnosed with Asperger Syndrome. Not long after, her mom purchased and renovated a nearby home. This spry, older woman has become "everyone's grandmother" and is well known for her noodle pasta, a mushroom and spinach dish which she creates for potluck suppers. Mel so likes the dish that she makes it for his birthday and while it's sometimes hard for one with autism to display acknowledgement and appreciation in person, she will often find flowers on her doorstep.

Mary Lou has another two-family house on Brooklyn where she rents the first floor to a sign language interpreter and the second floor to a younger woman with challenges, who is learning to live independently and receives a lot of support from the community. People interviewed said any number of times how the community and specifically Mary Lou looks to support others.

Not too long ago, the director of Northern Berkshire Community Coalition moved to Brooklyn Street. The coalition is a strong supporter of neighborhoods, connecting neighbors, convening meetings to work with local issues, and promoting programs for area youth.

Mary Lou and Sherry are also active community volunteers. Mary Lou wants to be a child's court advocate and has signed up for training. Sherry helps with the welcoming committee preparing personal "door-step" baskets for new residents, adapting the baskets to their new neighbors' needs or hobbies: for the gardener, the basket may include seeds and tools; for a young family, the basket would have toys.

The inclusiveness of the community continues to attract people to the Brooklyn Street neighborhood. All are welcome. Both Mary Lou and Sherry have answered inquiries from across the country on how the Brooklyn Street lifestyle is working. They readily admit it's a work-in-progress but are encouraged by community support and the closeness that is developing between neighbors. Always open to new recruits, often Mary Lou or Sherry can be overheard saying, "I know where you can find an apartment!"

The neighborhood has had its challenges. Initially some were concerned about being so inclusive and welcoming/seeking all types of people to live in their neighborhood. Those few doubters have changed their minds and have come to see the community's outreach as a vital support for all. The community has also been greatly encouraged by the successful rehabilitation of deserted and foreclosed houses.

Mary Lou continues to be recognized as BSN's unofficial leader. Her openness, sparkplug personality, and desire for an all-inclusive community is a magnet for people. While still in the development stage, Brooklyn Street Neighbors has come a long way in meeting its mission *to create a sustainable, multigenerational, life-sharing community within North Adams that includes persons with disabilities, families, and friends.*

JOHN AGOSTINI

This long-serving western Massachusetts Superior Court Judge has, through the course of his career, rendered judgments on such nefarious cases as mob killings and local murders to domestic violence, human trafficking, and sexual assaults involving the Catholic Church. Court records show a wide diversity of cases in criminal and civil categories.

John Agostini is a quiet, self-effacing man, brought up in Williamstown. He has established a reputation as an honorable, upright justice, always in search of the truth. He has presided over nearly six hundred trials and served the Commonwealth of Massachusetts with dignity.

John Anthony Agostini was born on September 24, 1953, at the Putnam Memorial Hospital in Bennington, Vermont. His parents were Frank A. Agostini and Susan Del Tatto Agostini. Frank, born in 1914, had served in the U.S. Navy during World War II operating a Landing Ship, Tank (LST) participating in amphibious actions in the Pacific Theater. He was in the Battle of Okinawa and his ship fought off and survived furious *kamikaze* attacks. Frank was one of the first Americans to enter Japan immediately after the war at the seaport of Nagasaki.

Returning home, Frank attended Union College in Schenectady, New York, and then Boston University Law School. As a solo practitioner, Frank practiced law for many years from his downtown office, helping people contend with wills, real estate transactions, and occasionally divorces. He was a major influence on his family, seldom went out, and enjoyed being a homebody. Frank passed away in 1976 at age of sixty-three.

Susan Del Tatto was slightly younger than Frank, born in 1919. A daughter of Italian immigrants, Susan did not speak English when she first went to grammar school at five years old. That did not hold her back: Susan was a member of the first graduating class of Bennington College with a degree in government and worked briefly in Washington, D.C., under the Secretary of Labor, Frances Perkins, then returned to Bennington and worked in the college's administration department.

She married Frank in 1939. Later, she was the homemaker for the couple's five children, two girls and three boys. Independent and focused, "she ran the house, prepared the food, and worked in her husband's office part-time," recalls John. Both parents were major influences on their children's lives, providing direction and motivation. Discipline was usually not needed, since the children worried more about doing something to hurt their parents. Susan passed away at the age of seventy-eight.

John's paternal grandfather, Victor Agostini, was born sometime in the late 1880s or early 1890s in Tyrol, a mountainous region of northern Italy near the Austrian border. Victor and his wife Katherine immigrated in the 1920s via Ellis Island. The couple had two children, John's father and a younger brother. Katherine died at a young age, so John did not know his grandmother. Initially, neither grandparent spoke English although Victor, very entrepreneurial, opened an insurance agency and a macaroni factory in North Adams before the Great Depression.

It appears as though Victor did not attend college but graduated from Boston University Law School and became a lawyer at forty-five years old. He moved to Bennington, where requirements for lawyers were less rigorous, and became a referee for bankruptcy courts. At one point, he returned to Williamstown and opened his own practice. Always inquisitive, as an inventor, he registered five patents, including a gun rack for a Jeep that he tried to sell to the Army and a fishing lure retriever.

John's maternal grandparents were Carlo and Elmira Del Tatto, who immigrated as a married couple from Italy. The young couple did not pass through Ellis Island since Carlo was recruited directly by a marble quarry in Vermont. His ability to work with marble was well known throughout the industry. Pictures from the time period show Carlo laying the cornerstone in the old part of the Clark Art Museum, which is all marble. A family story recounts that one of Carlo's first gifts to Elmira was an Italian-English dictionary so she could learn her new country's language.

THE EARLY YEARS

John attended Mitchell Elementary school in Williamstown through sixth grade. The family lived behind the elementary school, and he and his friends rode their bikes everywhere, adhering to Mom's instruction to be home by 4:00 p.m. John hunted and fished a little with his older brother, but his real interest was sports.

He played Pee Wee football, basketball, hockey, and baseball in the town's Little League and Babe Ruth League. John Barrett, the current Massachusetts State Representative, coached John; even today Agostini calls him "Coach Barrett" whenever he sees him.

John's dad got home from his law office at 4:30 p.m., and family suppers were always at 6:00 p.m. It was important that everyone was there. His father, easygoing and social, always enjoyed discussing politics with the kids. John's mom prepared the food; Italian dishes were popular with her. Thursday nights meant spaghetti with Italian bread. The bread man would drop off a loaf in the morning, usually putting it on top of the family's car; otherwise, Major, their collie, would start barking. The collie was an important member of the family and often walked to Frank's law office, one time even wandering into court where Frank was meeting on the enactment of a new leash law.

Friday nights usually meant fish or a pasta-and-butter meal. Baked beans often made her menu, and the family knew three nights later the meal would be Pasta Fagioli (fazool), pasta and beans. Another of her specialties was *gnocchi*, fluffy dumplings made with potatoes and flour, steamed, and served with butter and cheese. Susan also cooked pork roasts and soups. There were no leftovers with a family of seven. Once or twice a year for a special occasion, the family would eat out. The fifteen years' difference in age from oldest to the youngest made dining out a challenge.

Family vacations were generally local. They rented a cabin for a month at Lake Shaftsbury State Park in Vermont, with John's mom and older sisters managing the group of youngsters. The family also vacationed in the Harwich area of Cape Cod. Red Sox home games were another family pastime.

John attended Mount Greylock Regional School from seventh grade through his senior year of high school. While occasionally participating in the school's musicals, John was primarily an athlete, playing football, basketball, and baseball. In football, his best sport, he was a running back on offense and linebacker on defense.

At five-foot-ten inches, he played center for the basketball team. John admits he probably "wasn't a great player," and one season the team only won one game. Baseball saw him playing out-field, catcher, and sometimes third base. He specifically remembers a major influence on him in the eighth grade when Coach John Allen encouraged him to try out for football. Agostini says, "Coach Allen saw something in me when I was working out in the weight room and asked, '*Why aren't you playing football?*' Coach Allen was very influential and respected for the way he treated people."

John tried out for football and made the team in the eighth grade. He remains close to Coach Allen today.

When growing up, John's first job was caddying at the Taconic Golf Club. He remembers exactly what he would earn to carry one golfer's bag: $3.25. With a tip, a youngster might make $5.00. Carrying two bags earned you $8.00 with the possibility of a $4.00 tip. This local rite-of-passage put him in contact with many boys from North Adams and Williamstown with whom he would later compete.

In high school (and later in life), one of John's favorite eater-ies was Friendly's restaurant on State Road. He loved their big beef burger and chocolate shake. During this time period, he found a new part-time job as a plumber's assistant, running errands for the plumbers, getting their tools, and drilling installation holes in new housing. John liked the job and says he learned a lot. He isn't sheep-ish about admitting he developed a certain "competency in cleaning up sewerage spills in basements . . . after a while, I didn't really notice the smell."

Always a focused, serious student, John did have an incident with his older brother's car. One night, Alan lent John his prized possession, a 1966 dark green Mustang. Alan gave him two cautions: "stay away from hills, my clutch is going" and "don't have a car full of kids." John called Alan later that night, stuck on Bull Hill road in Lanesborough with a burnt-out clutch and a car full of kids.

In 1972, John was accepted at Williams College. One of its biggest attractions was knowing he could play on the football team. He played on the freshman team and then varsity for his last three years as a defensive back. At the time, Division III football was limited to the last week in August to the second week in November, reducing the impact on his studies. He also played several years on the lacrosse team.

Majoring in physics and astronomy, John's extracurricular activities were limited to serving on the honor discipline committee for two years and participating in radio plays, although he is the first to admit he was "not the greatest thespian."

He worked part-time jobs at the college, including cleaning dishes in the cafeteria, working in the business office, and serving as a teaching assistant helping other physics students with labs and reviewing class notes. In the summers, he painted houses or worked in the shipping department at General Photo.

John initially wanted to be a professional athlete, then over time his objective changed to becoming a physics teacher. In his senior year, his goal changed one more time, and he decided to become a lawyer, like his dad. John graduated from Williams College in 1976 with a bachelor's degree in physics and astronomy, *cum laude*.

After having lived all his life in the northeast, he decided to apply to law schools out of the area and was accepted at Washington and Lee University School of Law in Lexington, Virginia, located in the beautiful Shenandoah Valley. John thrived in the small school environment. Although his studies were all-consuming and there was little time for activities, he did manage to help as the graduate assistant football coach. John graduated from W&L in 1979.

That same year, John began his law career in the Berkshire DA's office as an Assistant District Attorney. Shortly after, he became an associate, and then a partner, in the firm of Cain, Hibbard, Myers & Cook where, for the next twenty years, he worked long hours involved in civil litigation cases.

THE JUDICIARY

Talking with John, he acknowledges one of his proudest professional achievements was being admitted to the fellowship in the American College of Trial Lawyers at the age of forty-five. Not long after this accomplishment, John decided to apply for a judgeship. He hoped that receiving the fellowship, complemented by his criminal and civil law background, would give him a good chance of being selected. After twenty years in private practice, John thought he would like to change from mostly civil litigation and long hours of work to a broad offering of criminal and civil cases.

He forwarded his application and was interviewed by the Judicial Nomination Committee, which in turn submitted a slate of recommended candidates to the governor. In 2002, Governor Jane Swift, a former North Adams resident, appointed John Agostini at the age of forty-nine to the position of Associate Justice of Superior Court.

John readily admits he enjoys serving as a judge: No more advocating for one side or another or trying to slant the facts to meet individual client expectations. His focus was now based on "obtaining the facts, considering the law (precedents), determining the issue, and crafting a solution."

The judge still uses his extensive law library for deeper research.

There are thirteen counties in the State of Massachusetts. Each county has a Superior Court. Western Massachusetts, where John is assigned, has four Superior Courts. They are located in Hampden County (Springfield), Hampshire County (Northampton), Franklin County (Greenfield), and Berkshire County (Pittsfield). Judges have no permanent location and rotate between the four sites. John spends six months in Pittsfield and then three months each at the other courts.

Come autumn 2021, he will have been a judge for twenty years. Up until the recent pandemic, he tried cases between 9:00 a.m. and 1:00 p.m., then the afternoon was reserved to hear motions or pleas. Serious cases, he explains, can take one to three weeks to adjudicate, while less serious trials can be completed in three to five days. Eighty percent of his trials are criminal and involve serious felonies such as murder, rape, armed robbery, sexual assault, or human trafficking.

His civil trials normally involve contract disputes, zoning or real estate issues, product liability claims, or medical issues. Often two citizens are suing each other or companies are seeking relief from other corporations.

With pandemic concerns, trials were postponed beginning March 2020, and juries are just now being impaneled over a year later. During this time, the Massachusetts Supreme Court agreed to allow dangerous offenders to be jailed indefinitely. This long pause in meting out justice created a sizeable backlog of criminal cases.

I asked John what traits help him as a judge, and he said, "the need for patience, understanding, and at times a sense of humor . . . . I am witness to lots of things that people had to go through and when you have the whole picture [you] begin to see life differently." For John, ministering over the many serious trials has heightened his sense and concern for humanity.

John notes that over the past twenty years, cases seem to be more complex, technology has sped up the trial process, and the number of cases seems to have increased and are of a more serious nature. His most difficult recent cases involved technicalities lacking precedents in law or murder cases. At the time we talked, there were seven murder trials pending in Berkshire County.

Being a judge requires ongoing training; for a number of years John and others have participated in training programs in Massachusetts that emphasized ferreting out implicit biases. In this training, participants are reminded that in the search for truth, facts and relevance are important, and it's not a person's race, religion, sexual orientation, accent, or whether they are well dressed or not so well dressed that determines who is being truthful.

Massachusetts judges have their performance reviewed every three years. This comprehensive review includes completed questionnaires from the court staff and attorneys who appear before the judges. The information is collated, assigned ratings ranging from excellent to poor, and includes comments. The contents are reviewed with each individual judge by their boss, Chief Judge of Superior Court.

After participating in hundreds of criminal trials, John has seen a wide variety of viciousness, mayhem, and utter stupidity. He continues to control his emotions, keep a straight face, and search for the truth. I asked John about some of his more notable trials, and we discussed a few.

He was assigned to oversee the civil litigation against the Catholic Church where predatory priests had been protected by the institution. It involved over a hundred individual civil lawsuits against the Church. The suits included litigation and damages. The cases were of a more recent nature since Massachusetts has a three-year limitation on these types of charges.

The stories from claimants directly, or their affidavits, were particularly sad. Often when a sexual incident occurred, the child might complain to his parents or the church, not be believed, and many times the victim would be referred back to the priest for counseling. The Church was thought to be above reproach and stood for faith and trust. John and the lawyers categorized the claims in those cases by those that would accept a settlement and those that would not. Most were settled out of court, a few went to trial, and final settlements were paid by the church and its insurance companies.

Other cases involved the Church suing its own insurance agencies when coverage was initially denied, since the companies considered the predatory acts intentional and outside the boundaries of coverage. On a more serious occasion, John sentenced a former priest to twenty years in prison for raping two altar boys. He has helped lift document restrictions to determine whether another priest was involved in a boy's murder.

John notes that in Massachusetts when defendants are charged with murder, it is often the jury that decides its classification. If determined to be premeditated, the murder is considered first-degree; if lacking premeditation although with malice, the murder would be considered second-degree; and the third possible classification, manslaughter, involves recklessness with intent to harm.

Another one of John's more interesting trials involved the Gambino crime family, a syndicate that allegedly controls many of the illegal activities in Springfield. The family's boss in Springfield had been killed by an assassin, who was captured and then himself targeted for retaliation by the mob and his own employers. The state provided heavy court security as the trial was getting underway. Jurors were bused to the courthouse, but at the last minute, the assassin decided to cooperate with the FBI, and the case never went to trial.

One of the worst and most senseless crimes John had to adjudicate was a double homicide involving an elderly couple. Two youths who broke into what they thought was an empty house found an elderly couple at home, both in fragile health. The thieves decided to kill them and eliminate witnesses to their crime. The killers, a boy and a girl, fled and were captured in Virginia and returned to Massachusetts for trial. After separate trials, they were both found guilty and sentenced to life in prison. The murders were senseless and brutal.

Judge Agostini at his desk, where he makes deliberations.

John has handled a number of cases involving daylight shoot-outs on the streets, which seem to be more prevalent as of late and often injure innocent bystanders. One incident occurred at a Springfield housing project where four shooters ambushed their victim. One shooter, hidden in a dumpster, jumped out and killed a person. Two perpetrators were tried and both convicted of first-degree murder, which in Massachusetts results in a sentence of life without parole.

Discussing the case made me think of court security. John acknowledged that security has been heightened and has become more sophisticated over the years. Strong precautions are taken at times depending upon the case and intelligence-gathering that might indicate such things as gang affiliations.

"Generally, trials run smoothly," explains John. "Criminals understand the system and how it works." Seldom are court officers armed. In rare cases, armed state troopers or plain-clothes detectives are present. John's never been threatened but has received a few letters from persons disappointed with his decisions.

I didn't know this, but often the most dangerous court is considered Family and Probate. Normally its defendants have not been involved with the court system before, and when emotional decisions are made concerning children, responses can be unpredictable. Criminals are prepared for the consequences of their actions; family court participants are not.

Some of John's criminal cases could almost be considered humorous. As an example, he mentioned a Cumberland Farms robbery where four ski-masked, armed men stole money from the cash register and then started taking merchandise from the shelves. One robber noticed a kiosk of sunglasses with a viewing mirror. He took off his mask to try on a pair of glasses and preened in front of the mirror. His efforts were captured by the store's video recorder. He was identified by the police, captured, convicted, and went to jail. He was the only robber convicted.

In another instance, a drug dealer was arrested by police and brought to the police station. Under audio and video surveillance, he was offered a phone call. Forcefully, the defendant told the nearby patrolman to give him some distance for his phone call. He called his girlfriend and told her where the money and drugs were located and instructed her to retrieve and hide them. The entire conversation was recorded by police, and the criminal and his girlfriend were found guilty.

Sometimes even the more routine cases provide a moment of drama. During the closing argument of a simple motor vehicle accident case, the defense attorney began to garble her summation, went quiet, and fell to her side, hitting her head on the edge of the table. There was blood everywhere; luckily, two jurors were medical professionals and rushed to the attorney's aid. An ambulance was called, and she recovered from what was determined to be an epileptic seizure.

John's more locally relevant cases involved the Berkshire Museum and its ability to sell its artwork, including several Norman Rockwell paintings, because of financial difficulties. He ruled they could sell them. In another case, he ruled Tennessee Gas should be allowed an easement through Otis State Forest finding that federal law superseded state law. He also permitted the Stockbridge Bowl Association to use herbicides to treat a portion of the lake to deal with weed infestation. His decision on the Friendly's Ice Cream Company and the effects of the diminution of its value on its stockholders became a Harvard case study.

From a civic standpoint, John has served on Williams College's Advisory Board on Shareholder's Responsibility and been involved in reconstructing and updating some of Mount Greylock High School's athletic fields. He has coached, directed, and served as president of a Little League organization. In his community, he has also served on the Williamstown finance committee, elementary school building committee, and the economic development committee. In recognition of his distinguished community service, John is a recipient of Williamstown's highest honor, The Faith Scarborough Award.

Professionally, he has been president of the Berkshire Bar Association and for twenty years a member of the Western Massachusetts Pro Bono Referral Panel.

John lists his most satisfying personal accomplishment

as raising three boys with his wife, Nancy. Nancy has worked as a homemaker, a substitute teacher, a social worker at the Massachusetts Society for the Prevention of Cruelty to Children, and also as a court investigator. Several of their sons followed in their father's footsteps as football and baseball athletes.

Measured and thoughtful in his conversation, John likes to say, "You never have to apologize for something not said." He has also been described as empathetic, humble, possessor of a good sense of humor, and a man who does what he sets out to do. He is careful about his interactions with others to ensure his actions will reflect well on the court and avoid conflicts of interest.

John usually has coffee at his older brother Alan's house every Saturday morning, where the brothers can freely discuss local and national politics, always with a relaxed sense of humor.

In 2023, John's term as a judge will expire when he reaches the mandatory retirement age of seventy. He has no specific retirement plans yet and continues to focus, as he has for decades, on delivering justice in western Massachusetts.

DICK ALCOMBRIGHT

Former four-term Mayor of North Adams Dick Alcombright has found his greatest satisfaction in raising his very young granddaughter, Milania, and caring for his mom, Bernice, in her late nineties. It's been quite a change from his more recent mayoral duties.

Born on December 14, 1953, at the North Adams Hospital to Daniel F. Alcombright, Jr., and Bernice Owczarski Alcombright, Dick inherited his work ethic and civic duty from his Irish dad, born in 1923, who served in World War II as an Army sergeant in Italy, then worked twenty-five years at Williams College as the Supervisor of Custodial Operations. Daniel was also a city councilman for over thirty years and a strong supporter of the education, police, and fire departments. At his funeral, in tribute the fire department lined up its vehicles and the firemen saluted the funeral procession as it passed the station.

Bernice Alcombright was born in Adams in 1923 to parents who'd emigrated from Poland. Initially, Bernice stayed home to raise her four children, but in 1951, she opened a hair salon in a first-floor garage stall that her husband converted for her business. The salon was open for over sixty years, closing in 2017 when she was 93 years old. Bernice, who suffers from congestive heart failure, often joked that she would close her salon through attrition "when she or her clients died off."

Growing up, for Dick, was centered around "faith, sports, and ethnicity." He played at neighborhood playgrounds in the Blackinton and Greylock sections with his buddies. They would pool money to buy 25- or 30-cent Wiffle balls at West's Variety Store, then were off to the field to play endless baseball, using the gloves of whoever was batting for their bases and playing till the streetlights came on. This early love for baseball had Dick playing in Little League and Babe Ruth.

When the boys weren't at the playground, they might swim in Dick's above-ground pool at his home. Dick and his brothers and sister grew up at 1547 Massachusetts Avenue where his mom still lives. From the outside, the house appears to be almost four stories. The family lived in the downstairs apartment, had a renter on the second floor, and a full-size attic on the third floor.

He attended kindergarten at Greylock Grammar School and then used his yellow coach bus tickets to travel to St. Joseph's School from first to ninth grade. For the remainder of high school, he attended McCann Technical School, graduating in 1971 with a business diploma. Always the genial kid, he still remembers his two bus drivers, Bill and Gene.

While at McCann, Dick played three sports: football, basketball, and baseball. He was the catcher on the Hornets' baseball team and the center on its football team. During high school, his social life centered on teammates and his part-time job. His baseball chums indicate that he either hit home runs or struck out, probably fewer home runs. Dick always enjoyed a pick-up basketball game. One day, he decided he wanted to be able to dunk the ball. Undaunted, he bought some books, exercised with weights on his calves, taught himself to dunk, and did it once.

Once in a while, he might be the designated driver when his friends went over the line to New York State. Dick was never much of a drinker in high school or college, and even now he seldom partakes.

After high school, Dick drew the number three under the military draft lottery and went to Springfield for his physical, where he received a temporary medical deferment. The gruff sergeant present at the physical told him to work on the medical issue (essentially, to shape up or we will shape you up). Shortly afterwards, President Nixon called off the draft, negating his enlistment. Dick doesn't regret not going in the military but feels like he might have missed out on something.

During this time period, he attended and graduated from

College of St. Joseph in Bennington, Vermont, with an associate's degree in accounting. He is also a graduate of the National Association of Mutual Savings Banks School of Banking at Fairfield University and remembers his first exposure to computers being an IBM mainframe.

Over his lifetime, Dick has stayed involved with his faith, serving as an altar boy from eight to eighteen years old at the Incarnation Church and as a lector at Holy Family and Notre Dame churches. He has also been a member of church finance committees.

From age fifteen through twenty-four, Dick worked at Denelli's Gas Station pumping gas, changing tires, and checking customers' oil. He enjoyed doing the minor mechanical work of installing brakes and shocks.

For four summers, he worked cutting grass for the Buildings and Grounds department at Williams College. His first car was a worn out 1960 Plymouth Valiant. He got it for free and kept it at Denelli's while working on it. It took a year to get it running and his boss John Denelli let Dick put the parts on his account across the street at Adams Auto Parts.

Family supper occurred around 5:00 p.m. when Dad got home from work. Usually, the goal was to get the family fed, caught up on the day's events, and back out the door to the kids' activities. Mom cooked, although when Dick was about 10 years old, he started helping cook the evening meal when she would be busy in her beauty shop. She often prepped the food in the morning, maybe making spaghetti sauce, and Dick would cook the pasta and warm the bread. His brothers and sister helped with the cooking and dishes.

They were a meat and potato family: "everything went better with gravy." But Friday night was always meatless. The family loved "fish snacks" which consisted of two slices of potato, a piece of whitefish tooth-picked in the middle, battered and fried in Crisco. Their backup was fish sticks or a pasta meal. A special treat would be eating fish snacks at the Boston fish market.

Meals always included a tasty dessert. Dick's mom made chocolate cakes with vanilla frosting and pudding with whipped cream.

Sometimes they imported chocolate cake or Boston cream pies from Molly's (a bakery in North Adams across from Jack's Hot Dog Stand) or apple squares from the Polish bakery in Adams.

Mom was the family's disciplinarian. Brought up in a traditional, strict, Polish Catholic environment, while extremely loving, her episodes of disciplining kids were "memorable." She kept an Aldo's Paint and Wallpaper Store yardstick on the molding above the kitchen door for miscreants. It was a sturdy, old fashioned stick, three feet long, one-and-a-half inches wide and a half-inch thick. (She would never say "wait until your father gets home." Dad was too laid back!)

Many summers, the Alcombright family vacationed for one week in Savoy, renting a cottage at Windsor Pond. A large pavilion with a snack bar and a pool table welcomed teens to hang out when they were not swimming.

As a young boy, the biggest treat for Dick was traveling to Boston for a Red Sox v. Yankees baseball game. He remembers staying overnight at the Boston Howard Johnson hotel and the aura of Fenway Park. The crowds seemed to be mostly men and kids. In the late fifties, some men still wore dress hats, and he distinctly remembers a lot of cigar smoke.

STARTING YOUNG AT THE BANK

At nineteen, Dick joined the North Adams Hoosac Bank and throughout the next thirty-plus years held positions of increasing responsibility as the bank grew. He started as a teller and later worked in lending and accounting and helped with informational technology conversions. Most of his experiences were in retail versus the operational part of banking. In bank jargon, it's called "front-facing," meaning dealing directly with the customer through deposits, customer service, new accounts, and lending. The bank was Dick's first exposure to charitable work that began a lifelong avocation. He was initially involved in United Way Campaigns and the Fall Foliage Festival as part of a team that made floats for the parade.

Dick lived in Adams in the early 1980s in a three-family

tenement that his grandfather owned. He relocated to East Quincy Street in North Adams and returned to Adams for several years. Currently Dick lives on Williams Street in North Adams. During his early years, he refereed high school sports and played in a men's adult basketball league.

While working at the bank, Dick served nine years as a North Adams city council member and nineteen years as a member of the McCann Technical School Committee. He has also held leadership roles with an array of local organizations, including Northern Berkshire United Way, YMCA, Berkshire Rides, Northern Berkshire Community Coalition, Hospice of Northern Berkshire, Tri-Parish Finance Council, and the Massachusetts Municipal Associations Opioid Addiction and Overdose Prevention Task Force.

POLITICAL LIFE

After being on the city council for nine years, attending bi-monthly meetings, Dick saw things he would like to change in city government. In his opinion, there were certain fiscal issues such as budgeting and spending, and other dynamics that could be improved. So, he ran against

Awards and memorabilia collected throughout Dick Alcombright's years in public service.

a long-time incumbent, won, and was sworn in on New Year's Day 2010. He served four successive terms through the end of 2017.

The mayor's position has fifteen direct reports and is time-consuming. Reporting to the office were Police and Fire Chiefs, departmental heads, administrative offices, Commissioner of Public Services, Superintendent of Schools, and an administrative assistant. Dick's management style was a cultural change for people. He followed a very successful, type A, many-term mayor with his more relaxed "banker's" personality, frequently visiting people's offices to see how they were doing, soliciting opinions, and being available to discuss the smallest of issues: transparent, in some people's opinion, to his detriment.

Dick has never had much time for personal reading. His reading has focused on banking and political periodicals, legislation, compliance, or various statutes associated with his jobs. After a busy day at work (which also included a lot of reading) and a busy home life, there was little time left.

Dick, a heavy-set man, was always noted for his breakfast, which consisted of a diet soda and a peanut-buttered bagel from Dunkin Donuts. His busy day relegated him to sandwiches (Subway franchise was located across the street) or treks to the downstairs vending machines. Lunch meetings were most often at the Boston Sea Foods restaurant and any necessary dinners were frequently held at Grazie.

ACCOMPLISHMENTS

Dick was fifty-six years old when he entered office. "I grew more in the eight years of being mayor than my previous 56 years of life," he acknowledges. Before becoming mayor, he had served on the city council and various boards and commissions, but as mayor he became more personally involved with people from different walks of life and communities such as LGBTQ+, military veterans, and those with mental health challenges.

Each interaction broadened his perspective, and he considered each a growth experience. They sensitized him to the needs and concerns of others. One couple he met wanted to discuss a "Juneteenth" celebration. He had to admit to them that he didn't know what Juneteenth was, and when they told him, he thanked them for educating him and began helping them.

Dick thought his temperament was just like his dad's. His dad was very slow to anger and not much of a worrier. There could be a tense budget or council meeting, but ten or fifteen minutes after it ended, he would head home to enjoy his other life. He often said, "Life's too short. I leave my work at work. I don't get angry often, but can be passionate defending a school or town proposal."

He is proud of the city's more notable accomplishments, including balancing the budget, moving the city's credit rating from an A-minus with a negative outlook to an A in 2016 with a stable outlook. Promoting tax incentives that often turned "at risk" properties, close to being torn down, to tax-producing entities and operating companies was a "double win" in his mind. He was very willing to do short-term investing for long-term growth as evidenced by the new Tourists Hotel, and efforts at the Greylock Mill and Crane Stationery.

He also presided over the city's successful conversion of the old Drury High School to Colegrove Elementary School (kindergarten through fifth grade) and the consolidation of the Public Services Department into one location at Hodges Crossroads. Bringing the various city departments into one location greatly improved communications and cooperation.

Grants to city and private development projects included those that benefited the Colegrove Park Elementary School, MASS MoCA, Scenic Rail Trail, the Greylock Mill, the Extreme Model Rail and Contemporary Architecture Museum, the Hoosic River Revival Project, the Berkshire Bike Path, and a variety of public recreational amenities.

In 2017, Dick decided not to run in the 2018 mayoral election, primarily for family reasons. While not ready to permanently retire, he wanted to provide day-to-day care for his young granddaughter and mother. Coincidentally, as he contemplated running for reelection, the CEO of MountainOne Bank called him and ultimately offered him his current job, Vice President of Local Business and Customer Relations. Prior to becoming mayor, Dick had worked over thirty-five years for MountainOne companies.

BANK AND FAMILY LIFE BALANCE

The bank is considerate of his family caretaker activities. "Not a night goes by when I'm not thankful," he says of his work in customer development, where he works with the bank's clients reviewing their relationships. He solicits feedback on his bank's performance and how they could serve the customer better. Dick also attends many public forums, keeping the bank abreast of local developments and potential new customers. There is no better community ambassador.

Dick's personality has always meshed well with people; he is warm, easy to get along with, outgoing, empathetic, selfless, a good listener, and witty. He communicates well and is known as an excellent speaker. His ability to retain information (his forte is processing financial data) makes him a requested speaker at public functions or events.

Seated at his MountainOne desk, Dick Alcombright is ready for the next customer.

He sees his grandchildren frequently, one of whom lives with him. As he thinks about his future, Dick's focus is on his aging mom and her immediate needs and the raising of a healthy, happy, independent granddaughter. He considers these his life's work. Dick has always been involved in the care of his mother, her house, and her personal needs. He checks on her daily and takes her to most of her medical appointments. His brother says for many years Dickie was unselfishly "the heart and soul of taking care of Mom" and that "he is the reason she is still alive."

For relaxation, he enjoys hiking in the woods with his granddaughter. They enjoy walks near Peck's Falls on the Appalachian Trail or navigating the two-and-a-half-mile loop around the Fish Pond. They frequent Mauserts Pond at Clarksburg State Park, and also hike the four-mile trail in Hopkins Forest maintained by Williams College. He's begun returning to the gym as the pandemic concerns diminish.

Still involved in the community, he chairs the Berkshire Community Action Council helping in the areas of addiction, prevention, and recovery. He's served on the Northern Berkshire Community Coalition's RX/Heroin Workgroup and the Berkshire Opioid Abuse Prevention Response Programs. He is a member of the Attorney General's Family Advisory Council and the HEALing Communities Study Advisory Board.

Dick has been honored for his work and dedication by a number of organizations, among them the Berkshire Community Action Council, BCArc, Berkshire Regional Planning Commission, Brien Center, Child Care of the Berkshires, Mass Association of School Committees, National Alliance on Mental Illness, Northern Berkshire Community Coalition, Northern Berkshire United Way, UCP of Berkshire County, and the Salvation Army.

He has received an honorary doctorate from Massachusetts College of Liberal Arts, but he is still a down-to-earth guy with a keen sense of humor that some say he got from his dad. He enjoys the simplest of jokes and has a very funny delivery, courtesy of his love for Looney Tunes. To this day, Dick remembers many of the cartoons he watched as a youth and still finds time for an occasional episode. Get him alone and if you're lucky you'll catch his voice imitation of Sylvester the Cat, Yosemite Sam, and Tweety Bird.

When asked, "What is the kindest thing someone ever did for you," Dick answers without pause: his greatest gifts have been his children and grandchildren, and they are a "gift that keeps on giving."

JOHN & JANE ALLEN

This renowned coach and well-respected educator have, as a couple, affected the lives of thousands of athletes and students for over forty years. To illustrate how broad is their sphere of influence, sixteen of the thirty-five subjects in this book have had a direct connection with one or both of them, John through his decades of coaching and Jane through her work as a teacher, principal, and Town selectman. If Williamstown had a "best-known couple," the Allens would be it.

John Allen was born at the North Adams Hospital on December 22, 1938. His parents were Robert and Irma (Campedelli) Allen. They had two children, John and Zelda.

John's dad was born in 1910 in Fitchburg, Massachusetts, and came to North Adams as part of the Civilian Conservation Corps founded by Franklin D. Roosevelt. He helped build a camp at Savoy Mountain State Forest. During World War II, Bob served in the U.S. Army in the South Pacific. For much of his life he worked for the Clark Biscuit Company in North Adams as a driver and eventually retired from General Electric.

John's mom, Irma, also born in North Adams, worked as a housewife and as a capacitor assembler for the Sprague Electric Company on Beaver Street. The family lived on Hooker Street in what was known as the Italian section of North Adams.

Little is known about John's paternal grandparents, Robert and Edith Lilly Allen. John never met them but believes they came from Fitchburg. His maternal grandparents, John and Francesca Campedelli, emigrated from Italy in the early 1900s, met and married in North Adams, and John worked on the Hoosac Tunnel. He passed away in 1941 and Francesca in 1972.

Jane (Brooks) Allen, an only child, was born on January 12,

1939, at the W. B. Plunkett Hospital in Adams. She recalls a brief stay at the same hospital years later to have her tonsils removed. Her dad, Lindon Brooks, was born in 1900 in South Boston, grew up in Maine, and worked his whole life for the JJ Newberry Company. Mary, Jane's mom, was a housewife and an avid volunteer and worked at the North Adams Hospital as a nurse's aide and at the blood clinic.

Lindon and Mary had met in Pennsylvania when he was managing the local JJ Newberry store. They were married in Boston, then moved to North Adams when Lindon was assigned to the store on Main Street. He managed the North Adams branch from the 1930s until his retirement.

Jane's paternal grandparents were James and Grace (Babcock) Brooks. James was born on Prince Edward Island in Canada, and Grace was born in Maine. They married and lived in Maine while he worked for the Penobscot Chemical Fiber Company. Jane and her parents visited them in the summers.

Jane's maternal grandparents were John Yensensky and Anna Sofka. They immigrated separately to the United States from Hungary via Ellis Island. Passenger records from the vessel *Spaarndam* indicate that John embarked from Rotterdam and arrived in the U.S. on November 28, 1899. The ship's log misspells his name and records him as *Johann Jesensky*, age seventeen, from a small town called Sarpalak, which may no longer exist. John and Anna met in Pennsylvania and married. John worked most of his life in the coal mines, while Anna managed the home. Anna died in childbirth when Jane's mother Mary was only two years old.

A MASSACHUSETTS CHILDHOOD

John Allen attended Haskins Elementary School, pre-kindergarten through the eighth grade. Across town, Jane, less than two months younger than John, attended Brayton Elementary School.

The Allens were active parishioners of Saint Anthony Church (now known as St. Elizabeth of Hungary Church) and for vacations frequented his aunt's house in Revere Beach where he enjoyed swimming, fishing with his dad, and the roller coaster on the boardwalk.

Jane grew up on the State Road across from Fort Massachusetts, and the Brooks family worshipped at the First Baptist Church. They vacationed often in Maine at her grandparents', which allowed her dad to enjoy his favorite sport, fishing.

Both attended Drury High School and were in the 1957 graduating class. John was a three-sport star athlete, receiving thirteen athletic letters for four years on the varsity team in baseball, basketball, and football and one year of track. He was a catcher on the baseball team and awarded the Mack Award in his sophomore year. The award is given to the player with the highest batting average: John's was .402. Also, he achieved All Berkshire Honors in football, basketball, and baseball. John's yearbook bio mentions the nickname *Bugsy*, used mostly when quarterbacking the football team. Most people called him Johnny. (Aside from enumerating his many sports accomplishments, the yearbook also notes that he loves to Bop.)

Jane's yearbook shows that she was in Nu Sigma, part of the academic Honor Society. She served as Student Government President, played basketball, and skied. Most of all, she says she "loved cheerleading for four years." Her yearbook bio mentions driving a "clunk-a-mobile," which was her father's old car. "I can't see far" alludes to her nearsightedness and aversion to wearing her glasses. Jane fondly remembers, as President of the Student Council, something of a kerfuffle after the Student Council proposed to combine the boys' and girls' lunchrooms. The Council thought mixing the groups would create a better atmosphere for both sexes. After some initial administration resistance, the proposal was accepted and implemented.

John usually had part-time summer jobs with the city or state. One summer he did some "rip-rap" work on the Hoosic River. The young men would roll boulders down the embankment and bury them in place as part of the flood control project, to prevent erosion. He remembers his boss supervising this dangerous work from the other side of the river.

John also worked one summer at Sprague on Beaver Street, where his mom was employed, and most summers he played baseball as a Little Leaguer and in Babe Ruth league. When he was older, he played without pay in semi-pro leagues. In fall and winter, he played church league basketball for Saint Anthony's and was a frequent visitor at the local YMCA, swimming, playing basketball, and shooting pool.

During the school year, Jane worked for her dad on Saturdays at Newberry's, most of the time selling merchandise at the counters, ranging from hats to popcorn. Sometimes she would be assigned office work. She also belonged to the Hi-Y Club, a service organization sponsored by the YMCA.

Although the young couple shared an English class, they first met at a Drury High Saturday night dance, right after a football game. The girls were standing in a group chatting, and John walked up and asked Jane to dance. They began dating regularly and attended school proms together.

Both graduated from Drury in 1957 and John headed to Holy Cross College where he would receive a bachelor's degree in education. Tragedy struck in his freshman year when his mom died unexpectedly from a heart ailment.

John played varsity football for Holy Cross, on offense as a halfback and on defense as a safety. On the school's varsity baseball team, he earned an All-East catcher award and subsequently tried out for the Washington Senators. Sadly, a knee injury in his senior year of college ended any hopes of a professional career.

Both John and Jane graduated in 1961. While he was in the Boston area attending Holy Cross, Jane had matriculated at Keuka College in New York and transferred in her junior year to North Adams State College where she received a bachelor's degree in elementary education. She later completed a master's degree in educational administration from the State University of New York at Albany.

The high school sweethearts, who had been dating across states for four years, were married shortly after their graduations, on August 12, 1961. The wedding rites took place at St. Anthony's

Church in North Adams, presided over by the Reverend J.J. Ryan, a member of the Holy Cross faculty.

THE TEACHING LIFE BEGINS

Their first jobs as teachers were in Chelmsford, Massachusetts. Jane taught at the elementary school and John taught civics courses and was the assistant high school football coach. Their first of three children, Tracy, was born in 1962; Jane was required by state law, at three months of pregnancy, to quit her job. Their second daughter, Terry, was in born in 1963.

Reflecting back, Jane's desire to be an educator started with her "first-grade teacher needing to leave the room and putting me in charge of the reading group. I took the responsibilities seriously and still remember sitting in the teacher's big chair. That's where it began." She notes that back in the late 1950s, "occupations were somewhat limited for women to teaching and nursing."

John was anxious to move on with his career. He jokes, "I applied for every head coaching job in the state." He was hired by Mount Greylock Regional High School in Williamstown in 1964 as a part-time PE teacher and full-time coach. Initially, John coached the basketball team, worked as the assistant football coach, and led the baseball team (John Barrett, currently a Massachusetts State Representative, was the student captain of that team).

Shortly after their arrival in Williamstown, their third daughter Mary Jane was born. During this time period, John received his master's in education from North Adams State College (now Massachusetts College of Liberal Arts). John coached basketball until 1966 when he became the school's athletic director and head football coach. He also continued to coach the baseball team until 1974. His busy schedule revolved around late-morning or early-afternoon physical education classes and then team practices and games.

Jane eventually resumed her career teaching the first and sixth grades at Williamstown Elementary, and remained there for over a decade.

Though physically small, her first graders made a big impression. One of Jane's students for whom learning was difficult struggled with timed math tests and yet one day scored a 100 percent. The class, knowing the student was struggling, gave its classmate a standing ovation after lunch.

Another time, her first graders were reading in a circle around Jane. One boy mentioned that he remembered the story from last year, then suddenly realized he had just let everyone know he was repeating the grade. Before anyone could say something, one of the brightest students said, "I'm repeating first grade also, I just wasn't ready for second grade." This surprised everyone and not another word was said.

One of Jane's students who had a difficult year, on his last day of school in line for the bus, turned around and thanked everyone for a great school year. This had never happened before, and the memory still brings tears to Jane's eyes. As the youngest kids in the school, their sweet honesty was endearing.

In their early years of marriage, John worked a summer job as the Waterfront Director at Camp Eagle on October Mountain in Lenox and at Camp Chesterfield in Chesterfield, Massachusetts. Jane and the girls vacationed at the camps, enjoying the amenities while he worked. The girls loved the routine, living in a cabin, waking at reveille, eating in the mess hall, canoeing and sailing with their parents, and swimming in the lake.

"At a young age, all three became great swimmers," recalls Jane.

After Camp Eagle, for many summers the family vacationed in Rhode Island with friends. Spending a week in an oceanfront cottage, the girls would build sandcastles, dig for clams, body surf, and ride the carousel at Watch Hill. Other summer pastimes included Jane's parents taking the girls and their friends to Lake George. They'd dock their cabin cruiser in a small bay, sleep overnight, and the kids would enjoy the use of the grandparent's dinghy. John and Jane also stayed there a number of times.

Naturally their girls played many sports, winter and summer. Everyone skied, and all the girls ran track. Tracy swam, Mary Jane liked downhill skiing and soccer, and Terry enjoyed cross-country skiing and field hockey. The local newspaper once featured three

Allen family members winning prizes at annual Berkshire County cross-country citizens' ski championships. Jane was third in her class, while John and Terry placed first in the parent-child combined race. Terry also took first in her class.

The family had a special tradition of spending Christmas Eve with friends that had kids the same ages as the girls. The menu was always the same: stuffed mushrooms, ham, lasagna, chicken tetrazzini, and Texas sheet cake for dessert. Adults gathered at one table and eleven children sat at card tables. The boys were always mixed in with the girls to try and limit their rowdiness.

John loves Italian food, and the family would enjoy their visits to Florini's restaurant in downtown North Adams. On occasion, they dined at the Howard Johnson restaurant in Williamstown, and more recently would cross state lines for a spontaneous breakfast at the Blue Bell diner in Bennington.

A LEGACY SET IN STONE

John coached Mount Greylock football for almost forty years, from 1964 until he retired in 2003. During this hectic time period, the family supported his efforts by late suppers after football practice and before John's nighttime Athletic Director responsibilities. Jane's days were equally busy, often bicycling to work, then to girls' games, and home to cook simple pasta pre-game meals.

Football practices were Monday through Friday, with lighter practices before and after games. Initially the football field had no floodlights, so only day games were played. Classes at Mount Greylock got out at 3:00 p.m., and the team needed to be on the field ready to go at 3:15 p.m. Practices ended at 5:00 p.m., and Saturday games were at 1:00 p.m.

Early in his coaching career, he and Jane began a team tradition of cooking a spaghetti-and-meatball dinner at their house for the Mt. Greylock senior players at the end of each season. Another tradition was holding mini-reunions with John's Holy Cross classmates and their families. Each year, the reunions rotated between four households.

Over time, Mount Greylock's teams excelled at football, running, cross-country skiing, and wrestling. The football team competed in the Intercounty League composed of schools their size, and won three football championships. At one point, Mount Greylock was moved to the Kosior League to face more difficult competitors such as Springfield and Pittsfield high schools, and won six more championships. John was voted Berkshire County Coach of the Year in 1967 and 1980 during his 7-0 winning seasons.

Mount Greylock's players carry Coach Allen off the field, celebrating another win.

As the years passed by, former players going back to the 1960s with the help of the school organized the John T. Allen Day on October 20, 1990, and began celebrations at an afternoon game against Pittsfield rivals. Red baseball caps proclaiming John T. Allen Day were everywhere; the students dedicated the stone marker near the field to John. The plaque there reads: "Dedicated October 20, 1990, by football alumni and friends in appreciation of John Allen's ability to teach football, instill values, and for being a role model for Mt. Greylock students. His legacy is, so to speak, set in stone."

The Mounties beat Pittsfield 20-6 to complete John's surprise party. Then everyone celebrated the dedication and victory at the Williams Inn after the game. Over two hundred and twenty-five people from twenty-one states participated in the tribute dinner honoring John. Those present spoke emotionally of their respect for this humble and unpretentious man.

Players from politicians to police chiefs described John's desire and effort to have them believe in themselves and put forth maximum effort in whatever they do. It's been said that John's record of "producing winning people, not winning games, truly marks him as an educator." Many consider him a trusted friend who provided them direction in their lives. He is often seen as a father figure.

Friends and former players sent letters of congratulations and gratitude for John's influence on their lives. As one former player said, "Your success is measured not in wins or losses, but in young men; young men who have, with your help, made successful transition to adulthood. By such a measure, you are the most successful coach in Massachusetts."

Another player wrote, "I credit knowing and being associated with you as having instilled the notion in my head that there isn't much I can't do if I am willing to work hard and pay the price. For that I am extremely grateful."

One of the most poignant letters said, "I don't think there are words which adequately say how thankful I am that I had a coach that could turn my life around that way you did."

Another said: "My sons never met John Allen, but in their father, they see him every day." One former player described him as "approachable, humble, disciplined, and a tough coach . . . and somehow always seeming to impart a lesson on life . . . he was beloved." His calm, reserved, focused nature only asked for the player's commitment to do his best.

John was a student of football and loved the game, and this intensity transferred to his teams. Players remember a sheet hung up in the locker room listing every play from the previous game. There were red circles around a player's name and the play that was missed. When the team watched the post-game film, his observations were almost always right. John's style was not to berate anyone; he would simply say, "On this play you should have . . . "

One player recalled, "He never expected anything more than for you to do your best and when teaching you he expected you to understand and put his directions into effect."

His signs in the locker room are legendary. One read IT DOESN'T

MATTER THE SIZE OF THE DOG IN THE FIGHT, RATHER THE SIZE OF THE FIGHT IN THE DOG. Another read WHEN THE GOING GETS TOUGH, THE TOUGH GET GOING. As one player said, "He would repeat these clichés, looking you in the eye, and make you a believer."

The Mount Greylock School Committee authorized the placing of the stone plaque on the playing field but rejected naming the field after John. Tongue-in-cheek, friends joked that it would be easier to make this tribute to John if he were already dead. Yet his players and friends persisted, and on July 7, 1995, the new soccer/football field was officially named *John T. Allen Field.*

John and Jane celebrate the fiftieth anniversary of the Mount Greylock 1967 championship, joined by former players Pete King (far left) and Dick Cummings (far right).

The evening dedication ceremony coincided with the installation of a lighting system, new bleachers, and a scoreboard with John's name on it. John was singled out to turn on the lights for the first time, then he walked on the field through a line of thirty of his former players. Jane and his three daughters were there for the dedication. The installation of lights meant a lot because the Mounties could now play night games.

A close friend said, "John loves all aspects of football: analyzing, the contact, and competing." They would often pre-game scout other teams together, John with his clipboard and stubby pencil scribbling down x's and o's for the different plays. It usually looked like an ancient etching by the time he was done.

John asked a friend whom he saw videotaping Greylock games if he would want to tape them for the team to use as pre-game reviews. The friend agreed, and John said, "There is $200 in the budget for someone to film." The friend agreed, and over the many years he has filmed, he hasn't seen a nickel of the money. It became a running joke with him and John. When asked about the $200,

John would say, "It's an investment in your future—I'm holding it for your future."

In appreciation of John's contributions, former players helped create The John T. Allen Fund. The endowment makes grants for initiatives at Mount Greylock that broaden students' experiences and horizons, enrich athletic programs, or help develop character aspects such as self-sacrifice, team spirit, work ethic, pride, and the desire to achieve one's full potential.

THE BITTERSWEET JOY OF RETIREMENT

While John devoted his life to helping student athletes, Jane has also had a successful forty-year career in education. After teaching in the Williamstown schools, she became principal in the Central Berkshire Regional School District of the former Crane Community School of Windsor and Cummington while also directing the Title I program for the district. She then served as principal at Kittredge School in Hinsdale and the Clarksburg Elementary School.

John and Jane Allen vacationing in Colorado in 2009.

As principal, when she had a difficult day or things weren't going her way, she knew she could always go to the kindergarten for a boost, the place where kids gave everyone unconditional love and hugs were plentiful.

In June 2001, when she retired, a group of community residents created the Jane Allen Fund to assist in renovations of Murdock Hall at her alma mater, Massachusetts College of Liberal Arts. In her honor, a classroom is named after Jane. In 2002, at the school's commencement Jane was again recognized for her achievements in education, and given a honorary degree of Doctorate of Pedagogy.

John retired from Mount Greylock in 2003, although he volunteered to help coach the Williams College football and baseball program for a number of years before finally retiring.

After her retirement, Jane, not one to be idle, became a Williamstown selectman for twelve years. Serving under a Town Manager, the group was instrumental in helping to create affordable housing in Williamstown. The impetus began when many residents of the upscale Spruces Mobile Park were displaced when the park was destroyed by Hurricane Irene. The elected officials also supported the repurposing of several mills for additional local housing.

The Spruces site, no longer useable for housing, has become Town property and is a walking/dog park. John and Jane walk there almost every day.

In 2006, "because of excellence and service to the Town of Williamstown," Jane was honored by Williamstown residents and presented the Faith R. Scarborough Award. It was noted additionally, "You made an extraordinary effort to ensure each student received the best education possible . . . ."

The couple, now retired, are well known in their community, and appreciation runs deep for their forty years of service. They are genuine role models.

Since retirement, John occasionally plays golf and meets daily with his cronies, often for coffee at the Tunnel City coffee shop on Spring Street. John, Jane, and the girls often celebrate family reunions and have visited Alaska, Denver, Rhode Island, and Florida. Family has been everything. Jane notes, "John visited my mother every day when she was in the nursing home next to the high school recovering from a stroke. He'd spend the noon time pushing her wheelchair or sitting and talking with her on the porch."

Kindness in this community is constantly being paid forward.

"Probably one of the kindest things anyone has done for John," recalls Jane, "is honoring him with the naming of the football field at Mount Greylock. It was a persistent effort on the part of his players coupled with the efforts of parents of his former players . . . . It was a true labor of love!"

JOHN BARRETT III

Massachusetts State Representative John Barrett is one of the most well-known public figures in Berkshire County, where he served as mayor of North Adams for a record twenty-six years and is currently the area's representative to the Massachusetts Legislature as the State Representative for the 1ˢᵗ Berkshire District. During his forty-five years in public service, he earned a reputation as someone who sets and accomplishes his goals. Hardly soft spoken, at times he is known to play hardball when it comes to getting things done. Juxtaposed with those attributes is his deep caring for the City of North Adams, his Berkshire County constituency, and all those he represents.

Leadership skills were first shown during John Barrett's senior year of high school when he was elected captain of the Mount Greylock baseball team. His coach, John Allen, was one of the first to recognize John's leadership ability. John was known in high school to be less than a serious student. Long after John graduated, his former coach would often say he was one of his best team captains. This was no small praise coming from a renowned coach like John Allen. On more than one occasion, Coach Allen would become involved in one of John's campaigns, including the 2017 race for state representative.

This early leadership position kicked off many years of service as a storied public servant, working on countless boards and commissions. Most likely, John has held more elected and appointed positions than anyone else in the history of Berkshire County. He was recently reappointed to a second term on the MCLA Board of Trustees, his alma mater. During his long career, many from around the state have sought his advice.

John was born in Bennington, Vermont, on May 16, 1947. His parents were John Barrett Jr., formerly of Lawrence, Massachusetts, and Venice Lee Fressola of North Adams.

His paternal grandparents, John and Bridget Barrett, emigrated from County Cork, Ireland, in the early 1900s. He never knew his grandparents, both of whom died prior to his father's twelfth birthday.

Maternal grandparents Michael and Marguerite Fressola hailed from Naples and Atena Lucana, a small, Southern Italian town near Salerno. The two met after arriving in the United States, married in Manhattan in 1909, and moved to Williamstown, where Michael owned a cobbler shop on Spring Street and Marguerite raised their children and also cleaned houses.

John's father, John Jr., worked as the second chef at the Paradise restaurant in Bennington before the family moved to Williamstown in 1953 when his parents purchased the Dinner Bell restaurant in the Colonial Shopping Center. After three years, his father sold the restaurant and returned to Bennington, buying the New Englander restaurant. The restaurant was beloved for its curb service, popular in the 1950s and 60s. After two years, he sold the New Englander and purchased the former Rosa Restaurant in North Adams. The purchase meant a lot to John's father since he first worked at the Rosa when he arrived in North Adams in 1938.

Over the next seven years, John's mother and father owned and operated Lyn's restaurant on the south side of North Adams' Main Street, across from the Boston Store. The long, narrow space had thirty-five stools (no booths) and during busy hours was crowded with employees from Hunter Machine, Sprague Electric, *The Transcript,* and others who worked downtown. Often, hopeful diners would stand behind a stool waiting for a turn to eat, an efficient business model.

John began working at Lyn's in the seventh grade and continued for the next seven years. Despite his young age, with double sessions at school, he was able to work two years from 6:00 to 10:00 a.m., waiting on customers, placing orders, washing dishes, and anything else needed by his dad. It was a transitional time for him as he learned much about the people of North Adams. Though not always happy about getting up early for work, he is the first to acknowledge he learned a great deal about the people who came into his father's restaurant.

What he admired most about the people he met was their commitment to making sure their children had opportunities that they never had, especially getting a good education. He never forgot those hardworking men and women. Throughout his political career, he made sure they had a voice and always considered how his decisions would impact their lives.

His dad started having traditional holiday meals for those in need or lonely. At Christmastime, he would cook turkeys at his restaurant downtown and then bring them to the American Legion. He, along with the Legion commander Bill Callahan, started the Annual Christmas Day Dinner in the early 1960s with just one turkey. At its peak, over six hundred Christmas dinners were served. To this day, the American Legion continues to host the annual dinner. On Thanksgiving, his father would open his restaurant to the needy for breakfast and then provide a bag lunch.

It's a little-known fact, but John's parents wanted to name the restaurant after one of their children. His mom decided that "John" had a bathroom connotation, so it became Lyn's, dropping one "n" of his sister's name to fit on the neon sign.

The popular restaurant was razed during urban renewal. John's dad continued to work as a chef both at Williams College and the Richmond Hotel.

Another memorable job for John was caddying at the Taconic Golf Course in Williamstown. He carried golf bags, shagged golf balls, worked the driving range, cleaned clubs, hustled carts, shined shoes, and worked in the pro shop. "Growing up" on the course allowed him to meet people from all walks of life, the rich, the famous, and not-so-famous. Over the years, he had the opportunity to play with many celebrities including Luis Tiant, the famous Boston Red Sox pitcher, and George Shultz, the former U.S. Secretary of State, as well as many others. His most enjoyable time has been playing golf with friends he grew up with at Taconic.

FAMILY LIFE

Family vacations were few and far between in the restaurant business. When his parents owned the New Englander, they were able to take time off during the winter months. His parents wanted both him and his sister to visit historic locations and learn about their country. Twice in the late 1950s, they took three weeks in February and drove to Florida, which meant traveling up and down the East Coast, visiting historic places such as Monticello, Williamsburg, Mount Vernon, St. Augustine, and the nation's capital, touring its monuments. John felt these visits to Washington kicked off his interest in politics.

The high-water mark of their vacation was visiting the Red Sox training camp in Sarasota, Florida, and mingling with the ball players. They enjoyed days of watching practices and exhibition games. John's sister, Lynn, got Ted Williams to autograph a baseball. One notable impression from the Sarasota trips was the blatant discrimination shown to Black ballplayers who could not travel on buses with white players or stay in the same hotels, and were required to use separate bathrooms and water fountains.

Family suppers were often dictated by which restaurant his parents owned. When his parents owned the Dinner Bell, the family ate together on Tuesday nights. His dad did most of the cooking, and usually it was hot dogs and baked beans. With an Irish father, one would expect meals with meat, potatoes, and vegetables; however, those meals were reserved for holidays. Fish was also another entree his dad loved to cook. He also had a specialty of Welsh rarebit, a favorite of neither John nor his sister.

His mother's side of the family specialized in Italian fare. Sometimes Uncle Jerry would bring over some homemade Italian sauce when he made a batch, but their dad always felt his meals were better and had more protein. John's favorite meal was his grandmother's special tomato sauce, brewed for twelve hours and served with fresh-made raviolis and pastry. John's grandmother played an important role in his upbringing but unfortunately passed away when he was twelve years old.

Both parents strongly encouraged getting a college education. His mother would often say to him, "They can take everything away from you except an education." As children of immigrants, John's dad finished the eighth grade and his mom high school, yet both parents were business-savvy, well-read, and often suggested that the best job would be a teacher with the benefit of having summers off.

Growing up, sports were the center of John's life. As a youngster, he was always around a ball field playing or attending games. His parents always knew where he was in the afternoons: at the ball field or in the gym. At ten, he finagled his way into managing Williamstown High School sports teams. John was active in sports, although baseball was his favorite. He loved playing Little League and Babe Ruth baseball.

The highlight of playing Little League was the night the famous Hall of Famer Yankee Joe DiMaggio showed up at one of his games. Randy Trabold, *The Transcript*'s renowned photographer and a good friend of John's father, had arranged the amazing visit and took a picture of Joe giving John bunting tips. It was quite an evening. John still remembers how nice Joe was with all the kids, making sure each got an autograph.

The young Barrett, getting tips from the great Joe DiMaggio.

John graduated from Mount Greylock High School in 1965. With his mom still encouraging a teaching career, he enrolled at North Adams State College, where he received a bachelor's degree in education in 1969 (BSE) and later a master's degree in education in 1973. During his time at college, he was elected President of the Student Government and awarded the Distinguished Student Community Award.

After graduation, John spent the next 14 years as an elementary teacher. His first two years of teaching were in the elementary school in Pownal, Vermont, and 12 years at Johnson Elementary School in North Adams. Parallel to his teaching years, John became involved in politics and community service.

In 1971, he worked on Mayor Bianco's successful campaign. The mayor, appreciating John's doggedness, asked him to serve on the Airport Commission. John responded that he had never flown in a plane. The mayor said he wasn't looking for a passenger but someone to get things done. John joined, and later served for two years as chairman of the commission. Under his stewardship, the airport became a vital component of the North Adams economy.

POLITICAL LIFE

In 1972, John was elected, at the age of twenty-four, to the Democratic State Committee, holding the post for twelve years. In 1975, he was elected to the McCann School Board and served eight years, including a term as chairman. In 1976, he was elected to the Berkshire County Commission, which brought many duties. He gathered broad experience as a commissioner within the court system, jails, tourism, and economic development.

In 1983, John was elected mayor of North Adams and became one of the longest-serving mayors in Massachusetts' history, serving for 26 years. For several of those years he held the title of Dean of the Massachusetts Mayors. Being mayor was a high-water mark of his career, a position in which he most felt most comfortable. He enjoyed and felt well-suited to the job. Little did he know how chaotic his first six months in office would be, contending first with a major snowstorm and then a devastating announcement that the city's largest employer, the Sprague Electric Company, was moving its headquarters. Not long afterwards, the company announced it was moving its entire operation out of the city.

With a lot of intense negotiations, Sprague committed to keeping 600 jobs in the city for the next seven years. John later convinced Crane and Company to move into an empty building in Hardman Industrial Park, which eventually employed more than 400 people in the facility.

Not long after John was elected to the mayor's office, he married the former Eileen Chapman. Upon returning from their honeymoon, Eileen was diagnosed with breast cancer. The disease was rapacious over the next few years, and she finally succumbed to it in 1990. At the time, John started the Eileen A. Barrett Foundation, a support group initiated by Eileen that has helped many area cancer patients and their families deal with the terrible disease.

Without Eileen, John, already very busy, threw himself into his work.

ACCOMPLISHMENTS

Leading his numerous accomplishments was the opening of the Massachusetts Museum of Contemporary Arts, known as MASS MoCA. Once convinced of its viability, John fought relentlessly to promote and secure the idea to convert 28 mill buildings totaling 840,000 square feet and fill them with art.

After a fourteen-year effort, the city was able to secure $35 million from the state and transformed old Sprague Electric buildings into a now well-known art mecca that attracts 250,000 visitors a year from around the world. The downtown renaissance also draws millions of dollars in business investments, helping refurbish buildings and establish new restaurants, hotels, and businesses, all while supporting 300 local jobs.

During a Williams College commencement ceremony, the former three-term mayor of New York, Michael Bloomberg, lauded John's bold, persistent efforts to convert an old electronics plant to the nationally known MASS MoCA.

During John's administration, considerable planning and effort went into the much-needed reconfiguration of Drury High School. With state funds secured by John's administration, the

John Barrett, in front of the renovated Drury High School.

$22 million major renovation eliminated an "open classroom model." Updated classrooms with internet connections along with a new band room and auditorium produced an improved learning environment for the Drury students.

John came up with the novel idea of attaching the new Brayton Elementary School to the existing YMCA building, greatly assisting the financially struggling city's YMCA. The efforts, mostly financed by state monies, is credited with saving the city's YMCA, which was on the verge of bankruptcy. The YMCA now has a viable leasing arrangement with the city.

The North Adams Public Library, housed in the well-known Blackinton mansion, was expanded and renovated over 15 months, with a $5 million state grant and private donations. The 10,000-foot addition was creatively added, preserving the building's historical appearance.

The Veterans Memorial Wall project created a new war memorial with a monument and honor roll that lists the names of all local veterans etched in stone, surrounded by a plaza of flags. The project was completed with local and state funds, and it serves as a beautiful gateway to the City of North Adams.

One of John's last acts as mayor was renaming the Vietnam Veterans Skating Rink to the Peter W. Foote Vietnam Veterans Memorial Skating Rink. Pete, a 1965 Drury High School graduate and star athlete, was awarded the Silver Star for rescuing a wounded comrade, and ultimately was the only native of North Adams who lost his life in the Vietnam War. John and Pete were teammates on a local American Legion baseball team. John thought Pete was one of the best all-around athletes to ever graduate from Drury.

The Barrett administration is also credited with bringing the SteepleCats, a collegiate summer baseball team, to North Adams. With the help of Fay Vincent, the former baseball commissioner and a friend of John's, the SteepleCats began playing at Joe Wolfe Field in 2002.

John has always focused on rebuilding the community's sense of pride. He's lived up to his conviction that "in order to attract, you have to be attractive." Efforts to beautify the city included resurfacing streets and sidewalks, building neighborhood play-grounds, and preserving the historic Mohawk Theater as well as the state armory building. He oversaw the construction of Western Gateway Heritage State Park, a restoration project of the city's former railroad yard, listed on the National Register of Historic Places. The Park features exhibits about the area, including the Hoosac Tunnel Museum, which recreates the story of this nine-teenth-century engineering feat.

For two terms, John was president of the Massachusetts Mayors' Association and then served as vice-president for seven-teen years. His participation likely gave North Adams, one of the smallest cities and furthest from the state capital, a larger voice than it might have warranted. It also put him in a position to hear new ideas and quickly adapt them if they would improve his city.

"I'm fortunate to still be in elected office after all these years—being able to help people every day is most rewarding," says John. He readily admits he may not always "be the easiest person to be around." One thing is certain. He is fiercely loyal to the City of North Adams and its residents. As mayor, he was always available, visiting neighborhood organizations, riding on snowplows late in the evening to check on service, and sharing his phone number with everyone.

John is seen by some as strong-willed and determined. His sister, who regards him highly, describes John as a type-A personality who doesn't like to give instruc-tions twice. He's scrappy, independent, driven, decisive, knows what he wants, and "got it from mom," the family disciplinar-ian. Others describe him as brash, stubborn, and hard-fighting, never bashful about rebuking his critics.

Representative Barrett in a recent photo.

John has admitted that "in order to make a good omelet you have to break a few eggs." His skill in setting and accomplishing goals has served the city well. His is a convincing, charming person-ality that can react quickly to situations. In 2009, a local newspaper described him as blunt, sometimes uncompromising, sometimes with an abrasive style but nonetheless one who gets results. *The Transcript*'s Opinion section noted, "tough times call for a tough mayor."

After the mayoral position ended, John consulted with the mayor of Pittsfield for a while, after which the mayor asked him to assume the role of Executive Director of the Berkshire Works Career Center, a position he held for three years. More recently, he was appointed by the governor to serve on the Massachusetts College of Liberal Arts Board of Trustees. Upon reflection, John jokingly calls himself the "accidental state representative." On a number of occasions, he has not sought out political positions but was asked if he would consider running for them, finding himself first as mayor, an office he never aspired to, and then later as a state representative.

In 2017, when State Representative Gailanne Cariddi unexpectantly passed away, he was encouraged to run for the vacant seat. Contemplating running for the office, he remembered that his number-one priority was to help people like those he had served in his dad's restaurant. John decided to run, and was elected 1st Berkshire District State Representative, a willing freshman among 160 representatives. John was reelected in 2018 and again in 2020. He has already fulfilled one of his campaign promises regarding the Greylock Glen project in the Town of Adams. After years of discussion, a $6.5 million grant has been awarded to begin the first phase of construction, which includes the Greylock Glen Welcoming Center.

John has never forgotten the customers he served at Lyn's many years ago and takes pride in knowing that he has been able to serve for over fifty years as "a voice for the people, especially for those not being heard." Each day his work might range from helping a community in his district to working with a constituent with an unemployment issue to assisting citizens trying to navigate state regulations.

During one of John's campaigns for mayor, a North Adams man was standing outside the polling place holding a Barrett sign in the rain. When asked by a bystander why he was standing in the pouring rain, he replied: "John stood up for North Adams when Sprague's pulled out of the city, and he went to bat for all of us in the city, so the least I can do is stand in the rain for him."

A fitting tribute to a longstanding public servant.

DAN BOSLEY

Dan Bosley is most recently known for serving as President of the SteepleCats, the popular collegiate summer baseball team based in North Adams. Prior to the SteepleCats, Dan served twelve terms as State Representative for the 1st Berkshire District, working successfully over a period of twenty-four years on Commonwealth issues as diverse as electricity regulation, MASS MoCA, funding for adult education, and workforce development. His community efforts continue through his work with the New England Clean Energy Council and with Soldier On, a non-profit organization that provides need-based housing to veterans and other organizations.

When I first contacted Dan, he spoke of three "heroes" in his life that he admired and who had influenced him. The first was San Francisco ball player Willie Mays, in Dan's opinion one of the best center field-ers to ever play the game. Willie's zest for the sport, positive attitude, and extraordinary ability always resonated with Dan, even more so later in life when he learned of Mays' struggles with adversity.

The second was singer/songwriter and philanthropist Harry Chapin. Dan met him once at an acoustic concert at Williams College. He and his friends talked with Chapin over a drink at the River House restaurant. Dan thought his music was powerful and encouraged people to get involved and help others. Notably, Chapin cofounded World Hunger Year, an organization dedicated to end hunger and poverty.

But the third, and greatest, influence was his maternal grandfa-ther, Harry Beer, an immigrant from England, and an ardent patriot with whom Dan spent much time. Dan credits the genesis of his interest in others and a life of public service to Harry Beer.

When Dan's paternal ancestors immigrated from Canada in the 1800s, they Americanized their last name, Beausoleil, to Bosley, and so it was that in December 1953, Dan Bosley was born at the North Adams Hospital to Edward William "Pat" Bosley and Dorothy Beer Bosley. Dan was the oldest of three children.

Pat Bosley had been born in Readsboro, Vermont, on March 16, 1931. He was nicknamed Pat because he was born close to St. Patrick's Day. He became a sergeant in the U.S. Army and a Korean War combat veteran. He then worked seventeen years at the Deerfield Glassine in Monroe Bridge and twenty-plus years at several other paper manufacturing companies.

Dan's mom, Dorothy, born in 1928, is still living. She came from a family of seven children, four boys and three girls. Several of her brothers served in World War II. She was always self-assured, somewhat of a free spirit, and never shy about voicing her opinions. She worked in production at Greylock Mills and Sprague Electric for some years and married Pat Bosley in 1950.

When Dan was nine, his parents separated, and he seldom saw his father the rest of his life. Dorothy was left with three children, ages nine, five, and three. She worked tirelessly, supporting the family through odd jobs, often cleaning, and at one point completed a certified nurse's aide program at McCann Technical School, then worked at local assisted-living homes.

While money was always tight, Dorothy continued to be resolute and upbeat. She was an avid supporter of Drury High School, enjoyed writing letters to the editor of the local newspaper, and crafted poetry in her spare time. At one point in her seventies, she worked as a tour guide on Mount Greylock. She drove a car well into her eighties.

Dan's maternal grandparents were Harry and Estelle (Stella) Phillips Beer. Harry was born in Cornwall, England, in November 1887. After emigrating from the U.K., he worked as a stationary engineer at the Greylock Division of the Berkshire Fine Spinning Associates in North Adams. Stella, born in Victory Mills, N.Y., in 1895, traces her heritage back to the *Mayflower*. The couple met in North Adams, married in 1915 in Bennington, Vermont, and lived in North Adams most of their lives. They had seven children and were married 63 years when Estelle passed away in 1979. Harry followed her with his passing in 1985.

When Dan was growing up, he was fascinated with his grandfather, who was by then in his seventies. Harry would regale him with stories about the majesty of England, his native land. Repeating the oft-used cliché, "the sun never sets on the British Empire," he could remember when England ruled 25 percent of the world's population. More importantly, he would tell Dan how proud he was to be an American and how pleased he was to be able to own his home in this land of opportunity.

Dan remembers that Harry had no middle name. As an example of Harry's patriotic fervor, when he read somewhere that Harry S. Truman did not have a middle name but was given an initial by his parents, Harry Beer likewise began using an S.

Harry had encyclopedic knowledge, and Dan felt he could always go to him for answers about anything. They would meet at Harry's tool shed that also became Dan's fortress/hideaway and talk about history and ancestry. Harry would show Dan how various tools worked and entertain him with stories from his collection of U.S. history books. Harry, who had always been inquisitive and fascinated by knowledge, kept little spiral notebooks to record his learnings. The notebooks reveal a diversity of topics, ranging from what's the best type of soil to grow certain plants to how to build a stone wall. To this day, Dan treasures Harry's notebooks.

Dan's maternal great-grandparents, who brought Harry to the United States, were Samuel and Mary Jane Beer. Samuel had been a miner in England and died shortly after his arrival in the U.S. from black lung disease. His widow, Mary Jane, opened a boardinghouse and eventually married one of her guests, Louis Lacatelli, who had emigrated from Italy.

Other than faint childhood memories of his paternal grandparents William and Myrtle "Pit" Bosley, Dan only saw his grandfather once later in life, although he was able to reconnect with his aunts and uncles on that side of the family. William worked as a laborer at the Deerfield Glassine Company until his retirement and managed a 150-acre farm. Myrtle passed away in 1973 at the age of 58, and William followed in 1978 at 69 years of age.

GROWING UP

Most of Dan's life was spent in the Town of Florida, Massachusetts. He attended Monroe Bridge Elementary School in first grade, where there were two people in his class. It was then on to Mark Hopkins for second grade, and he transferred to Florida Consolidated School for third and fourth grades, Houghton Elementary for fifth grade, and finally back to Florida Consolidated for middle school. Often, class sizes were under ten children.

When Dan was nine years old, their rented house caught fire in the middle of the night. He, his mom, and his sister were sleeping upstairs. The fire blocked the front stairway exit and the family frantically proceeded down the back stairway, only to find the door locked. Dan, who always seemed to have his baseball bat and glove with him, with great presence of mind quickly broke the window with his bat, draped a blanket over the glass and the family escaped. The house was destroyed, and the family spent several days searching for a new residence.

Dan spent most of his time outdoors when he was growing up. He and his friends rode their bikes everywhere. At an early age, they would ride from the Hoosac Tunnel section of Florida to Monroe and back, a distance of five or six miles. They spent many hours in the woods camping and hiking, often leaving home on Saturday and returning Sunday. Their life consisted of tents, blankets, campfires, and a transistor radio to listen to the Red Sox. Food was often provided by Steve, who worked at the local Burger Chef. Out-of-date, reheated, or cold hamburgers were perfect for their overnight trips.

Usually, Dan's younger brother Ron tagged along with the group of chums. They'd make their own baseball diamonds in open fields, swim, and float on rubber rafts in the nearby Deerfield River or the Sherman Dam in Monroe. They loved to walk along railroad tracks and explore the nearby old soapstone mine.

Dan, being the eldest, was often responsible for Ron, especially when their mom was working. When Dan coached at the YMCA, Ron was right there beside him. Once when hiking, Ron was attacked by a German Shepherd. Dan chased the dog away, wrapped Ron's bloody head, and brought him to the hospital for stitches. Dan was twelve and Ron was six years old.

They shared a bedroom, so Ron knew how much Dan loved his DC and Marvel comics, and it was no secret that he was a fanatical Batman fan. His caped Batman outfit and autographed pictures were prized possessions. As they grew older, on Sunday nights they would secretly listen and laugh uproariously to the *Dr. Demento* comedy show on their transistor radio.

FAMILY LIFE

With Dan's mom often working, Harry and Estelle, his grandparents who lived in North Adams, would often babysit. That was fine with the kids. Grandpa had a great sense of humor, and Grandma loved to cook. She made great chicken and dumplings, and her strawberry rhubarb and hand-picked blueberries made delicious pies. Estelle also made birthday cakes for each grandchild. When not cooking, she was always ready for a card game of Pitch.

While the family didn't share a lot of meals, their mom made her own spaghetti sauce and meatballs and also made an English meal called "pasty," a delicious, crusted meat and potato pie. There were few lengthy family vacations, although several times they boated and picnicked at their aunt's cottage at Lake Winnipesaukee in New Hampshire.

Dan's first job was working for the Town of Florida at age thirteen. He was on the road crew, clearing brush from the roadways. He also cleaned a nearby church and did odd jobs at Whitcomb Summit.

He attended Drury High School for four years and enjoyed managing the three athletic teams: baseball, basketball, and football. He belonged to the Future Scientists of America and fondly remembers a trip to Mexico to study Mayan ruins. He played the bass drum in the band his sophomore year.

Dan and his friend Steve were announcers for the Drury High School radio station. The air waves couldn't project far beyond school property, but they enjoyed playing promotional music. The radio booth was located over the stage, which put them in a position to help the musical stage crew.

During high school, Dan began working at Bear Swamp, a hydroelectric construction project on Florida Mountain. He worked for a security agency, driving a truck, standing guard, and even once directing traffic. When not working, he'd find time to hang out at McDonald's, go to the drive-in, bowl, or play his much-loved baseball on the nearby North Adams State College fields.

Dan graduated from Drury High in 1972. He matriculated at North Adams State College (Massachusetts College of Liberal Arts) and declared an English major for one semester before changing to history and political science. His grandfather's influence and the charged political times of the 1970s made the choice easy.

During college, he continued to work at Bear Swamp. When that job ended, he found employment as a janitor with Excelsior Printing. In his free time, he played flag football and intramural basketball and always made time for a pick-up baseball game. Dan graduated in 1976 with a bachelor's degree in history and political science.

CAREER

Dan's first full-time job was selling cars for Shapiro Chevrolet and Oldsmobile on Union Street in North Adams. Shapiro's sent him to "sales school" in Framingham, and the courses on closing deals and reading body language have been helpful throughout his career.

From the late 1970s to the early 1980s, Dan helped manage a tool-and-die business and led a sales organization that became involved with government contracts. In 1983, he was appointed Executive Director of the Northern Berkshire Development Corporation and also served on the North Adams City Council. This was the beginning of his involvement in politics. Dan also recalls working on John Barrett's 1982 campaign for state representative.

In 1986, Dan ran and won the state representative seat for 1st Berkshire District and served in that role for the next twenty-four years. During his twelve two-year terms, he won three elections and ran unopposed nine times. Dan describes this as his "best job." He loved "being in the room" where decisions are made that help people's lives. He also proudly noted that the Massachusetts House of Representatives "is the oldest continuous elected democratic body in the Western hemisphere."

As Representative Bosley, he worked at the State House on Beacon Hill in Boston, a three-hour commute from North Adams. As a freshman, he found his office to be a "bull-pen like" conference room with two used desks, one aide, and little privacy.

Early on, he travelled back and forth to North Adams two and three times a week. With formal sessions on Mondays through Wednesdays and planning sessions on Thursday, it wasn't long before he found a nearby studio apartment. He would leave North Adams for Boston on Sunday night, returning Thursday evening or Friday morning to meet with local constituents. There were often casual meetings on the weekends, whenever people would seek him out.

Much of the allotted salary and per diem was absorbed by meals, apartment rent, and travel. Dan usually would drive his car for about two years before high mileage necessitated a trade-in. During the commuting years, he drove Fords, Mercurys, and a few Toyota RAV4s.

As legislative and committee responsibilities grew, Dan's office accommodations improved; eventually he had ten staffers and a number of college interns supporting his efforts.

In the early 1990s, Dan was appointed to the important Joint Committee on Labor and Workforce Development. His responsibilities included discussion and work on unemployment issues and best practices for job creation. His knowledge and experiences quickly found him in demand by other countries, and various groups supported trips to South Africa, Mexico, Israel, China, and Canada to discuss economic and job development prospects.

Twice he went to Russia and another time to Brazil. In Russia, on an exchange program, he taught classes at a local university.

Dan was appointed to chair the Joint Committee on Government Regulations in the mid-1990s. This central position required almost all state regulations to pass through his committee, providing him the opportunity to meet a broad swath of elected officials and work with them across multiple issues.

Government regulations work could be as mundane as determining barber and liquor licenses, but the chairman who appointed Dan

Dan Bosley speaking at a trade forum in China.

wanted him to focus on electricity regulations and the questions surrounding native tribes' interest in gambling casinos. Dan's work within the electrical industry determined that high costs were due to an aging structure, little encouragement on increasing capacity, and the restricted ability to pay off improvements. After months of efforts and research, the committee wrote one of the nation's first electrical restructuring bills that encouraged competition. The increased capacity reduced consumer electrical costs by 15 percent in the first two years after the bill was introduced.

Work on the casinos required diligent research and travel to determine the best outcome. He wrote a detailed paper on the pros and cons of the introduction of casinos and submitted it. For most of his tenure, casinos were voted down by the representatives, then finally passed toward the end of his appointment.

During Dan's time as a representative, he received his master's degree in public policy from the University of Massachusetts, as well as several fellowships. In 2001, he was awarded an Honorary Doctor of Laws from his alma mater, MCLA.

Dan likes to say his twenty-four years in office were "book-ended" by several significant events. As a freshman, it was the successful passing of a bill that provided $35 million for the creation of the future MASS MoCA. Before leaving office, it was obtaining $55 million for the new MCLA laboratory. He is also most proud of his involvement in the 1993 Education Reform Bill that created $4 million in funding for a state-wide literacy program. The bill gave a network of institutions across the state capital support for reading encouragement, obtaining general equivalency degrees, and English as a Second Language (ESL) programs. Over the years, realizing the bill's effectiveness, under Dan's watchful eye, its budget has grown to $30 million.

Dan Bosley and his daughter Stephanie share a few moments with the late U.S. Congressman John Lewis.

Aside from the many bills Dan has written or supported, he's pleased by what might be considered minor accomplishments to some people, like the installation of a traffic light at the intersection near the Pedrin's Dairy Bar on Curran Highway. After several motor vehicle fatalities, there have been no fatalities there in the twenty-plus years since the light was installed.

THE STEEPLECATS

After leaving office in 2011, Dan was selected to be President of the North Adams SteepleCats, a local member of the New England Collegiate Baseball League. The North Adams *Transcript* noted the Cats "couldn't have done better than to call in Dan Bosley from the bullpen to take over during its 10th anniversary season."

"An avid baseball fan, [Bosley] brings vast knowledge of the region and its players, and the know-how to get things done," wrote *The Transcript*.

Dan's lifelong love of baseball was now able to manifest itself in working with the Cats, helping field a great team, providing entertainment for residents, and displaying talented college players as an example to kids of the possibility of reaching the big leagues. The Cats fielded between twenty-five and thirty major-league aspiring players each year, most often college freshman, sophomores, or juniors. Ten of the Cats' players have moved on to the majors.

Although his duties were primarily administrative from mid-April to the end of July, he found himself almost always at Joe Wolfe Field, whether working with the concession volunteers, obtaining the necessary licenses, making sure the field was in good shape, or painting the stands.

Off-field, and before the playing season, he worked hard on fundraising, searching for housing for coaches and broadcasters, helping volunteers, and finding and supporting host families for players. He was responsible for players' paperwork and yearly updates on concession merchandise (T-shirts, hats, balls, bats, etc.). He also needed to secure interns from local colleges to clean the stands and help with game scripts for the broadcaster.

It was a family effort: Laura, Dan's wife, spent many nights cooking hot sausages and other items for the concession stand, which she helped run for a number of years. Dan enjoyed meeting Craig Biggio, the former second-baseman with the Houston Astros, now a Hall-of-Famer. Biggio's son had an opportunity to play for the SteepleCats. Dan treasures an autographed picture taken with Craig.

Two of the SteepleCats' biggest fans, Craig Biggio and Dan Bosley, at the ballpark.

About the same time Dan became the SteepleCats President, he started the Dan Bosley Consulting Service, counseling clients on a variety of government and program issues, including budgetary and funding needs. He works with clean-energy and veteran-housing groups and has consulted on establishing a World War II museum.

Dan chairs the Board of Trustees for MountainOne Financial, a banking, insurance, and financial services company. He attends monthly board and committee meetings involved in auditing, good governance and compliance, credit, and emerging technologies.

At the top of his list of hobbies is watching sports, followed by ancestry research. He has read all of Steven King's novels and enjoys mysteries by David Baldacci. Around the house, Dan landscapes and gardens. He also has a small collection of items from the countries he visited, including Olympic buttons from China and South African tribal masks.

When thinking of the important people in his life, Dan is quick to credit his wife, Laura, for her ongoing, unfailing support at his many events, and he has fond memories of his daughter, Stephanie, accompanying him to the State House as a child, which he believes led to her involvement helping people in need. When I asked this long-serving public leader what were some of the things people had done for *him*, he said, "I remember many of the things that people did for my family when we were poor growing up . . . . [L]ife is full of little kindnesses . . . we just need to take time to recognize them."

STANLEY L. BROWN

From the Model T era until the 21st century, Brown's Garage was where Berkshire families had their cars serviced. Founded just six years after the famous Mohawk Trail opened in 1914, Brown's Garage (and the Brown family) helped travelers and locals continue on their way for nearly a century.

Stanley Brown lives in Drury, a genial little village within the slightly larger town of Florida, Massachusetts. The village was named after Nathan Drury, one of its first settlers and one of the initial donors of the Drury Academy, which became today's Drury High School. The Town of Florida had at the 2010 census a population of 750 people, not too far off from its 1860 census of 645.

Little towns like Florida, but with even smaller populations, form a string of contiguous villages dotting this remote area along picturesque Massachusetts Route 2, known as the Mohawk Trail. Florida shares its zip code of 01247 with North Adams, then there's the town of Drury with 01343, while the nearby villages of Hoosac Tunnel and Rowe share 01367.

The Brown family has been in Berkshire County for at least nine generations and is proud of its heritage. Stanley's great-great-grandfather settled in Florida, Massachusetts, in 1810. A distant relative on his father's side had sailed to America on the *Mayflower*.

Stanley Lincoln Brown was born at the North Adams Hospital on February 12, 1934, President Lincoln's birthday, and Stanley's mother named him accordingly. Stanley's parents, Harold Ellsworth Brown and Sarah Belle (Gifford) had, themselves, been born at home, he in 1899 and Sarah in 1909. They married in 1926 when Harold was twenty-seven and Sarah eighteen. The young couple had seven children, three girls and four boys. They had good luck with holiday birthdays; another child was born on the Fourth of July and yet another on November 11, Armistice Day.

As a young man, Harold had shown a strong interest in cars. He took auto repair correspondence courses, obtained his chauffeur's license, and drove taxis for Grundy's Garage in Williamstown. When the Mohawk Trail was being built, the state purchased some of his grandfather's land, and Harold, spotting an opportunity, purchased a single lot from his father and built a one-stall garage.

Sarah had come from a large farm family of ten children. As a young girl, she worked on the farm and delivered farm products like vegetables, beef, pork, and chickens to the stores in North Adams. During World War ll, she worked at the Sprague Electric Company soldering condensers.

Jerome Brown and Mary Ruberg were Stan's paternal grandparents. Jerome was born at home in Florida, Massachusetts, and Mary in Colrain, Massachusetts, sometime after the Civil War. Jerome was a blacksmith, farmer, and teacher; Mary was a homemaker. They had seven children, six boys and one girl. Stan's maternal grandparents were Jessie and Abbie Gifford. Jessie was a farmer and sold firewood. Abbie was a homemaker.

Stan's parents initially lived in a modest house across from the garage where they had a small vegetable garden, raised laying hens for eggs and meat plus hogs for slaughter. Later, the couple purchased and moved to a nearby farm where they had dairy cattle and grew potatoes, squash, pumpkins, beans, carrots, and beets. His mom could often be seen boiling and canning meat and vegetables in her many Mason jars.

Stanley attended one of Florida's five one-room schoolhouses, walking to and from school. His family lived nearby in a house his dad built close to the garage. Some years later, they moved to a larger farmhouse. Stan remembers as a little kid how they butchered pigs in the fall when it was cool. Once killed, the animal's carcasses were lifted up and put in large kettles of scalding water, which helped remove their coarse hair. Eventually meat was salted and stored in a crock in the cellar.

THE TRAIL BEGINS, BROWN'S GARAGE THRIVES

In 1914, local residents were pleased to see the Mohawk Trail being built. Initially, it was not a hard surface, yet it was much better and smoother than the dirt roads at that time. In the late 1920s, the Trail was widened and given a hard-topped surface. Crushed stone, excavated from the central shaft of the famous Hoosac Tunnel, was used as a base, and the surface was tarred.

In the mid-1930s, the State assumed winter upkeep. Prior to that, the steepest part of the road from Florida to the Western Summit had been shoveled by hand and often remained closed for long periods of time. Now there was a concerted effort to keep the road open year-round. Initially, the Mohawk Trail ran from Greenfield to Williamstown, a distance of forty-five miles. During the era of Brown's Garage, it was extended an additional 24 miles to include the Town of Orange. The Trail's beautiful scenery became a magnet for tourists and provided plenty of business for the Browns.

Harold opened Brown's Garage in 1920 and operated it for the next twenty-six years. In 1947, he sold it to his brother-in-law, Frank Gifford, who operated the garage for another twenty-five years, until 1972. At that time, Frank sold the station to Stanley, who operated it until the garage closed in 2003. All in all, it enjoyed over eighty years of family ownership.

At ten years old, Stan began working in his dad's garage. His chores were menial, but he loved it. He filled water and oil cans, scraped carbon off engine heads, cleaned parts with solvent, and went to the nearby brook, in back of the garage, to immerse flat tires in water and look for leaks. He also tended a long line of cars needing water for their radiators.

Stan had daily farm work, too, and earned extra money working at his uncle's sawmill, shoveling sawdust and stacking lumber. One day, he returned home to find the barn hit by lightning and on fire. He rushed inside, and with his pocketknife cut the leather restraining collars off five calves. Three made it out safely.

When he turned fifteen, he began working for the Town of Florida in the summers, cutting brush with scythes along the town's roads. Stan attended Drury High School, making the one-hour multi-stop trip off the mountain. Often it was his uncle who drove the small, yellow, four-wheel-drive bus. Stan, who always had an eye for vehicles, remembers it was a Dodge power wagon built on a bus chassis, an indomitable piece of transportation for the winter weather.

When Stan turned sixteen, he bought his first car from his cousin for $35, an old 1930 Model A Ford. The black coupe with a rumble seat became his senior-year transportation.

Stanley, as the proud owner of a slightly used Model A Ford.

In high school, Stan was on the Pro Merito Honor Society, President of Nu Sigma academic society in his junior year, the class photographer, and a member of the engineering club. He did not play sports, as there was little time between his ten-mile ride home, chores, and studies.

During high school, he continued working at the sawmill, but his main chores involved feeding and watering the family's cattle and milking cows. In the summer, he delivered milk and produce to restaurants and stores along the Mohawk Trail. In addition, he cut, baled, and stored hay and chopped turnips and rutabagas into animal feed.

The 1951 senior high school yearbook description of Stan reads: "You wouldn't know that Stanley was even in the classroom if you waited to hear from him, but his marks let you know that he is there, for they are always of the highest grade—a very good worker." His

Class Personality describes him as "Most Versatile," referring to his ability with machines, knowledge of woodworking, metal fabrication, and electricity, most of it gained while working with his dad.

Stan was accepted at the University of Massachusetts and attended the agricultural school, receiving an associate's degree in 1953. He enjoyed driving his Model A the fifty miles to the Amherst campus and then to Vermont for his six-month farm internship. At a solid speed of fifty miles an hour, the car was dependable transportation. Always the tinkerer, after using the Model A for four years, he converted it into a "doodlebug" (a homemade tractor) and mowed lawns with it.

After graduation, Stan worked as a carpenter, building homes for several years. He liked the jack-of-all-trades work and learning more about plumbing and electrical at a time when permitting was not required.

In 1956, Stan was drafted into the Army and attended basic training at Fort Dix, New Jersey. He was assigned to infantry and went to Fort Campbell, Kentucky, for parachute training with the 101st Airborne Division. During training, he developed a stress fracture, but the Army doctor said he could still parachute. Disaster struck on his first jump. He landed roughly and broke his right hip at the top of the femur. Hospitalized for six months, he was transferred to Fort Knox and retrained to be a company clerk. Stan was honorably discharged in November 1958.

Although the hip nagged him, he resumed working as a carpenter. During this time, he met Maralyn Domin, a North Adams native. The couple married in 1959 and had two girls and two boys. From the early 1960s until the early '70s, Stan worked for the James Hunter Machine Company in North Adams in the order department.

When he was at Fort Knox, Stan had taken flying lessons on weekends. After discharge, he took more lessons at Harriman Airport in North Adams, soloed, and received his private pilot's license in 1968. His obvious next step was to purchase a plane. Photographs show Stanley, a proud owner, standing near his 1939 three-wheeled, single-engine Stinson monoplane, bluish in tone with the white registration number N-21186 stenciled along the fuselage. He sold the Stinson in 1976.

Over the years, Stan flew a Cessna from the airport in North Adams to deliver parts for the Hunter Machine Company to customers in Rhode Island and Connecticut. He was delighted to be flying for work and accruing his required flight time.

ALL IN THE FAMILY

When Stan's uncle decided to retire in 1972, Stan bought Brown's Garage. He felt confident having had the experience of working for his dad, and after some auto correspondence courses and mechanical training while enrolled at UMass, he was ready.

Harold had built the garage in 1920 with the help of his brothers and the use of one of their sawmills. The building was all wood with a concrete floor, and a sloped front-to-back, flat, tarpaper roof. The garage was rebuilt in 1941, and then again in 1964 after it burnt to the ground. The Town's only fire truck was just too far away to get there in time. The building Stan bought was built with cinder-block walls and a sloped, rubber-membraned roof.

The building itself, identified by the large BROWN'S GARAGE sign in front, is small, about thirty-six feet square, with two bays featuring drive-in lifts and manual, spring-assisted, twelve-foot glass-paned overhead doors able to accommodate most vehicles. The only other room is a 12' x 20' office. For most of the time Stanley has owned it, the building has been painted red, white, and blue. The station initially pumped Mobil gas.

Older pictures show a neon Mobil oil sign on the side of the building, with the street side of the garage festooned with signs offering Kendall 1000-mile oil, safe Bowes tire service, and a PAUSE AND DRINK COCA COLA sign. Quarts of Mobil oil stand ready to be called into service in racks on each side of the office door.

When Harold first opened his business, it was at the height of the Model T era, and auto touring was becoming very popular, especially in summer and fall. As the road and cars improved, tourist traffic became more prevalent, and Brown's Garage became a

Stanley and his son, Steven, installing a new Brown's Garage sign, circa 1999.

beacon for thirsty radiators at the top of a long hill. It's hard to imagine, but in the late 1920s before the Trail was being plowed, Stan's father and buddies who wanted to drive to North Adams would shovel a narrow path to the Western Summit to reach the plowed highway.

In the 1920s, '30s and even into the '40s, Harold dealt mainly with adjusting and repairing transmission bands, oil systems, and tire repairs on Model Ts and Model As. In a curious adaptation for the area, some early Model Ts would be modified by replacing the front tires with skis to deliver mail in remote areas like Florida.

As described by Stanley, the early Model Ts had cast-iron engines with a splash-oil system versus an oil pump. Small paddles from the system splashed oil on connecting rods in the cylinders. If a tourist's car was low on oil while climbing the steep hill coming from Greenfield, the connecting rod would burn out in the number-one cylinder. Stan's dad always kept spares.

"It got so he and a helper would team up and work the top and bottom of the engine at the same time and have the motorist back on the road in short order," recalls Stan. After accumulating 100 burnt-out rods, Harold would send them to Springfield to be re-babbitted. Later Model As solved this problem by adding an oil pump. Harold also spent considerable service time adjusting Model T transmission bands that helped brake the car and control its speed. The bands, via certain floorboard pedals, controlled the car's gears, shifting it from low to neutral to high.

During the more than 30 years that Stanley ran the business, his main service work was in replacing brakes, doing tune-ups and working with suspension systems, and installing shock absorbers and springs. Often working alone, he occasionally was assisted by his sons or daughters with repairs or paperwork. Maralyn had the responsibility of picking up replacement parts in North Adams, Pittsfield, Greenfield, or Albany, New York.

Engineering with Empathy

Servicing vehicles evolved over the years from when Stanley helped his father repair flat tires, fill radiators, and tighten bands on Model T transmissions. In the 1970s, Stan was dealing with drum brakes, points, condensers, and distributors, and just prior to retirement, he was replacing disc brakes and needed special diagnostic equipment to work with cars' computer systems.

For many years, Brown's Garage sold Mobil gas, and the company provided outside signage and once painted the garage grey. Stan remembers when gas was $0.19/gallon in 1950, and by 1970 it was $0.40/gallon. Over the years, his profit per gallon ranged from $0.05 to $0.10.

In the 1990s, Mobil relinquished pump ownership to Stan. He installed new pumps and began buying gas from a local distributor. A combination of influences led to his retirement in 2003. His injured hip/pelvis continued to nag him, especially when stretched out on the floor repairing cars in the cold winter weather. It was also challenging complying with costly and time-consuming Environmental Protection Agency requests to upgrade pumps and replace soil contaminated over the many years.

Stan has a trove of good memories helping stranded or desperate drivers. He gleefully recalls taking mice out of air filters or removing seeds, cleverly stashed by a squirrel, from a large Pontiac's heater system. Another time he helped a tourist who had tied his wobbly exhaust system to the drive shaft with a wire, which quickly wrapped around the shaft and pulled apart the entire system.

Sometimes all he needed to offer were kind words when customers would stop at the isolated garage and ask when would they *ever* be out of the wilderness or *please* where was the nearest restaurant. Another time a customer with a flat tire started crying when she found out she had been driving the wrong way on the Trail for many miles and would be awfully late for an appointment.

BEYOND THE GARAGE

Stan continues to stay very busy. He has worked on centennial and bicentennial committees for his church and the Town. He works with Florida's Historical Commission and has become a local authority on the Town's history, giving presentations at the senior center. He has helped to locate graves of the Town's first settlers, scattered about in eighteen different cemeteries, and places gravestone information on the *Find a Grave* website.

For some time, Stan and his family belonged to the Berkshire Gas & Steam Engine Association, a club organized by individuals interested in antique gas and steam engines. They enjoy displaying and working with old engines. The family would attend summer meetings and autumn displays, sometimes trailering a 1932 Farmall or 1942 Ford tractor to the show. On one occasion, they exhibited an engine belonging to an antique drag saw.

Stan always enthused about club members who would make parts for old engines, especially when they could duplicate needed items by using cast parts borrowed from other engines. Mechanics would also make patterns, casting them with aluminum. Stan learned the casting process by using a homemade propane-fired furnace and sand from the nearby Deerfield River. He would take the equipment and materials needed to the club's annual shows and offer to make needed parts for members' exhibits. At one point, he made trivets depicting the association, sold them, and donated the proceeds to the club.

Always patriotic, he dressed up as Uncle Sam at the town's bicentennial celebration and a number of other times, including the local Fall Foliage Festival's 50th anniversary. In 2014, in a parade celebrating the 100th anniversary of the Mohawk Trail, Stan and Maralyn drove a Model T Ford, later donating it to the Model T Ford Museum in Richmond, Indiana, in memory of his father and the Mohawk Trail.

He and Maralyn continue to live on what was his father's farm in a solar-paneled house that Stan built in 1962. His daughters, daughter-in-law, sister, and nephew all live nearby in this circular family compound. They all continue to use Brown's Garage to work on their vehicles. After all, it's only a mile away.

Stan's most cherished memory of working at the garage? "How grateful people were to have me fix their car and be able to get back on the road," he recalls, marveling too that through eighty years of service in all types of weather, neither he, his dad, nor his uncle was ever injured. He added, "Best of all, I still have all ten fingers!"

MAGGY BUTTON

A lifelong North Adams native and a cornerstone of the local newspaper where she has worked for over forty-five years, Maggy Button has written hundreds of news articles on northern Berkshire society. As a well-known city editor of The Berkshire Eagle, *she understands, appreciates, and loves the local culture.*

She is a repository of information about people, places to eat, and local culture. She is always willing to share her information. Her news articles are warm, informative, sometimes personal, and almost always contain a touch of her humor. Maggy, as she is known, was born, raised, and educated in North Adams. Except for a brief time at graduate school, she has lived most of her life on Foucher Avenue in the Greylock section of town and worked for *The Transcript* of North Adams and *The Berkshire Eagle*, always editing and reporting on local news.

Margaret Ruth Ebert was born in May 1953 at the North Adams Hospital. An only child, her parents were Harry and Ruth (Kean) Ebert, predominately of German, Welsh, and English ancestry.

Harry was born in 1916 in Stamford, Vermont, and served in the U.S. Army during World War II in the South Pacific with C Company, the 242nd Engineers Battalion. As a corporal, he drove a DUKW, a two-and-a-half ton, six-wheeled amphibious vehicle, helping his team build bridges and roads in the effort to liberate Guam, Okinawa, and the Philippines.

Returning home, he met and married Ruth Kean in August 1946 and worked for Railway Express Agency for thirty-six years. He then worked eleven years for the Simmons Funeral Home as a driver and pallbearer before retiring. Harry was a fifty-year member and past Master of the Masons. He devoted time to Naomi Chapter 17, Order of the Eastern Star, an appendant body of the Masons that focuses on service and charity. He also served as an advisor for the associated girls' social club.

Maggy's mom, Ruth Agnes Kean, was born in 1912 in North Adams. She attended Drury High School, was a homemaker, and worked as a bookkeeper at Aldo's Paint and Wallpaper Store. Ruth was an accomplished organist and played for the Blackinton Union Church, the Simmons Funeral Home, and provided background music for the Kiwanis and Rotary clubs. She was a matron for Naomi Chapter 17 of the Eastern Star and also advised the young girls' club.

She and Harry were married almost forty-six years when they passed away in 1992, less than three months apart.

Maggy's paternal grandparents were Henry Augustus and Nellie (Bishop) Ebert. Henry, who used his middle name Augustus, was born in 1875 in Stamford, Vermont, and worked as a blacksmith for many years, passing away abruptly in 1934. There are several interesting news articles involving Henry, one about a band of traveling gypsies who were arrested for stealing $175 from him.

Nellie, Henry's first wife, was born in 1876 in Readsboro, and married Henry in January 1905 at the Methodist Church. Nellie passed away in 1916 at forty-two years old. She was the mother of their two sons, Carroll and Harry. Henry's second wife, Flora, outlived him and died in 1948.

Maggy's maternal grandparents were Fred and Ida (Wylie) Kean. Fred, born in Williamstown in 1881, lived most of his life in North Adams. He was employed as a foreman at the James Hunter Machine Company for thirty-five years, and he was a lifelong member of the Methodist Episcopal Church. Fred passed away in 1933 at the age of fifty-two.

Ida, born in 1885, emigrated from Germany at six months old with her mother and three sisters. She was employed for many years at Strong-Hewatt & Company in Clarksburg, and was working as a finish seamstress upon her retirement. She was deeply involved in her church, First United Methodist. She served as president of the Ladies Aid Society and was active in the church's choral group. Her prized possession was an amethyst ring presented to her father for rescuing people from a fire in the mid-nineteenth century in Germany. She gave the ring to Maggy before passing away in 1969 at the age of eighty-four.

EARLY LIFE

The Ebert family briefly lived on the corner of Lawrence Avenue and Corinth Street, until Maggy was in the 3rd grade. The family then moved to East Main Street right across from Drury High School and finally settled on Holbrook Street. Ida, her grandmother, stayed with the family and Maggy has fond memories of walking to Ida's sister's house for cookies and ginger ale. Ida also loved listening to the Red Sox on the radio and kept track of the scoring with her homemade scorecards. When Maggy's parents went out, Grandma would babysit and they would watch TV, play board games, dress her paper dolls, and color. It was the only grandparent she knew; how she loved her!

Grandma taught Maggy, at an early age, how to knit. She also passed on to Maggy several of her most delightful recipes, one for Puff candy and another one for gingerbread cookies. When it came time for schooling, the choice was simple: Maggy walked the half-block to Mark Hopkins Elementary School where she attended kindergarten through eighth grade. She and her friends often used its playground to play Wiffle ball, hide and seek, or ride their bikes. At home, she enjoyed her Barbie dolls, a recent introduction by Mattel, and her stamp collection, which she still has today.

On Sundays, her mom played the organ at Blackinton Union Church; Maggy and her dad attended the First United Methodist Church where she enjoyed participating in youth groups from junior high through high school.

With her father and mother involved in the Order of the Eastern Star, Maggy became an active member of an associated group, the International Order of Rainbow Girls. Open to young girls over the age of twelve, the Order offered leadership training and encouraged charity through community service. Years ago, when Maggy was a member, entrance requirements were rigorous by today's standards and not always inclusive.

Maggy attended Drury High School, and her quiet personality limited her involvement in any particular group, although she developed three or four close friends and still sees them today. She was an active member of the Spanish and Pep clubs and coincidentally the newspaper staff. Her most rebellious action was joining a group of student protestors in an effort to raise attention concerning the old school's poor indoor climate conditions. Maggy graduated in 1971.

Following this, she attended Quinnipiac College in Hamden, Connecticut, majoring in physical therapy. After a semester, she was determined to change her major. Missing her hometown, she transferred to North Adams State College, now Massachusetts College of Liberal Arts, and decided to major in English. She was on the newspaper staff throughout college, and this association made her realize how much she enjoyed journalism. She graduated in 1975.

After graduation, Maggy was accepted into Boston University's prestigious Master of Science in Journalism program and completed her degree in 1976. In order to support herself, she worked part-time for the Boston Ballet and for a financial firm. Maggy loved Boston and all of its entertainments, although she continued to miss the quietness of her small town.

CAREER ADVANCEMENT FOR A HOMETOWN GIRL

With her affinity for North Adams, Maggy once said: "I never aspired to work at *The Boston Globe, The New York Times,* or *The Washington Post* . . . I just wanted to come home and work at my hometown newspaper." She had warm memories as a child gazing from the sidewalk into the basement windows of the *Transcript* building when it was located on Bank Street, watching newspapers roll off the old lithograph presses. During the city's urban redevelopment, the paper relocated to American Legion Drive. Interestingly, Maggy has the original "Bank Street" sign proudly displayed in her living room.

Maggy returned home and accepted a part-time job in the *Transcript*'s advertising department in 1976. It wasn't the intrepid reporter's role she was seeking, but at least she was now working for *The Transcript*. At that time, the paper, established in 1843, had been owned by the Hardman family for over seventy years, and it quickly felt like home to her. Several years later, her position became full-time and she found herself immersed in taking ads over the phone, designing special ads for her own customer accounts, and a myriad of other duties.

While working at *The Transcript,* Maggy went on a blind date arranged by a co-worker. She had just broken up with her boyfriend and had no one to take to the *Transcript*'s Christmas party. Maggy was in a fix. With this in mind, she had a trial lunch date at Friendly's on State Road. The December date was successful, and she and Guy Button attended the party. Several years later, in 1981, they were married. Maggy was unaware that Guy had gone home and told his mom, "that's the girl I'm going to marry."

Guy and Maggy soon purchased a home in Greylock and their son, David, was born while they lived there. The family vacationed at Disney World in Orlando from the time David was two years old until high school and usually spent one week in the summer at Hampton Beach, in a roadside motel or a beach cottage. On occasion, they might drive to Ohio to visit with Guy's brother. Both parents were strong supporters of David's athletic activities and spent a lot of time watching swimming competitions and high school football.

After eleven years at *The Transcript*, Maggy was promoted to an editor's position in 1987. She moved to the newsroom. Initially, she was concerned that never holding a reporter's position would be a detriment to editing others' stories. It wasn't, and it hasn't been for the last thirty-four years. Her promotion came about in a curious way. After telling her Managing Editor a number of funny personal stories, he encouraged her to put them in writing. That became Maggy's foray into human interest articles, which she describes as her "whimsy column." The personal stories she told her boss ranged from living within the local airport's landing pattern, her wildly fluctuating home mortgage rate, and even included a story about when Guy lost his job.

After seventy-eight years of family ownership, *The Transcript* was sold in 1976 and has been resold a number of times over the past years as the newspaper industry has contracted with local papers acquired by large chains. In 2014, *The Transcript* was shuttered, and North Adams lost its hometown newspaper. Many employees were transferred to *The Berkshire Eagle*, a longstanding, well respected newspaper based in Pittsfield that now reports the news for North Adams and other northern-area towns.

After being based for many years on American Legion Drive in North Adams, the printing operation of *The Transcript* had been moved to *The Berkshire Eagle* years prior to *The Transcript*'s closure. Maggy moved to the *Eagle*'s newsroom, transferring to the Features Department, and she began commuting to Pittsfield.

© Dennis Pregent, 2021

Maggy working out of her home office, 2021.

Over the years, Maggy wrote hundreds of weekly, bi-weekly, and monthly articles for *The Transcript*, and continues to do so for *The Berkshire Eagle*. She has established herself in newspaper columns on people, recipes, restaurants, bars, wineries, coffee houses, kitchen tips, book reviews, landscaping, weddings, pastries, popcorn, veggies, fruits, and the perfect grilled cheese.

Her kitchen tips column, called "Kitchen Comfort," is all about making things easier in the kitchen. Tips, old wisdom, and tricks-of-the trade make the section indispensable as she writes in a clever manner about things as mundane as coring a head of lettuce, or cleaning pans, or handling leaky faucets. Her articles on food have covered the spectrum, from turkey leftovers, holiday cookies, and dieting to Whoopie pies and bean recipes. They usually include one of her recipes, some how-to instructions, and often a touch of humor.

In her current role as the Assistant Editor of Features, she has written numerous fascinating articles on theater, arts, concerts, and restaurants.

Some years ago, when her husband's employment appeared threatened, Maggy began working part-time at the Big Y supermarket as a cashier. Though at the time it seemed necessary, now the job simply allows her a forum to socialize with familiar customers, reconnect with high school and college friends, meet people from different countries, and gather content for her articles.

Over a four-year span, Maggy suffered two significant setbacks in her life. In 2009, her home, where she had lived for over thirty years, caught fire and the interior was totally destroyed. A local neighbor raised the alarm, and the family barely escaped with the clothes on their backs and a few personal items, including their photo albums.

Much more tragically, in 2013 after thirty-one years of marriage, her husband Guy died from a number of medical complications. She and their son, David, still grieve his absence. Guy was funny, a joker, and always ready with a wisecrack. He often volunteered to be a timer at David's swim meets, or both he and Maggy would help out at T-Ball games.

When asked about the kindest thing that ever happened to her, she quickly remembers the support received from *The Berkshire Eagle* and Big Y after the house fire and when Guy passed away. When their home was destroyed, they lived with close friends for two weeks and neighbors gave them a place to live, rent free, for six months. Other friends purchased items for them, gave donations, and a neighbor set up a fund at a local bank.

COMMUNITY AND HUMAN INTEREST

Maggy continues to write interesting and acclaimed articles for the *Eagle*. One of her more recent stories was an in-depth series of articles on Appalachian Trail hikers who pass through northern

Berkshire. After three months of investigation, interviews, and research, she wrote engaging, personal stories on hikers that traverse the 90 miles of trail that passes through the Berkshires. She interviewed them at nearby grocery stores as they picked up supplies, gave them rides, and on occasion even fed them lunch at her home, causing neighbors to wonder about her strange visitors.

She finds subject matter where most of us wouldn't look. Some time ago, she wrote a story on Drury High School's "Lineman Hat" tradition. Over the years, at the end of the football season, a senior lineman would sign his name on a vintage hat and pass the hat to a hardworking underclass lineman. Maggy decided to research and talk to the people whose names were written on the hat, some as long as sixty years ago.

This great human-interest story became another front-page article in *The Transcript*. Over the years, she has received hundreds of compliments on her articles via phone calls, emails, congratulatory cards, and personal letters.

COURTESY MAGGY BUTTON

Maggy still enjoys knitting and has used her skill to make baby buntings for new parents and assorted mittens, hats, and scarfs for others over the years. More recently she knitted an afghan for herself.

Reading on a broad number of topics is a good hobby for a writer. She is currently reading the *Lord of the Rings* trilogy. Maggy also enjoys cooking and baking, interests inherited

Maggy contemplating her next newspaper article.

from her mother. Some of her specialties are giant cookies with surprise ingredients, meat pies using her mother-in-law's special recipe, potato salad, and Chinese cole slaw. She has a beloved collection of recipes from her mother, mother-in-law, sister-in-law, grandmother, co-workers, and friends.

She enjoys going out with friends and co-workers. Favorite haunts include Renee's Diner for breakfast or lunch, and there is always the historic Norad Mill cafeteria or the Freight Yard Pub.

With one of her closest friends, Susan, she watches *I Love Lucy* reruns. Susan is clearly Lucy, and Maggy has determined she is Ethel. They both love the Christmas season and own collections of Christmas movies. They plan to host a viewing marathon one day.

Susan told me Maggy is enamored with covered bridges, has visited quite a few, and even written an article about them. She hasn't told many people, but one of her fondest wishes is to see a moose someday. And, by the way, she loves white wine and dark chocolate.

In my conversations with Maggy, it was easy to see why her friends describe her as bubbly yet shy, occasionally direct, hard-working, sometimes a procrastinator, and always a faithful friend. Maggy's personality and accessible writing style have produced hundreds of extraordinary articles over the past forty-five years for thousands of grateful readers of *The Transcript* and *The Berkshire Eagle*.

GEORGE CANALES

It wouldn't be an exaggeration to call George Canales Northern Berkshire's "Mr. Baseball." For almost three decades he coached the McCann Technical School baseball team, the Hornets, and co-founded the well-known, ever popular LaFesta Baseball Exchange.

Born George Albert Canales on November 12, 1944, in Somerville, Massachusetts, George was the youngest of five boys born to Cecilio and Cordelia (Lefavre) Canales. His family lived on Washington Street right next door to Harvard University.

Cecilio, George's father, was a world-renowned baker, having crafted three of President Kennedy's birthday cakes. He emigrated in the early twentieth century from Spain, where his father and three brothers raised bulls for the arena. Cordelia was born in Williamstown, Massachusetts.

George's siblings, Rudy, Junior, Richie, and Dan, were born over a ten-year time span. Tragedy struck the family early when three-year-old Junior, just when his mom's back was turned, pulled a boiling kettle off the stove and was scalded to death. Some years later, when George was ten years old, his father abandoned the family. Cordelia and the four boys travelled by train from Boston to Williamstown to live with her parents. George's memories of his dad are vague and fragmented.

George attended Williamstown Grammar School, and his life revolved around sports, playing at the Youth Center on Cole Avenue with his buddies John, Butch, and Harry. They could be found either on the basketball court, playing pool, or out back playing "pick-up" baseball.

He attended Mount Greylock Regional High School, lettering in the three major sports: football, basketball, and baseball. Few people know that in the eighth grade, just shy of six feet tall and lightning fast, he was recruited by Mount Greylock's high school football coach to play their home games. George played the split-end position on the football varsity squad for four years, three years of varsity basketball, and was on the varsity baseball team his final two years.

With their dad gone, George's oldest brother Rudy attended all of his home or away games, and in many ways became a surrogate father, someone George loved and respected. When George was a teenager, Rudy asked him to help him coach his baseball team, and George attributes this experience to his future coaching aspirations.

Between school and sports, he found time to stock shelves and bag groceries at Eddie's Supermarket on Cole Avenue. George graduated from Mount Greylock in 1964 and worked for several years at General Cable as a laboratory technician. He also enlisted in the National Guard, though during basic training he aggravated a football injury and was medically released from service.

It was during this time period that he met and married Nancy Fulginiti. Nancy was born on September 15, 1946, at the North Adams Hospital to Samuel and Mae "Betty" (O'Neill) Fulginiti. Samuel worked many years at the Cornish Wire Company in Williamstown and Mae worked at the Sprague Electric Company. It was often said in jest that her Italian father and Irish mother made for a fiery combination.

Nancy and George met for the first time in the summer of 1966 at the local teenage gathering spot, the parking lot at Friendly's Ice Cream on State Road. Nancy and her friends loved to go there for ice cream and coincidentally they knew many of the guys that hung out there with their "hot" cars.

George and Nancy were married on July 22, 1967, at Saint Anthony's Church in North Adams (now known as Saint Elizabeth of Hungary). They currently reside in North Adams and have three children and six grandchildren.

George had a thirty-three-year career at the General Electric Company in Pittsfield. He worked as a shipper and dispatcher in the transformer division, and in his last six years, he was assigned to naval ordnance assembly. In 2000, General Electric's ongoing workforce reduction eliminated George's position. Not ready to retire, he began working locally in the Museum of Contemporary Art's maintenance department until retiring in 2007.

LOVE OF THE GAME

George has been an official scorekeeper for over twenty-five years for boys' and girls' basketball games and also serves on the McCann School Committee. George coached the McCann junior varsity baseball team for several years and the varsity baseball team for twenty-three years, from 1985 to 2008. He still helps his son coach a Northern Berkshire Youth League team.

McCann's baseball team was the Hornets. They wore white uniforms with green lettering for home games and green uniforms with yellow lettering for away games. Pre-season practices and try-outs were held at the field beside McCann Technical School. One player remembered "the field was a little bumpy and rocky but we kicked the rocks away." Games were played from April through June, with home games at Joe Wolfe Field.

Early in the program there wasn't a lot of interest in baseball. The small school played against local large public schools like Hoosac Valley, Drury, and Pittsfield High, often getting trounced. When their schedule was adjusted and the school began playing against other regional/vocational schools, the team became more competitive. As one player said early on, "If you tried out for the team, you made the team." As the team began winning, securing a spot became more difficult.

George's love of the game and working with kids was motivating to him. This was fortunate considering the effort George expended, working from 7:00 a.m. to 3:30 p.m. at GE in Pittsfield, then quickly travelling more than 20 miles to McCann for daily afternoon practices or games. George's time was so constricted that he would go to work early, stay late, or work on weekends to ensure he could make games and practices, even using vacation days when necessary.

The season's ten home and ten away games plus practices made for a busy season. On out-of-town game nights, George got home around 9:00 p.m. from a day that started at 5:00 a.m. For their considerable efforts, most coaches received a stipend of $1,000 to $1,500 annually. As one former player noted, "Coach Canales was always there for practices. When we got to the gym he was already there. His office *was* the gym. If you needed to talk to him, he would just meet you away from the group."

The team's regional games required the Hornets to travel by bus to towns and cities up and down the scenic Mohawk Trail. They competed against schools such as Pioneer Valley, Frontier, Mohawk Regional, and Athol High School. Out-of-town games meant one-to-two-hour drives in a faded yellow bus.

Over the years, George's coaching style emerged as *instructive*. While not a strict coach, he said, "When I talked, players needed to listen, and when they talked, I needed to listen." He said that he focused on "what needs to be done and how to do it correctly—harping or screaming at players does not work." One of his fellow coaches said, "George is a player's coach. He is most excited about teaching kids the game, helping them improve and develop."

Although he does not talk a lot about wins and losses, anyone will tell you he is competitive. He had his players run through plays until everyone understood. He strived for players' continued improvement, his patience tested by those not paying attention. One player said, "We knew when he was upset when he argued with the umpire or became quiet and started pacing back and forth in front of the dugout."

George Canales' trophy room, dedicated to a life of coaching, includes baseballs from decades of LaFesta games.

On occasion, he would throw his hat in the dirt, objecting to an umpire's questionable call.

When players made mental mistakes, he would encourage them to "shake it off" and not let one error affect the rest of the game. He had a reservoir of patience as long as his players were giving 100 percent effort. Others noticed that he treated his players as though they were his kids.

George's team practices were always evolving. He would research what good teams were doing and was always willing to try something new, especially if it would stimulate practices. Several of his favorite drills were pitching miniature Wiffle balls to players to hit with a broomstick, then switching to a regulation-size baseball and bat, which in contrast seemed the size of a beach ball, improving the team's hitting prowess.

Often, he would have eight players on one side of the field throw to eight players on the other side of the field. With six to eight balls in the air, one needed to be quick and always alert. His over-the-shoulder drill had a person stand behind the batter and throw a ball over his shoulder so the batter could hit it on the descent. He thought it important to keep players engaged through batting practice, fielding exercises, and base running drills.

After coaching all these years, George has plenty of anecdotes. Once, his scrappy team with a tall, strong pitcher almost beat another regional school in a home game. The visitor's pitcher was being scouted by the big leagues, who were at the game to judge his performance. McCann narrowly lost in a 2-1 ballgame. The close outcome must have irritated the opposing coach. Next time, just before their arrival, that coach used a bulldozer to level the pitcher's mound, trying to take away any advantage the Hornets might have. George complained to the umpire and the mound was rebuilt. It took two hours to bring back the dirt and stamp the mound down, but the field was restored. The Hornets still lost.

Sometimes the team played on less than optimum turf. One away game was delayed for over an hour because a farmer's tractor had broken down. Once fixed, he was able to cut his corn, which was outfield. Another time, the team was relegated to playing on top of a former landfill, running uphill from first to second base.

Away games usually included a stop on the way home at a

fast-food restaurant, often Taco Bell, KFC, McDonald's, or Burger Chef. Once when they stopped at a Burger King, the manager came out of the restaurant as the team was getting back on the bus and wanted to shake George's hand. He said, "My restaurant is cleaner now after your team has eaten." George always made sure everyone picked up after themselves. It was also the team's practice to have two players rotate on cleaning up the bus when they arrived home.

LaFesta Exchange

The other baseball track in George's life has been the LaFesta Baseball Exchange. George, John Lipa, and Tony Abuisi are co-founders of LaFesta, now in its thirtieth year of existence. John and Tony were looking to have a closer connection with friends who lived in Boston's North End, while also bolstering youth attraction to Saint Anthony church's long-running LaFesta Festival.

The three men met with their Boston friends and decided baseball was a common interest of everyone. Over time, the church's LaFesta activities faded, but the baseball exchange quickly became very popular. Each city would sponsor a team with players selected by their Babe Ruth League coaches. Selections were not normally All-Stars, but they could be. Most players were thirteen, fourteen, or fifteen years old, and each team selected fifteen players to represent their city. Over the years, one of the most notable and outstanding players was a talented one-armed outfielder.

George was selected to coach the North Adams team for the first three years. Later, others took his place, while he and his family became one of the Exchange's strongest group of supporters. The first game took place in North Adams in 1991 at Joe Wolfe Field. Several weeks later, the North Adams team travelled to Boston's North End to play at Puopolo Field. This reciprocity has continued for thirty years, although recent games were postponed due to the COVID-19 virus.

Today's exchange games are played on the weekends, with players staying at local hotels. There are usually two games, one Saturday night and one Sunday afternoon. Games are heavily promoted, with a World Series aura, and during the North Adams games, Joe Wolfe Field has the feel of a major league ballpark with announcers, player introductions, national anthem, and merchandise sales. Visiting players are well entertained by their hosts. In North Adams, the players might mingle during a cookout at Windsor Lake, navigate a challenging rope course, or play Wiffle ball and touch football. They are also interviewed by local TV stations.

To date, 104 games have been played, with a gratifying display of sportsmanship such as congratulating other team members on great plays, shaking hands, hugging, and the establishment of longtime friendships. The Exchange participation has broadened recently to include players from Adams and Williamstown, as well as Bennington, Vermont. The camaraderie is notable. One year North Adams' team parents noticed Boston's catcher's equipment was very worn. Unsolicited, the group pooled their money, and purchased brand new equipment for the Boston catcher including a mask, chest protector, shin guards, and a helmet.

At the 2016 Exchange game in Boston, Mayor Walsh presented a "George Canales Way" sign that now hangs in North Boston near the ballpark.

The LaFesta Baseball Exchange has become a family weekend affair for the Canales family. Its fourteen members, children, grandchildren, and in-laws help with setting up and manning food booths, selling tickets, and selling shirts. George and Nancy even have a dedicated LaFesta room in their house featuring a trophy ball from a North Adams triple play, a first pitched ball from the inaugural Exchange game, and signed team baseballs from both teams for each year of play. For George, it continues to be less about wins and losses, more about relationships.

THERE'S COACHING IN THE GENES

Coaching is contagious in the Canales family, and their three boys, Mike, David, and Jason, all attended McCann. As one said, "It's a rite of passage for a Canales. It's in our genes." Mike coached girls' basketball for years, David coached baseball, basketball, and lacrosse, and Jason has coached baseball and hockey teams.

Over all the years, their mom Nancy was a mainstay of support, attending most games, juggling the three boys when George was at a game, and working as a cake decorator at the Adams Super Market. It seemed like there were always extra kids at supper who loved her legendary lasagna, spaghetti, and homemade Whoopie pies.

At the age of seventy-six, George coaches more infrequently, although he quickly accepts any opportunities to see his grandkids. There's the annual weeklong Cape Cod trip, road trips to North Carolina beaches, or cruising to Jamaica, Mexico, or the Dominican Republic. On one of their recent beach trips, while walking with a granddaughter on the beach, George decided to retire from coaching and watch his grandchildren grow up.

In the meantime, he and Nancy volunteer one day a week at the Tourist Booth on Union Street answering travelers' questions. They've enjoyed meeting people from across the globe. Both are involved and volunteer at the North Adams Historical Museum, where Nancy serves on the Board. Nancy continues to be active at the Mary Spitzer Senior Center on Ashland Street.

George remains on the city's Parks and Recreation Committee and attends monthly meetings. He is also a long-term McCann School Committee member, having served over twenty-five years. He was on the Board of Directors for the Babe Ruth League, and Nancy works at the food bank. As one of their sons said, "Helping and volunteering is just something the Canaleses do for their community."

George particularly enjoys staying connected with his former players. When one of them spots him in town and calls out *Coach Canales!,* George lights up and welcomes them over and wants to know what they are doing. He enjoys bragging on his former players, some of whom are working in government, serving as State Troopers or serving in the Armed Forces. He is proud of them.

One of the greatest tributes to George's years of coaching was when a player said, "George influenced my entire life. My wife and I adopted four children, and I'm able to teach them how to act or respond to situations calmly and with patience. George showed me how to teach baseball to young people, showed me patience, how to control my emotions, when its okay to speak out without being rude or offensive. He was a great example for young boys."

Still enjoying a "hot" car in retirement, George bought a black 2010 Mustang convertible in which he and Nancy can be seen cruising on nice days. If you see him, just shout, *Hey Coach!*

ALFRED CAPRONI

No one sees a town quite as clearly as its McDonald's manager. For over fifty years, Al Caproni has witnessed countless changes to North Adams' community and its businesses. His McDonald's is at the center of everything, both figuratively and literally. Located on Union Street, it's the terminus of the beautiful Mohawk Trail and a gateway to the City of North Adams.

Since 1968, Al Caproni has faithfully served customers through some of the most eventful years of North Adams' history. He's watched the evolution of the 1970s urban renewal project; the opening of the new Drury High School; and the closures of St. Joseph's High School, the Sprague Electric Company, *The Transcript*, and a number of churches. He has been there for the opening of MASS MoCA and mostly weathered the recent pandemic. Al has been ringside as the city's population declined from 19,000 in the 1970s to approximately 12,770 today.

The events occurring in North Adams over Al's fifty-year tenure also coincide with some of McDonald's greatest menu introductions, including the Filet-o-Fish and the Big Mac in the 1960s, the McDonald's Breakfast, Quarter Pounder, Egg McMuffin, and the highly popular Happy Meals of the '70s, and the critical invention of the Chicken Nugget in the early '80s.

EARLY LIFE

Alfred George Caproni Jr., was born at the old North Adams Hospital on January 9, 1945, toward the end of World War II. His father, Alfred Sr., was fighting in Europe and first met Alfred when he was 13 months old. Al grew up alongside his brother and sister on the 120-acre Seeger Farm on Walker Street owned by his grandparents.

Alfred Sr., originally from Boston, had first arrived in North Adams in the late 1930s as a member of the Civilian Conservation Corps (CCC), building the Florida Mountain prison camp and helping cut trails for the Thunderbolt Ski Trail on Mount Greylock. As a U.S. Army medic under General Patton's command, he fought across Europe after landing on Utah Beach, and participated in the Battle of the Bulge. Alfred worked several years at the Clark Biscuit Company before spending forty years at the Cascade Company in North Adams. He was an avid horticulturist and gardener, well known for raising strawberries. Alfred passed away in 2000.

While working at the Biscuit Company, Alfred met Gladys Hewitt Seeger, and they married in 1942. Gladys was born in North Adams, attended local schools, and graduated from Drury High School in 1939. She enjoyed canning and preserving fruits and vegetables and baking, specializing in strawberry pies. Gladys passed away in 1994.

Al's lineage is a mixture of Italian, Irish, German, and English. Al's paternal grandfather was Alfred Washington Caproni, born in 1883 in New York City. He moved to Lynn, Massachusetts, as a young man. He served as an auxiliary police officer for thirty years and was most well known as "Boston's # 1 baritone" for his vaudeville minstrel show performances. Alfred died in 1960.

Rose (Jennings) Caproni, Al's grandmother, was born in 1889 in Westport, Ireland. She emigrated by herself at the age of fourteen years old. Records indicate she passed herself off as eighteen to secure passage to the United States. In 1918 at the age of 28, she died from the Spanish Flu when her son, Alfred Sr., was only six years old.

Al's maternal grandfather, William Seeger, was born in Stamford, Vermont, in 1883. William worked a variety of jobs. He was a tax collector and later a game warden. After those jobs, he went to work at Hunter Machine and then as a dairy farmer for more than thirty years. He most loved trapping, and in vintage photos is pictured with fifteen fox pelts. Records show he also trapped mink and was paid $8 per pelt. A fellow trapper reportedly offered him $50 for his secret trap scent, which he declined. His grandchildren fondly remember him being willing to go fishing "at the drop of a hat." William died in 1959.

Al's grandmother, Elizabeth (Hewitt) Seeger, was born in 1889 in Clarksburg. She was a homemaker, canning and preserving much of the family's food. What they grew on the farm in the summer got the family through the winter. Records indicate that Elizabeth's ancestors fought in the Battle of Bennington during the Revolutionary War and bought land in North Adams in 1796. Her great-great-grandfather and his son fought with the Vermont Volunteers in a number of Civil War battles, including Gettysburg where the father was gunshot and recovered in Washington, D.C., before returning home.

GROWING UP

As a young boy, Al and his family lived on his grandparents' farm right next door to the original farmhouse his grandparents, the Seegers, occupied. The farm was a busy place, producing bushels of potatoes and corn, tomatoes, peas, and beans. His mother and grandmother spent much of their time canning their produce and storing it in Grandma's cool, dirt-floor cellar.

At eight years old, Al worked for Seeger's Dairy, helping his uncle deliver milk to their two hundred customers. He worked on the dairy route in the summer, school vacations, and holidays from 8:00 a.m. to 1:00 p.m., receiving two dollars a day.

Al and his brother, Roy, milked cows, cleaned stables, plowed fields, gathered hay, and dug up stones from the field. At nine years old, in the fourth grade, Al started buying his own clothes. As he got older, he delivered newspapers daily to his 112 customers, receiving a princely sum of $17 per week.

The close-knit family lived a busy life. Al's dad never stopped working between his job at Cascade and working on the farm or in the garden. He was a quiet man, although willing to talk to anyone, recalls Al. His mom did all the driving since his dad never had a driver's license, and she also handled the family's finances. Gladys was "kind, willing to do anything for any body and always saw the best in a person."

There was never a lot of money, so there were no vacations except for a once-yearly four-hour ride to visit his grandparents in Lynn, just north of Boston.

Suppers were basic fare—meat, potatoes, and vegetables— always hot and always at 5:00 p.m. Often for Sunday's meal, someone would go to nearby Uncle Walt's and grab a chicken to slaughter. Other meals would include hamburgers, steak, or stuffed peppers. The kids fondly remember her "porcupine" meals: breaded hamburger meatballs with rice sticking out and a special sauce with potatoes and vegetables. The family never ate out.

Al went to Houghton Elementary School through eighth grade, and when not in school or working, the kids played on the farm: camping in the woods, playing softball, baseball, or football in the fields, and in the winter, building a fire and playing hockey on the shallow pond behind the house.

One wintertime, Al cut his face badly when his sled broke through some crusted snow. His mom cleaned his bloody face and bandaged the cuts across his forehead. At fourteen, he had a much more serious incident. When using the farm tractor, dragging a stone boat behind it, pulling stones out of the plowed field, the trac- tor became off-balance and flipped over backwards on top of Alfred. His brother thought he was dead, but luckily Al fell between two furrows and crawled out the front of the tractor.

Al attended Drury High School and played football all four years. He was captain in his senior year and received All Western Massachusetts and All Berkshire Honorable recognition. He also received the Delnegro Memorial Trophy for his athletics. Al played basketball, baseball, and was involved in the reading club and sev- eral class plays. His mode of transportation and his pride and joy was a black, 1953 Chevy four-door sedan.

During his high school years, Al worked at Dutch Hill cooking hot dogs and hamburgers in the kitchen on Saturdays and Sundays. In the summers, he worked at Cascade Paper Company for $1.25 an hour in the receiving department. Al graduated in 1963.

After high school, Al briefly attended Berkshire Community College and then joined his dad working at Cascade Paper. During this time period, Al joined the local National Guard, training initially as a tanker and then an infantryman. He served seven years and was honorably discharged as a sergeant.

CAREER

In 1967, Al began working for North Adams State College (now Massachusetts College of Liberal Arts) in the maintenance department, grounds and facilities. Most of his responsibilities were outdoors and that suited him just fine. His duties, depending on the season, ranged from planting, mowing, and snow removal to cleaning classrooms.

In 1968, while working fulltime at the college, Al accepted a night job at McDonald's and commuted to the Pittsfield store for training before managing the new McDonald's in North Adams. The training was rigorous. At the time, the restaurant had no drive-thru service, which increased workload. Also, the employees needed to peel potatoes by hand. In May 1969, Al began working at the North Adams McDonald's five and six nights a week. Between the college, McDonald's, tending cows on the farm, and National Guard meetings, Al was busy.

Al did a lot of hiring at the new McDonald's, and one day a local college student interviewed for a summer job. Al was impressed by her apparent work ethic considering she had another job, and hired her almost immediately. He later said her dark eyes and hair, petite stature, and short black skirt may have influenced his decision. The young lady, Mary Ann Scerbo, began working the night shift with Al and by summer they were dating. She was also a North Adams native, graduating from Drury in 1967 and attending college in New York City. They were engaged in April 1970 and married at St. Anthony of Padua Church in North Adams on May 8, 1971.

The young couple lived near the family farm, and Al's schedule remained hectic. Early morning and midday cow feedings, work at the college, then McDonald's in his evenings. This is all in addition to plowing and planting on the farm, cutting logs for heat, tapping trees for the family's maple sugar business, and responding to late-night snow-plow calls at the college.

In 1978, the family built a home on a portion of the Seeger Farm, fulfilling a lifelong dream, and raised their two sons there.

THOSE GOLDEN ARCHES

During his fifty-four years at McDonald's, Al observed many changes within the business model. When he began in 1968, customer orders were written down on a pad, and the menu had five items: hamburger, French fries, shakes, coffee, and soda. To convert a hamburger to a cheeseburger, a slice of cheese was added for five cents.

Advertisements at the time said "Have a meal and get change for a dollar." At the time, a burger was ten cents, fries twelve cents, and a shake twenty cents. The marketing campaign progressed from the "Golden Arches" to "You Deserve a Break Today," to the famous catchy chorus, "two all-beef patties, special sauce, lettuce, cheese, pickles, onions on a sesame seed bun."

In the 1960s and early 1970s, with Drury and St. Joe's high schools nearby, McDonald's became the high-school hangout. Thursday through Sunday nights, there could be as many as two hundred students in the parking lot. A police officer was hired to be on-site Friday and Saturday nights to control crowds, traffic, and occasionally break up fights. When St. Joe's closed in 1974, and Drury moved to the edge of town, the young crowd receded.

Al, front and center, as he's been for over fifty years.

In the 1980s and 1990s, older clientele replaced the throngs of students. Small groups of three to seven people, often retirees, would come in to talk politics and have a coffee. Al noted, "Now there are always regulars in the early morning, mid-morning, and for lunch."

Over time, the composition of McDonald's forty-five part-time associates has changed. In the 1960s, most were high school or college students; today, more are adults. As the local economy struggled, and the minimum wage was raised, older people filled positions and today a number of day-shift associates have over twenty years of service. Associate training is done in-house, following specific guidelines provided by the corporate office that even include the precise way to "dress" a hamburger bun.

Al has been present for the successful introduction of many new menu items. The popular Big Mac came in 1968, and the breakfast menu was introduced in 1972. At the time, McDonald's was the only fast-food restaurant offering breakfast, and Al saw a great increase in customer traffic and volume of orders. Breakfasts appealed to a wide group of customers from business people and retirees to high schoolers on their way to class. According to a CNN profile of McDonald's history, by 1986, it was "responsible for serving one out of four breakfasts in the US that is not cooked at home."

Other notable menu introductions in the 1970s were the Quarter Pounder, Egg McMuffin, and the most popular Happy Meal. A young child could now get a hamburger, fries, and a drink for 99 cents and get the ever-popular toy. The toys often followed Disney movie promotions, such as *The Lion King* or *101 Dalmatians*, and children wanted to collect every figure within a series. Once a year, the store promoted miniature Barbie dolls and Hot Wheels in their Happy Meals. Over the years, Al has collected many of the Happy Meal toys, and at one point was able to purchase two unopened sets of *101 Dalmatians* figures.

In the 1980s, the instantly popular McNuggets were introduced, and store traffic again increased as people from all walks of life, many using coupons, would purchase ten- or twenty-count packs of nuggets. The store also embraced the relatively new "drive-thru" model in the late '80s and began offering salads which, like nuggets, became mainstays for the business.

The most popular item on the menu is the French fries. The store has been using the same Idaho producer for over fifty years, standardizing the size and moisture content of the potato, thus ensuring a uniform, delicious taste. Al's McDonald's, considered to be a small store, uses 40 cases of fries a week, in total more than 1,400 pounds. To ensure quality across the menu, McDonald's nationalized its suppliers for sourcing supplies such as dry goods, frozen food, and milk to maintain predictable taste among its thousands of stores.

Other high-volume menu items include hamburgers. The store uses 500 patties a day, roughly fourteen cases, or 3500 patties in one week. The store's other big seller is Chicken McNuggets. It serves over 8400 individual nuggets weekly.

Still hard at work, Al makes the ever-popular Egg McMuffin.

Al's own view of the store is literally night and day different! Midway through his tenure he went from late evenings to early mornings. He started at the North Adams store as the night shift manager, working 5:00 to 11:00 p.m. four nights a week, for twenty-seven years. When his schedule changed to nights at the college, for the next twenty-seven years he moved to first shift manager, covering 6:00 a.m. to 2:00 p.m.

Often when associates did not have a car or during inclement weather, Al would drive people home after the night shift ended at 1:00 a.m. Now on day shift, he will pick up employees before 6:00 a.m. if they don't have a ride. For many years, Al and his wife Mary Ann have given Christmas gifts to associates and hosted Christmas and Halloween parties at their home. The Halloween parties were especially popular with associates' children, featuring apple dunking, games, and costume activities.

With the advent of computer technology, drive-thru, and

twenty-four-hour service, filling customers' orders quickly is essential. Monitors are placed throughout the work areas to let each employee know the timing of when an order was placed and how long it took to fill it. The store's goal is 90 to 120 seconds to complete each order. When busy, drive-thru will process eighty to ninety cars an hour.

The recent pandemic has closed the lobby and reduced the number of employees necessary for cleaning. The pandemic has also shifted customers to McDonald's drive-thru, which now does 80 percent of the store's business versus 60 percent in the past. Mobile orders and pay apps have become popular, representing 20 percent of the store's volume. Computer generated orders appear on internal monitors and let the employees know when the customer is near the store and ready for pick-up. Surprisingly, computer orders are often over forty or fifty dollars.

FARM LIFE

In his personal time, Al and his family have belonged to the Massachusetts Maple Producers Association for over fifty years. Of the 200 members, only four or five have been making maple syrup this long. Al's entire family is involved in tapping trees in early March, using over 900 tree taps and an intricate web of plastic tubing and vacuum pumps. The family produces 175 to 200 gallons of maple syrup annually, and recently expanded production to include maple sugar candy. Some of the maple syrup products are given to friends though the bulk is sold via mail orders received from the internet. Business is good, and they usually sell out.

The family also has a sawmill operation on the farm. New equipment allows cutting of 30-inch diameter logs that can produce lumber from 2" x 4" all the way to 2" x 10". Most of the lumber is used on the farm. Some of it is planned for the new sugar house.

For over a quarter of a century, Al maintained seventeen honeybee colonies, producing up to 800 pounds of honey and selling out the same number of one-pound glass jars. At one point, while working two other jobs, Al decided to close the business. For most of Al's life, he has worked two, at times three, different jobs. He is approaching his fifty-fourth year at McDonald's and finally retired from the local college on his thirty-seventh anniversary. Now, the farm and its three horses, ducks, and numerous chickens keep him busy when he is not managing the restaurant.

When he attained fifty years of service at McDonald's, Al was the company's longest-serving manager in Massachusetts and the fifth-longest-serving nationwide. His faithful tenure was recognized in front-page news articles in newspapers across the country.

Al and Mary Ann, the college student he hired over fifty years ago, recently celebrated their fiftieth wedding anniversary. They and their two sons, who teach at Drury High School, and four grandchildren remain close and actively engaged in farm activities.

Al has no plans of retiring from McDonald's. Every day, he enjoys greeting customers he has known for thirty or forty years. After flipping thousands of hamburgers, he is still "Lovin' It."

"All in all, it's been fun, and I feel like it keeps me young," he says.

So, for the foreseeable future, he will continue his philosophy of high-quality customer service . . . and always keep the drive-thru moving.

JUSTYNA CARLSON

This diminutive, curly-white-haired grandmother has a serious, professorly countenance and a loving and caring personality. Justyna Carlson has devoted her life to teaching, her church, and numerous forms of public service ranging from preserving North Adams history to assisting in urban renewal projects. She is a volunteer extraordinaire.

Her story begins as Justyna Mary Steuer, an only child named after her Polish grandmother. Born June 14, 1944, at W. B. Plunkett Hospital in Adams to Edward Gordon Steuer and Julia Agnes (Kruszyna), little Justyna enjoyed a healthy delivery. Doctor McLaughlin, a general practitioner, was pleased.

Justyna's dad, Edward Steuer, was born in Adams, Massachusetts, the eighth and final child of Martin and Elizabeth Bailey Steuer who had moved from Brooklyn, New York, in the 1890s. The six boys and two girls were of German, English, Bavarian, and Irish descent. The first four children graduated from the eighth grade and worked in the Berkshire Mills, allowing the last four to attend high school. Edward graduated from Adams High School in 1923, and then from the five-year General Electric drafting program. Subsequently, he left GE and attended Fitchburg Normal School, earning a bachelor's degree. In his later years, he received a master's degree from North Adams State College.

He taught mechanical drawing at Greenfield High and married Julia Kruszyna in 1934. From 1940 to 1966, Edward taught shop and sheet metal classes at Drury High School. He volunteered for service in World War II but was medically disqualified due to color blindness.

Justyna's mom, Julia Kruszyna, was born to parents who had emigrated from Jasło, Poland, a small town southeast of Krakow.

103

The promise of jobs and better opportunities was their reason to start a new life in the United States. Recruiters sent to Poland from the Berkshire Mills attracted them to this area. Julia's father died when she was two and she was raised by her mother and stepfather, John Durda.

Julia worked in the Drury and Greylock school cafeterias, and at Pizzi's Dress Shop and Kwalitee Gift Shoppes until they closed. As an adult, Julia was very active in the community and church, serving on the Parent Teacher Association, the Cancer and Rosary Societies, the Visiting Nurses Association, and City Parent Council Group, to name just a few.

EARLY LIFE

The family moved in 1940 to North Adams, and Justyna grew up at 61 Elmwood Avenue. When, in her sixth-grade year, the family moved to 36 Cherry Street, she attended Mark Hopkins Grammar School, receiving upon graduation in 1958 the Balfour Plaque, an award bestowed for honor, loyalty, and achievement. Growing up, she remembers the playground at Mark Hopkins School to be the center of her life, from playing with her friends Joan, Paula, Lorraine, JoAnn, Leslie, and Kevin, to roller skating, riding bicycles, working on crafts in the city's summer programs, and ice skating in the winter.

© DENNIS PREGENT, 2021

Two significant events in these years had a lasting impact upon her life. Her seventh-grade teacher, recently returned from Mexico, was asked to introduce Spanish to her class. Acing a prequalifying test, Justyna began studying the language with books provided by the PTA and fell in

A vintage schoolroom at the North Adams Museum of History and Science, shown to the author by Justyna.

love with it. During the same time period, she began playing the organ at St. Francis of Assisi Church under the tutelage of Maria Weber, the church's accomplished organist. Justyna continues to play for church today—and has a master's degree in Spanish.

The family often vacationed in Atlantic City, New Jersey. They visited her aunt and uncle, eating at his restaurant, walking on the beach, and experiencing the amusement rides at Steel Pier. On one memorable vacation, the family travelled to Québec for one of her dad's fishing trips and had the chance to visit the Saint-Anne-de-Beaupré shrine. Justyna felt lucky to tag along with her dad, who served as a bus driver for Drury high school events, on the debating team's frequent road trips. Justyna attributes her love of driving and wanderlust for travelling to her dad.

Family life and supper conversations revolved around her dad's work at Drury or her mom's volunteer work. On weekends, Saturday was her father's time to hunt or fish, often with his brother. In the evening, Justyna's aunt and uncle would stop by, and the foursome would play canasta or cribbage. Sunday was family time, and Julia (an excellent cook) often prepared breaded veal cutlets, corn, and French fries.

Big extended family holiday gatherings with many cousins have been a long-standing tradition. Justyna, following in her mom's footsteps, brings boxes of home-baked sugar cookies for each family. Outside of family, her mom's cookies, known as Mrs. Steuer's butter cookies, have over the years been enjoyed by many friends and classmates.

Justyna clearly remembers Wednesday nights in 1955. The family would visit her cousin's house to watch black and white TV. Her dad's favorite show was *Superman*, and both families enjoyed watching Arthur Godfrey's talent show and Sid Caesar. It wasn't long before the family bought their own television.

Justyna has fond memories of competing alongside her mother in the annual Cummington Fair. Her mom won numerous ribbons for sewing and placed annually in the apple pie contests. She and Justyna competed in as many contests as they could for this once-a-year fest. They both participated in the box lunch competition that required competitors to pack a balanced, nutritious meal. Both were delighted that on one occasion Justyna won first place.

In late middle school, Justyna and her friend Linda loved attending Friday and Saturday night dances at Notre Dame School and the Masonic Temple. Mostly attended by teens and high schoolers, rock and roll music dominated, and The Twist, a dance introduced by Chubby Checker, prevailed. Often, reluctant boys were circumvented by girls dancing with girls.

When it was time for high school, most of her close friends attended St. Joseph's High School, the local Catholic school. She was slightly disappointed, but understood the need to attend Drury, the town's public school, where her dad taught classes.

Justyna attended Drury High School from 1958 to 1962 and it was a busy time. She was kept quite busy with her studies, twirling practice with the band, the Pro Merito Honor Society, and being president of the Future Teachers of America and the editor-in-chief of the yearbook her junior year. Summers often found her waitressing at the Taconic Golf Course in Williamstown, saving her money for college.

When she was six years old, Justyna had started taking baton lessons. She then twirled for four years in high school, captaining her senior year. As part of the band, the twirlers performed at Armory basketball games and Noel Field football games. Most memorable was leading the band down Main Street in the Fall Foliage Parade. Sometimes they performed out-of-state, although their standard non-school demonstrations were mostly on Memorial Day, marching/twirling over the weekend in Blackinton, Cheshire, and Adams.

Frequently, she'd return from a baton performance and have to run down the hill from school to play the church organ for May devotions. There was always some concern that a devout parishioner (or the Monsignor!) might not appreciate her gold mini-skirted twirling outfit. Luckily, the stairs to the choir loft were in the back of the church, and she was usually able to scamper up them without being seen.

Justyna attended Georgian Court College (now University) in Lakewood, New Jersey, where she was deeply involved in school activities. She graduated in 1966 with a bachelor of arts in Spanish and a minor in French. One of Justyna's sweetest memories while attending college was the "shoe scholarship" provided by her dad's part-time employer. The proprietor, pleased with her dad's work, promised to outfit her for four years with any shoes she needed.

Desiring to follow in her father's steps, she then attended the University of Massachusetts, receiving in 1967 a master's of arts in teaching, again a member of their honor society. In 1975, Justyna received a second master's degree, this one in Spanish, from Middlebury College. During college days, she continued to play the organ at church services and used her Spanish to host a Sunday school for migrant workers. She was also an active member of the National Federation of College Catholic Students, an organization that sponsored charitable activities.

Her first teaching position was at Immaculate Conception in San Antonio, Texas, as part of Catholic Lay Mission Corps working with missionaries teaching sixth-eighth grade Hispanic students. She taught some of the more difficult subjects: arithmetic, geometry, and algebra. In the evenings, using her Spanish, she taught citizenship courses.

After a year, she returned to Massachusetts and taught Spanish at Frontier Regional in South Deerfield where she started educational spring break trips, traveling to Spain the first year. The thirty students and adults visited Madrid, stopped at a monument called Valley of the Fallen, then on to the walled city of Avila, and the highlight of the trip, a visit to Toledo to view paintings by El Greco. During Easter, the travelers visited Greece, stopping in Athens, visiting the Parthenon temple there, going to the Oracle of Delphi shrine, and making a day trip to the port city of Piraeus.

In the early 1970s, Justyna had an opportunity to return to her alma mater, Georgian Court, as the Spanish, French, and Latin American Literature translation instructor while also working with the admissions office, meeting new applicants as the college's Director of Recruitment. Never one for idle time, during this period she attended the Harvard Admissions Institute, and spent one summer in Poland at Jagiellonian University in Krakow. Culturally it was an opportunity to study the language and tour the country. During this time, she also began studying for her second master's degree at Middlebury College and received certifications in English and History.

During her travels, she had a serious auto accident and decided to move closer to home. For the next five years, she served as the language coordinator and departmental supervisor for Mount Anthony Junior and Senior High Schools, commuting from North Adams to Bennington, Vermont. During these years she served as President of VFLA, the Vermont Foreign Language Association, as well as Vice President of NEFLA, the New England Foreign Language Association.

GIVING BACK IS A FULLTIME JOB

As happenstance would have it, one night she attended a potluck supper for singles at a Pittsfield church where she met and eventually married Gene Carlson, an electrical engineer from Montana. They were married in the summer of 1978, and had a daughter, Marissa Eilleen. They now reside at 32 Cherry Street, just a few doors from where she grew up.

After several years, Justyna returned to the work force as an adjunct Spanish professor at Massachusetts College of Liberal Arts and spent the next 23 years (1982-2005) on its faculty. For six of those years, she concurrently taught at Southern Vermont College in Bennington.

When time permits, Justyna likes collecting postcards, stamps, shot glasses, and magnets from their trips. She has collected postcards from all fifty states, has some hard-to-find cards of North Adams, a number from foreign countries, and Georgian Court.

Born on Flag Day, she enjoys decorating for the holidays. It all started in San Antonio when she was teaching, buying her own materials, and decorating her classrooms. Now she continues the hobby, hanging decorations in her windows and on her front door for most holidays. Often, she still uses classroom materials purchased so many years ago.

She and Gene continue to volunteer and participate in many social and civic programs. It's almost as if they needed to retire from paying jobs to be able to fit in all the volunteer work! They also enjoy watching their granddaughter, Ksena.

Church life is important to her. Justyna continues to play the organ at St. Elizabeth of Hungary church where she is also a lector, Eucharistic Minister, and an Adorer. She is active in the Catholic Daughters of America, a charitable organization, that represents local Catholic Parishes, selecting guest speakers and donating to charitable causes. Following in her mother's footsteps, she serves as Regent of Court Margaret #629 CDA, attends biennial conventions, and continues to be involved with the Spiritual Life Commission, helping set up retreats, train lectors, and organize Mass. In the meantime, she continues to be active in the National Catholic College Graduate Honor Society (known as Kappa Gamma Pi or KGP) as Western Massachusetts chapter president, Eastern Regent, IIVP, IVP and eventually in 1997-2001 National President of KGP. In 2017, she and Gene attended the National Convention in Philadelphia.

Justyna serves as secretary of the North Adams Historical Society and chair of the North Adams Historical Commission. Whether a docent at the North Adams Museum of History and Science, a volunteer at the Tourist Booth, or an usher at Massachusetts Museum of Contemporary Art, she contin-ues to promote North Adams.

At the museum, Justyna displays a portrait collection of the former mayors of North Adams, including John Barrett and Dick Alcombright, bottom right.

She and Gene volunteer to staff the snack bar for the SteepleCats, a group of skilled baseball players from high schools or colleges that play throughout New England. They particularly enjoy watching the games of these young, accomplished players, and by working in the snack shop, a $75 donation is made to the Historical Society.

As hosts of the "Young Americans" traveling musical troupe that comes to town for several days a year to find, rehearse, and encourage local youth musical talent, Justyna and Gene help them set up a community concert before the troupe moves on to their next destination. Often a student or chaperone will stay with them.

Just when you wonder how much more can one person do, Justyna and her daughter chair the inveterate Fall Foliage Leaf Hunt, seeking sponsors, making up clues and hiding leaves. She also has served as chair of the Drury Music Alumni Band, where former high school musicians meet every five years for a weekend of concerts and dinners.

She is complemented in her largesse by her husband, Gene, treasurer and board member of the North Adams Historical Society and docent at the North Adams Museum of History and Science, playing a major role in recently helping move the museum. He also serves as the editor of *Hoosac Trails*, the quarterly NAHS newsletter.

Gene, matching Justyna's civic spirit, continues to support the United Way, Al Nelson Food Pantry, St. Vincent de Paul, and MCLA where the family endowed the Nicastro Spanish/Italian award and the Schiff French award in honor of Justyna's mentors. Gene, with Justyna, financially supported the Haiti Plunge, a mission project in the mountains of Haiti. He has also spent many volunteer hours in archival work at the North Adams Public Library.

Their list of community involvements is daunting, always growing, and seems never-ending. It's quite possible no couple could match the level of philanthropy she and Gene have contributed. Rightly so, they received the Northern Berkshire Hero Award in 2019 for preserving the city's history and for community involvement. Justyna has also received the Women of Achievement award from Business and Professional Women.

When asked why she does all that she does, Justyna responded that a priest once told her, "From those to whom much has been given, much will be expected." She strongly believes she has been blessed with many life opportunities and wants to give back and help others. Justyna's and Gene's generosity in energy, spirit, and financial contributions to the community and others has been boundless.

MARTHA COAKLEY

Martha Coakley, a native of North Adams, was the first woman in Massachusetts to be elected Attorney General, the state's highest law enforcement position. Martha's reputation is that of a trailblazer with over thirty years of public service, especially as a strong advocate for women and children and consumers. She has spent most of her adult life in the public eye, in courtrooms or at homicide scenes, announcing indictments or convictions.

Martha wasn't always certain what her career would look like. She'd thought of being a journalist or a lawyer. She was a very good student and enjoyed competing and debating. She thrived on reading Nancy Drew novels and watching defense attorney Perry Mason successfully defend his clients on television.

She joined the debate team in high school and spent part of two summers at a Georgetown University debating institute. Martha loved debate, and it wasn't long before accolades started rolling in. Over several years, she took the first-place varsity speaker award in the Springfield Diocesan Debates, was a member of the second-ranked team in the diocese, and on the sixth-place team in the Massachusetts State Debating Tournament.

She was also first in the Diocesan Speech Festival in the girls' extemporaneous division and was selected to participate in national competitions in Chicago, Washington, and Florida. She won awards in the American Legion and VFW oratorical contests.

One of Martha's high school teachers described her as intelligent, one who loves to argue. And in an auspicious prediction of her future: "one of those students who spoke in paragraphs oftentimes . . . . Students can give very short answers, [but] she was one who could explicate what she was talking about."

Martha's story began on July 14, 1953, at Saint Luke's Hospital in Pittsfield. She was the third of five children, four girls and a boy, born to Edward J. and Phyllis (Laffey) Coakley with fifteen years spanning from oldest child to youngest.

Her father, Edward, was born in Rhode Island in 1921, graduated from Brown University, served as a Commissioned Naval Officer in World War II, and was recalled as a Naval Reserve Officer for Korea. He served six and a half years as a destroyer officer, leaving active duty with the rank of lieutenant commander.

He worked in the insurance business his whole life, first with Aetna in Springfield and then, moving to North Adams, joining and becoming a partner at the Geddes & Crippen Insurance agency in 1954. Eventually, he became part owner and president of the Coakley, Pierpan, Dolan & Collins Insurance Agency, serving businesses and individuals across the state. Edward passed away from a heart attack while playing golf in Williamstown in May 1993.

Phyllis Eileen Laffey, also from Rhode Island, was born in 1923 and married Edward in April 1946. They moved to North Adams in the 1950s and resided on Highland Avenue. Phyllis, a homemaker, was active in the Northern Berkshire community as a volunteer with the North Adams Hospital and the American Red Cross. She was a longtime member of the Rosary Sodality and the Catholic Daughters of the Americas Court Margaret, a well-known charitable organization. Phyllis passed away from acute leukemia in July 1995.

The family's only boy, Edward J. Coakley Jr., a graduate of Williams College and a talented pianist, expert historian, and accomplished skier, died at the young age of thirty-four in 1996.

Martha's paternal grandparents were William and Mabel McGovern Coakley. William was born in the United States in the late eighteen-hundreds and married Mabel after she emigrated from Ireland. The family lived in Pawtucket, Rhode Island, where William worked in blue-collar factory jobs and died at a young age. Mabel, a devoted homemaker, raised a family of three boys, one of whom was Martha's dad, Edward.

Martha's maternal grandparents were John and Mary (Elwood)

Laffey, both born in and emigrated from Ireland. They also lived in Pawtucket. Martha's mom was the youngest of their ten children.

Martha remembers making the three-hour trip with her family, from North Adams to Pawtucket, visiting "Gram" Coakley at her apartment. Gram would take the family to Newport Creamery for ice cream and, if there was time, enjoy playing Scrabble with the kids. She is remembered for saying "use a word three times and it's yours."

EARLY LIFE IN THE BERKSHIRES

Martha attended kindergarten at Mark Hopkins and then St. Joseph's schools through 11th grade. She lived on Highland Avenue not far from Mark Hopkins playground, where so many of her youthful activities occurred. She and her friends skated there when the city froze the rink. She also began snow skiing in third grade, a sport she enjoyed through high school and still enjoys today.

In the summer, she played hide and seek, cops and robbers, and seemed to be always nursing scraped knees from roller skate or bicycle falls. The friends would swim at the Fish Pond at the top of Bradley Street or walk to the nearby library. Martha was an avid reader. She also enjoyed going to nearby Fischlein's for groceries for her mom and, in the process, getting a candy bar or ice cream for herself. Once when she was six years old and trying to do another good deed, she clipped some tulips from a neighbor's yard and brought the lovely bouquet home to Mom. She had apologies to make.

Martha was a Brownie and a Girl Scout. One of her happiest times of the year was attending Girl Scout Camp Witawentin in the summer. The girls swam, boated, learned arts and crafts, hiked, cooked, and camped overnight. The camp lasted two weeks, and one time Martha was able to stay a whole month.

In the summertime, she remembers her entire family of five children and two adults packed into the back of the family's station wagon headed to Rye Beach, New Hampshire, for a July vacation. The vacations were special and usually included meeting up with cousins. The Coakleys rented a cottage a short distance from the ocean and every day they packed a lunch and walked to the beach to swim and raft. If it rained, they would head into Hampton Beach to see a Jerry Lewis movie, play arcade games, or hunt for souvenirs.

The family always said the Rosary going to and coming from the beach for safety while travelling. Martha described her childhood memories as "happy, easygoing, and loving."

The family went to 9:30 a.m. Mass on Sundays at St. Francis Church, and Martha sang in the children's choir, under Sister Anna Francis, from 3rd to 8th grade. Her dad belonged to the St. Vincent de Paul Society and had the kids help collect clothes and count donations for the needy. Martha's mother belonged to the Rosary Sodality. Sometimes Martha would accompany her dad when he went to daily Mass during Lent. At that time, the Mass was in Latin, and Martha still remembers some of the Latin prayers.

The close-knit family ate their evening meal every night at 5:30 p.m. when dad returned from his insurance office on Main Street. Her mom, not an avid cook, prepared meals ranging from "Gram's meatloaf" to chicken dishes or Friday's traditional no-meat meal, often Mrs. Paul's fish sticks. On Saturdays, the fare might simply be hot dogs and beans, while Sunday meals were more elaborate and included roasts, potatoes, and vegetables.

The children had no specific daily chores other than to make their beds and pick up their rooms. There were no weekly allowances. Everyone was expected and wanted to help out.

The family loved musicals: *Camelot, Hello, Dolly!, Oklahoma!, Sound of Music, Man of La Mancha*, many of them seen at the local Mohawk or Paramount theaters. Once the family even travelled to Broadway in New York City to see *George M!* They loved to sing the scores to musicals when traveling and one time sang the *Camelot* repertoire from North Adams to New York and back.

Martha entered St. Joseph's High School in 1967 and quickly became engaged in the school's activities. She joined the well-known debate club, became a member of the honor society, served two years as secretary of the Student Council, and as national delegate to their convention. In her junior year, she was chosen to represent the American Legion Auxiliary as Girls State delegate, all the while at St. Joseph's becoming a ranked and accomplished debater. At Girls State, she was elected "governor" for the session.

In early 1970, as talk of closing St. Joseph's increased, and funding and support for extracurricular activities seemed to be waning, Martha and her family decided she would transfer to Drury High School for her senior year. The transition was successful even though she needed to make up a number of physical education courses not available at St. Joe's. She continued speech competition, joined the ski club and class newspaper staff, and acted as Maria the Innkeeper's wife in the school's play *Man of La Mancha*. She graduated tenth in her class. She still has many friends from both St. Joe's and Drury High.

During high school, Martha's first job was scooping ice cream at Howard Johnson's in Williamstown. She worked in her dad's insurance office at a time when all car license plates expired on the same date. She would help his insurance customers with their renewals and exchanged old plates for new ones, a slow process the agency offered of renewing five plates at a time. As a high school senior and college freshman, she waitressed at Williamstown's 1896 House.

ADVANCED DEGREES

Martha entered Williams College in the fall of 1971, the first class of women to attend all four years. (Coeducation was adopted by the college in 1969.) She worked on the school newspaper, and became a host on the college radio station WCFM-91.9 "On Your Dial," initially reporting on news and sports. In her later years, she hosted a classical music program on Sunday nights. She belonged to the Cardinal Newman Society and attended Hootenanny Masses on weekends.

As a sophomore, she served on the search committee for a new college president. Following that interesting assignment, she worked with the Dean of Williams on women's issues concerning careers and health. Martha graduated in 1975 with a bachelor's degree in the History of Ideas, with honors, and was awarded the William Bradford Turner Citizenship Prize.

Considering careers in journalism or law, she decided law school offered more opportunities and flexibility for careers in the public or private sector.

Waitlisted at several prominent law schools, Martha decided to wait a year before attending Boston University Law School. During this time, she waitressed on Martha's Vineyard, substitute taught, and worked for *Martha '72,* a nonprofit cleaning and service company. During college and later in law school, Martha would vacation on Martha's Vineyard. Rested and relaxed, she entered law school in 1976.

At Boston University, Martha was on a committee involving women's organizations, served as a teaching assistant in public communications, and was on the National Moot Court Team. She was the class speaker at her 1979 graduation, receiving a Juris Doctorate in Law.

After graduation and until 1986, Martha worked for two private law firms primarily on civil cases, including defense work in personal injury incidents defending homeowners, drivers, or doctors in malpractice suits. She had an opportunity to do some *pro bono* work and at one point was elected the President of the Massachusetts Women's Bar Association.

Interested in trial work and public service, Martha joined the Middlesex District Attorney's office in 1986 as an Assistant District Attorney in Lowell, and shortly afterwards was asked to join the Boston Organized Crime Strike Force as a Special Attorney of the U.S. Department of Justice. Martha then returned to the DA's office in 1989 and was appointed Chief of the Child Abuse Prosecution Unit two years later. She remained in this position until 1997 when she resigned in order to campaign for Middlesex County District Attorney.

THE POLITICAL REALM

Martha refers to herself as an "accidental politician." After working as an Assistant District Attorney, she realized that to have a wider effect on the justice system and help a broader section of people, she would need to be in a position of higher authority and responsibilities. This was the beginning of a path that eventually led to becoming the Attorney General for Massachusetts.

While serving as an ADA, Martha was assigned a criminal case that made her name well known. The case concerned the prosecution of Louise Woodward, a nineteen-year-old British *au pair* accused of shaking an eight-month-old child to death. Coakley and the lead prosecutor convinced the jury to convict her of second-degree murder, which the judge ultimately reduced to manslaughter. *The Boston Globe* stated at the time, "Coakley's lucid presentation of complex medical testimony made her one of the nation's most recognized criminal lawyers." The case also revealed Martha's strong sense of empathy when, behind the scenes, she shed tears with the victim's father as he recounted taking his son off life support.

Bolstered by her experience and high name recognition, Martha ran for and was elected District Attorney for Middlesex County, the largest county in the Commonwealth, in 1998. During her campaign, she met Thomas O'Connor, a deputy superintendent for Cambridge Police, who visited her headquarters to contribute $100. They married two years later on Martha's Vineyard while Martha was serving as the District Attorney. She served in this role for eight years.

During her time as Middlesex County District Attorney, she oversaw several more high-profile cases. They included the prosecution of Michael McDermott, who shot and killed seven co-workers in Wakefield, Massachusetts. Using a rifle, pistol, and shotgun, he shot off thirty-seven rounds, shooting his victims in the back of the head. He was found guilty of seven counts of first-degree murder and is serving seven life sentences without the possibility of parole.

Another case involved the conviction of Thomas Junta, a hockey dad, of involuntary manslaughter after he attacked and killed another hockey father at a children's pick-up hockey game. The attack, witnessed by those children, drew much publicity in the area.

One of her more complex cases was trying Paul Shanley, a former priest who was convicted of raping a child. Shanley had been evaluated in the 1990s by the Church and found suspect of sexual encounters. The Church settled several related lawsuits and then transferred Shanley to another parish out-of-state. Ultimately, after testimonies, Shanley was convicted of raping a child while serving in a Middlesex County parish. He served twelve years in prison, was released in 2017, and died in 2020.

While she served as DA, the office established preventative measures for child abuse, and parameters for holding accountable those in violation. The department also enhanced its investigatory methods involving domestic violence and sexual assault issues.

With her successes, Martha ran for and was elected Attorney General of Massachusetts in November 2006. When she took office in January 2007, she became the first woman in state history to serve as attorney general. She was sworn in at the MASS MoCA in North Adams with a benediction by Fr. Jerome (Joseph) Day, her St. Joe's classmate. In her new role, she managed five diverse bureaus: Executive, Government, Criminal, Medicaid Fraud, and Labor with over five hundred employees and attorneys in the numerous divisions within each bureau.

The position of Attorney General, a four-year term, is one of six elected Constitutional offices within the State, among them Governor, Lt. Governor, Secretary of State, Treasurer, Auditor, and Attorney General.

Over the ensuing eight years, Martha was responsible for sponsoring many public policy pieces of legislation, ranging from a Guide to Consumer Credit that activated a hotline for helping people with financial difficulties to human trafficking statutes designed to change the lens on how people viewed prostitution. She strongly advocated that prostitution is not victimless, but truly a crime against women, often young girls.

Martha is credited with recovering over $600 million for the Commonwealth by settling the Big Dig lawsuit. Contractors for Boston's complex highway/tunnel project were held responsible for killing a passing motorist after the ceiling collapsed in the tunnel. The project, overdue and over budget, had been plagued by relentless water leaks.

During her years in office, in one of the first settlements of the time, she won lawsuits recovering over $400 million from Wall Street lenders making predatory home loans. The result kept thousands of people in their homes, reduced principal on certain loans, and financially assisted others who had already lost their homes.

Tom O'Connor and Martha Coakley with Michelle Obama in Boston at a 2014 event when Coakley is campaigning for Governor.

Under Martha's direction, the Medicaid Fraud Bureau recovered over $100 million from a series of fraudulent schemes ranging from overbilling the state for inflated drug prices and lab fees to unnecessary treatment, treatment not provided, or kickback efforts. Hundreds of indictments were issued in her ongoing efforts to protect the Medicaid program.

Politically experienced, competitive, knowing she could make a difference and affect even a wider group of people, Martha decided to run for U.S. Senate in 2009 to succeed the late Senator Ted Kennedy. As the Democratic nominee, Martha lost the election to the Republican candidate and subsequently was re-elected to serve in her role as Attorney General.

Though eligible for re-election as Attorney General in 2014, Martha decided to run for the open seat of Governor of Massachusetts. She and her running mate ran a widely respected campaign but were narrowly defeated, losing by two percentage points.

Martha has served as the President of the Massachusetts District Attorneys and Women's Bar Associations, been on the Board of Directors for the Dana Farber Cancer Institute, and was on the Board of Directors for the Middlesex Partnerships for Youth organization.

After leaving office in 2015, Martha attended the Harvard Kennedy Institute of Politics and then reentered private practice as a partner in a Boston-based law firm, working as an attorney and legal advisor. Her clients range from a fantasy sports website to a student loan company to an electronic cigarette maker.

LIFE AFTER POLITICS

Today she works as a consultant from her home, representing and advising clients while her husband, Tom O'Connor, retired from the police force, works for a private security company headed by a former police commissioner providing executive protection and site security services.

Martha and her husband, Tom, enjoying a sunny day on the slopes.

COURTESY MARTHA COAKLEY

Martha showing off their new puppy, Jefferson.

COURTESY MARTHA COAKLEY

She enjoys downhill skiing with Tom at Killington or Stowe resorts in Vermont, and they especially enjoy ski trips out west to Park City in Utah or Steamboat Springs in Colorado. Martha remains a voracious reader, working on three or four books at a time, more fiction than nonfiction, and enjoys historical biographies.

They enjoy walking their Labradors, a yellow male named Jefferson and a black female named Honor. Martha is involved with a capital campaign for the New England Assistance Dog Society (NEADS) that trains mostly Labradors for use by veterans or persons with emotional needs.

Martha's real relaxation comes in grocery shopping and preparing meals. She makes her own salads and is accomplished at pasta and sausage dishes, as well as fish, pork, and chicken. Their favorite food style is Italian, and the couple likes to frequent Italian restaurants in the North End of Boston. They have cut back on red meat but still enjoy a burger "now-and-then."

Her caring, pragmatic, self-confident, and strong personality has helped many people in the Commonwealth of Massachusetts. In her words, "Growing up in that small city [of North Adams], I had a very strong sense of discipline, education, and the need to work for things."

Martha has accomplished many firsts in her life, from graduating in the first Williams College class of four-year female students to being the first female District Attorney for Middlesex County, the first female Attorney General for Massachusetts, and the first female Democratic senatorial candidate in Massachusetts.

One supporter summed it up very simply: "She is a very caring person and has done a lot for the Commonwealth." Over her thirty-plus years of public service, Martha has garnered many accolades and awards from many different sources: Woman of the Year from the Center for Women in Politics, the Leila Robinson Award from the Women's Bar Association, and the Eleanor Roosevelt Award from the Massachusetts Democratic Party. These recognitions are well-earned and speak volumes.

LOIS DAUGHERTY

This mother of eight children, five girls and three boys, is a portrait of devotion and resilience. Lois Daugherty has parented, mostly alone, raising her children into adults who have then gone on to devote their careers to helping others. She is descended from one of the first African American property owners in North Adams, and her spirit spreads through the community exponentially.

On June 5, 1928, in North Adams, Lois Greene was born at home to Anthony Greene and Vivian Vanderburgh Greene. Anthony had been born in Washington, D.C., in 1900 and moved to Williamstown as a child. He graduated from Williamstown High School where he was a star athlete and played varsity football. Anthony worked for the Massachusetts State Highway Department for over forty years, receiving a gold watch when he retired in 1965. He lived nearly twenty more years, passing on in 1982.

Lois's mother, Vivian Vanderburgh (Lewis) Greene was born in Bennington, Vermont, in 1889 and married Anthony in 1919. The couple resided in North Adams for over fifty years and ultimately had seven children, two sons and five daughters. One son was killed in action during the Korean War. Vivian was a Gold Star mother and a member of the Veterans of Foreign Wars Auxiliary as well as the Military Order of the Cootie, the honor degree of the VFW.

Little is known about Lois's paternal grandparents, Charles and Margaret (Henry) Greene, who were born in the Virginias or Carolinas in the 1800s then moved to and resided in Washington, D.C.

Lois's maternal grandparents were Walter J. Lewis and Elizabeth Lewis Vanderburgh Dawkins. Vivian, Lois's mother, was raised by Elizabeth and her second husband Thomas Dawkins, who were married in 1908. Thomas Dawkins had been born in Union, South Carolina, and worked for forty-three years for the Pullman Company, most of that time as a porter on trains of the Harlem division of the Boston & Albany railroad. His route was between New York and North Adams, and the round trips are what attracted him to the North Adams area, although he had little time to enjoy its beauty, with traveling so often. He retired in July 1948 and passed away a decade later.

Thomas and Elizabeth were one of the first African American property owners in North Adams. Elizabeth managed their apartments on River Street and in the summertime she also rented rooms at their Walnut Street property to wealthy, Black New Yorkers. Elizabeth and Thomas lived on Walnut and Houghton Streets for most of their lives, Elizabeth passing away in 1966 at their home on Houghton Street.

Lois grew up on Washington Avenue with her parents and six siblings. There were five girls and two boys in the family. The yellow, two-story, slate-roofed house just off Ashland Street was in an area called "the swamp" because it flooded frequently, located at a low spot between Church and Ashland Streets.

Her childhood chores included washing the stairs, cleaning the kitchen, and general housekeeping with her older sister. The boys had paper routes and shoveled snow. Lois recalls, "I babysat, and any money earned was brought home and given to Mom." She spent a lot of time at the nearby YMCA, swimming, swinging from ropes, and playing ping-pong. Outside, it was riding bikes and playing hopscotch with the girls.

Her mom was the family's cook, and a good one. Vivian had little tolerance for others in her kitchen, not wanting the risk of wasting food while training novices. Breakfast was cereal or oatmeal. Anthony, working varied hours for the highway department, was usually gone for supper so mom and the kids ate spaghetti and meatballs, meatloaf, reheated hamburger, and different macaroni dishes. The best dessert was doughnuts made from scratch. The doughnut holes were reserved and used as a reward for children doing their chores.

Marcella, Lois's eldest sister, had the biggest influence on her. She babysat Lois, the youngest, and was a big help to Mom.

Marcella, very independent, left home and moved to Washington, D.C., to work at the Pentagon. She was Lois's role model.

Lois grew up in North Adams, attended Mark Hopkins elementary school, and went to Drury High School. She was an active, athletic, and fun-loving classmate. Lois was a guard on the school's girls basketball team and captained her sophomore year. Although wanting to pitch, she dominated as the baseball team's first baseman. Lois played both sports all four years of school. In addition, she played soccer, was on the bowling club, and served as homeroom vice president.

Nicknamed "Louie" in her senior yearbook, Lois was clearly beloved by her classmates, who wrote of her: "Sparkling personality—participated in all sports—life of the gym class—carefree nature—crazy antics—best candidate for the 'ping-pong' champion of 1947," referring to the years she spent playing ping-pong at the local YMCA. Her favorite teacher was Mr. Wellington Charles (whom the kids called Duke). Lois enjoyed his history course and his easygoing nature. Geography was another favorite subject. Math was the subject she likes the least, even today.

Lois started working at the Sprague Electric Company during the war years until someone discovered she was only fifteen years old. Returning to Sprague after high school, Lois worked there a number of years while playing on its basketball team, the Sprague Lassies. Lois played center guard for the Lassies, a semi-professional team that belonged to the Western Massachusetts Amateur Athletic Union (AAU). It was one of the most enjoyable times of her life, working and playing basketball. The team competed throughout western Massachusetts, playing in Westover, Fitchburg, and Lenox. The girls brought their basketball uniforms to work, changed near the end of their shift, and travelled by car to games. Sprague enjoyed the advertising and reimbursed the ladies for lost work time.

In August 1951, the family received tragic news that Lois's brother, Corporal Gordon Greene, was killed in action in Korea, the first North Adams man to die in the war. Gordon was twenty-six years old, a career soldier who had survived the grueling World

War II battles in North Africa and Anzio. He had reenlisted in 1946 and was a member of the heroic Negro Battalion of the 24th Infantry Regiment when killed.

MARRIAGE AND CHILDREN

In 1953, Lois married Carlton Daugherty at Saint John's Episcopal Church in North Adams. She left Sprague and moved to New York State where Carlton worked as a lathe operator for the General Electric Company in Schenectady. Carlton had been born in Albany, New York, in the 1920s and served in the U. S. Army during World War II. He worked for a time as a longshoreman on the Hudson River and later at the Saratoga Racetrack. While in the Saratoga area, Lois worked as a cook at nearby Skidmore College.

While living in New York, the family had four children and eventually returned to North Adams to be near family. Four more children were born. In 1960, the family lived in a small duplex on East Quincy Street, owned by her sister, and then moved to a tenement house on Crowley Avenue. Carlton worked as a school custodian, and after several years, he and Lois divorced.

Lois was now alone with eight children, ranging in age from teenager to infant, living in sub-standard housing on Crowley Avenue. The apartment had a living/dining room with a large kitchen on the first floor and on the second floor, one bathroom and three bedrooms. Lois and one daughter shared a bedroom, four girls in another, and the three boys in the last bedroom.

The two-story white clapboard tenement was frigid in winter, with stoves only in the living room and kitchen. The boys would seal off the back door with plastic to keep some of the heat in. One daughter remembers that with no heat upstairs, "in the morning we'd wash up in the bathroom and run downstairs and get dressed in the living room."

The kids did whatever chores their mother assigned, and always made their beds first thing. Since the family did not have a clothes washer or dryer, the older sister and brother took the laundry for nine people to the nearby laundromat. It was the younger boy's responsibility to burn the trash outside. Making eight school lunches five days a week was also a demanding effort.

In her early years, one daughter fondly remembers her mom sitting outside in the summer smoking Kent cigarettes. "A pack would last her forever. She didn't inhale and usually smoked only in the summer, mainly to keep the bugs away, " her daughter said.

With little money to spend, and food to stretch, Lois did all the cooking, mostly from memory. She cooked a meal the kids called "American Goulash," a mixture of elbow macaroni, meat and sauce. Saturdays was always hot dogs and mustard. In wintertime, breakfast needed to be inexpensive, hot, and filling: They ate a lot of hot cereal like Maltex oatmeal or Cream of Wheat. Yet Lois always seemed to find time to bake cakes, brownies, and the most fantastic chocolate chip cookies for her troop of kids.

Sunday meals were special. Lois often made cinnamon toast slathered with butter, cooked sausage, and they would have tea with condensed milk. Sunday dinners could be roast beef, leg of lamb, or Lois's great fried chicken and sometimes her acclaimed potato salad.

Most importantly, Lois made sure church was a central part of the family's life. They all walked and sat together at nearby Saint John's Episcopal Church for services and Sunday school, even through high school.

Growing up, the family could not afford vacations. Lois didn't even drive until later in life. The family played plenty of board and card games, and Lois would send the kids to the library at least weekly to check out books. Reading was important to her.

Every so often, Lois's brother Uncle Q took everyone to Riverside or Mountain Park for the day. Another treat the kids loved was accompanying their grandfather on his Saturday morning trips to the dump and having a chance to throw things in the landfill. Lois' parents were supportive—and grandma made the best doughnuts.

The Daughertys had plenty of playmates. Kids came from all around the neighborhood to play on Crowley Avenue, riding bikes or playing Wiffle ball games in the large parking lot near Ashkar Sales and the Jarisch Box Company and sliding in wintertime on the nearby hill. Best of all was playing at the railroad tracks, hiding and jumping around 55-gallon drums stacked 10 to 15 feet high. Like many parents, Lois's only instruction to her children was "be home when the streetlights come on."

Every summer, Lois enrolled the kids in the YMCA's Camp Stayhom. With packed lunches of bologna or sardine sandwiches, sometimes even thick ham and egg salad sandwiches, the kids would head off to the Y. There they learned to swim, enjoyed arts and crafts, took part in gymnastics or the basketball league, and sometimes they would go to Camp Clark at Windsor Lake for a sleep-out with the luxury of provided sleeping bags.

While the family received state aid, Lois was never one to think the system will take care of you. Life was not easy. She did not have a driver's license and needed to walk everywhere. She accepted the assistance for food and clothing for the children but also worked whenever possible. When the children were older, Lois went back to work at Drury High School and then retired from the Massachusetts College of Liberal Arts.

Lois had pride and discipline. The family was poor, but everyone went out of the house freshly scrubbed. Lois stressed a lot about having clean clothes. When the children were little, their grandmother sewed some of their clothes. Otherwise, most of the kids wore hand-me-downs or donations that Lois insisted be neat and tidy.

As one daughter put it, "Mom was tough but loving and did an excellent job with us." By herself, she was naturally the family's disciplinarian. There are several versions of her tool-of-choice, although all involve the use of a stick she kept in the kitchen corner for serious rule violators. Some say it was a laundry stick nicknamed "boonie;" others say it was a three-foot Bat Masterson cane one of the boys ordered from the popular TV western.

HOLIDAYS TO REMEMBER

One thing Lois loved was making the holidays special. Thanksgiving was always a big celebration. Usually, the family ate at their grandparents' house right across the street. There were grown-up and kids' tables and always plenty of food.

Christmas was particularly special. Late on Christmas Eve, Lois and the older children would pull a sled through the yard and around the house, leaving tracks in the snow to imitate Santa's sleigh and leave partially eaten apples to imitate reindeer feeding. Cocoa and doughnuts were left by the fireplace for Santa. In the morning, "she would line us up on the staircase youngest to oldest to proceed down the stairs to see what presents Santa had brought. We were always amazed when we turned the corner into the living room to see how many presents/toys there were."

The whole family together: back row, l-r, Alex, Dave, Marvin; middle row, l-r, Carla, Khaliah; front row, l-r, Jill, Terri, Wendi

Lois had spent months saving and buying items on store lay-away, making sure each child received one particular item he or she wanted, in addition to clothing.

Easter was one of the family's bigger celebrations. Lois would have one of the older boys put a stuffed bunny rabbit in the tree so the little children would find it in the morning, indicating the Easter Bunny had been there. Easter baskets were filled with candy with lots of jellybeans and everyone had new clothes for Easter including hats or bonnets. To this day, Lois still enjoys her black licorice jellybeans.

The kids always dressed up for Halloween in home-made out-fits. Over the years, there were firemen, cowboys, Indians, movie stars, and once there were three Supremes. When the kids got home, Lois had everyone dump their candy into a large yellow bowl. She would then equally distribute the candy. That wasn't an always popular decision, especially among the older children who had col-lected more.

Within the local community, Lois was a member (and one-time president) of the Merry Makers Club, an African American Women's society. The club planned children's activities such as recit-als, Christmas, and Halloween kids' parties. As part of the local Black community, the family had close ties to four or five families. Together they had parties at different people's homes, inviting sin-gles as well as couples. The group played cards and danced. When it was at Lois's house, Carla, the second oldest daughter, and her siblings would watch from upstairs. The same group, sometimes as many as sixty family members, would have great fun in nice weather picnicking at the Fish Pond or Mauserts from early morn-ing until dark.

A First Home

In the late 1960s and early 1970s, the City of North Adams embarked on a huge urban renewal project, tearing down blocks of buildings on the south side of Main Street. Homes and familiar stores were affected, and Lois and her family needed to move before their tenement was torn down.

With help and Lois's insistence on finding a decent place to live, in 1973 she bought her first house on Gregory Avenue. It had been a duplex but was converted to a single-family home. Now with twelve rooms, the family had plenty of space, although Lois was burdened with her first mortgage, still supporting eight children with some assistance. The children helped as they could, pitching in money earned from part-time jobs. One son said, "I turned over my earnings to Mom. She took care of everything, so I didn't need money, and she did it to run the household. We all gave her our money."

The move provided more room for the family but now they found themselves a cab-drive away from the YMCA, Nassif's, their drug store, grocery shopping, and their neighborhood friends. Lois stayed on Gregory Avenue for the next forty-three years. More recently, she moved to the Riverview City Apartments.

In her later years, Lois met William Nelson, an Army veteran who had served in a unit with the famed Tuskegee Airmen. He had moved to North Adams in the early 1960s. Not long after his arrival, in 1966, his Marine son was killed in action in Vietnam. William, known as "Pops" to Lois's children, initially worked at Arnold Print Works and subsequently retired in 1988 from James River Company as a steam engineer. He enjoyed driving immaculately kept Buicks and Pontiacs. The couple married in 1986, and Lois, in her fifties, learned how to drive. They were married for less than three years when "Pops" passed away from cancer in 1989.

Never one to sit still very long, over the years Lois has served on the Community Development Corporation and Legal Aid. People value her opinion and willingness to speak out on issues. She still enjoys sports and watches Celtics basketball and Patriots football.

Tragedy struck one more time when on December 22, 1995, Lois's son Marvin, a U. S. Air Force veteran and a registered nurse working at the Berkshire Medical Center, died from cancer and heart complications, leaving two young daughters.

Lois is the family's historian. In addition to passed-down family stories, their vital oral history, she is the keeper of the family's black-and-white photos. The kids are always able to find a picture of someone they are looking for. When asked what her biggest accomplishment in life was, she said, "My children."

Mostly by herself, Lois raised her eight children, all of whom graduated from high school, and among them earned seven bachelor's degrees, four master's degrees, and a doctorate. Their careers range from law/criminal justice, hospitality management, nursing, psychology, and education to a health educator and respite worker, dedicating their lives to serving others. Four currently live in North Adams near their mother.

One son beautifully summed up Lois's life when he said, "We never wanted for anything. I'm not sure how she did it all."

On graduation day, Lois and "Pops" are so proud of Alex, who has gone on to be an attorney.

FATHER JEROME "JOE" DAY

Two distinct threads run through the remarkable life of Jerome Day—his service to God's Word through his calling as a priest in the Catholic Church and his inspiration as a journalist and teacher. Day, better known to all as Father Joe, believes in his heart that he has been guided and touched by Christ. He considers it a "gift from God" that he has been able to pursue both journalism and his religious calling. Now, instead of editorializing for a newspaper, he is witnessing to his students and leading his congregation.

Father Joe's story begins with his birth in North Adams, Massachusetts, on September 4, 1953, to Charles Franklin Day and Marjorie (Costello) Day. Joe never really knew his father. Charles Day was born in 1903, in Clarksburg. He was an old New England Yankee raised by his grandfather (also named Charles) and step-grandmother. Joe's dad had been a contractor by trade. Although he built some houses, he was primarily involved with earth-moving machines in industrial work. In 1954, he died suddenly from a cerebral hemorrhage, leaving behind Marjorie and the two children, Katherine, by his first wife Genevieve, and one-year-old Joe.

Marjorie was born in 1912 in North Adams and met Charles when she was employed at Richmond Oil Company in Adams. Notably, her Irish ancestry can be traced back to cousins Charles and John Carroll, the former a signer of the Declaration of Independence and the latter the first bishop and archbishop of the Roman Catholic Church in America. Initially, Marjorie, by then widowed, was able to stay at home with Joe, but when he got older, she worked at the Adams Nursing Home (in North Adams) as the Director of Activities. Marjorie passed away in 1985.

Father Joe's Irish heritage runs strong and deep. His paternal grandfather, Charles Day, born in North Adams, was a farmer. The Day lineage stretches back to County Fermanagh in Northern Ireland, where records indicate his ancestors may have been "planters." Planters were a Protestant people encouraged to move from England to Ireland to populate the land and support the English king. The first Day immigrated to New England in 1752.

Father Joe's maternal grandparents Joe and Ellen (Walsh) Costello lived in Clarksburg, Massachusetts. They had each immigrated to the U.S. during the last part of the 19th century, and Joe worked as a policeman in New York. Ellen was Joe Costello's second wife. When his first wife died in the 1890s, he accompanied her body back to Ireland for burial as she'd wished. Though Joe Costello and his second wife had immigrated to the U.S. about the same time, and though they'd belonged to the same parish in Ireland, it took a party in Bennington, Vermont, to bring them together.

On subsequent Sundays, Joe Costello would bike the twenty-five miles from Bennington to Adams to court Ellen. Clearly this worked, because he won her hand and they married. Joe went on to become a carder at the Strong-Hewatt Company in Clarksburg for many years.

FAMILY LIFE

Father Joe was brought up on Rich Street in North Adams, on a farm that had been in his family for four generations. His parents, grandparents, and great-grandparents had all lived on the farm. The farmhouse is now in a Trust, providing Father Joe a place to stay during his visits to North Adams. About ten acres remain, with the rest of the forty acres long sold off.

Because Joe's father died when he was just a year old, his mother relied on the help of aunts and uncles. In the early 1960s, the house was reconfigured, and Joe's two aunts and one uncle came to live on the farm. For most of his young life it was essentially Joe, his mom, aunts, and the uncle living on Rich Street. His sister, Kay, who was older, had married and left home, moving across the street to a house her dad had built. Kay passed away in 2011.

The five of them settled into a routine and always ate their evening meal together at the family's old-fashioned square table, white-enameled and black-trimmed with chairs that had shiny black vinyl seats. He remembers evening meals were between 4:30 and 5:30 with his mom and her sister at opposite ends of the table while he sat across from his other aunt and his uncle.

Joe's mom did most of the cooking, preparing typical meals of the time: beans and franks with coleslaw, spaghetti and meatballs, fried or baked chicken, ham, turkey, and really great soups and stews. It was always fish sticks on Fridays. Joe distinctly remembers a particular meal contributed by his Aunt Agnes: hamburger and greyish mashed potatoes served with a small dollop of lard. He ate what was put in front of him, but he did not relish this meal.

Vacations were a family affair. They visited Niagara Falls and Canada, stopping along the way to see various shrines. They visited the town of Saint-Anne-de-Beaupré in Québec, Saint Joseph's Oratory in Montreal, and the shrine of Our Lady of La Salette in Enfield, New Hampshire. Providentially, later in life during Father Joe's graduate studies at McGill University in Montreal, he was housed at the rectory of Our Lady of La Salette.

Local trips included Lake George, Fort Ticonderoga, and also New York City to sightsee and watch the famous Rockettes. Two weeks every summer, Joe attended Camp Holy Cross in Goshen, Massachusetts.

EARLY CALL TO HIS VOCATION

Joe and his family belonged to the St. Francis of Assisi Parish, and he attended the associated St. Joseph's schools. He served as an altar boy from the third grade through high school. In his junior and senior years, he was the leader of the altar boy society, helping to initiate and train newcomers.

Joe's vocation as a priest was on his mind at an early age. At the farm, there was a huge barn. In a corner of the barn, Joe created a little church. He used a brandy snifter for a chalice, a gold-colored paten, and he "celebrated" Mass accompanied by scripture readings.

Not surprisingly for a young boy, the barn and its outbuildings also served as "fortresses" where he and his friends had chestnut and snowball battles. Their hideouts also extended to rusty old Dodge and Plymouth cars on the premises.

During his early life, Joe enjoyed fishing with friends at Windsor Lake. He always thought his meager catches cast doubts on whether any fish at all lived in the pond. He was a member of St. Francis Boy Scout Troop #36 and enjoyed the camaraderie and hiking and the outdoors. He achieved First Class rank before the troop eventually dissolved. On occasion, he vacationed with his cousins who had a cottage on a lake in New York where they swam and waterskied. This was a treat. At home, he skied cross-country and skated at the public rinks.

Joe readily talks about his idyllic childhood and how it was nourished by the Sisters of St. Joseph. "They were kind, intelligent, funny, caring, and great role models," he recalls. His fondness was reciprocated. The nuns loved him. A local paper ran a photo of Joe as a first grader removing money from his piggy bank to donate to the convent building fund.

Early on, school seemed to point Joe in the direction of journalism. In the fifth grade, he became the *Savio Headlines* editor, and in the eighth grade, when Sister Raymond Francis asked him what he would like to do with his life he said, "Live in North Adams and be the editor of *The Transcript*," the local newspaper that had been founded in 1843. This interest carried on through high school where he was a reporter and editor for the *Scribe* and then on into college where he worked for *The Saint Anselm Crier* and served two years as its editor.

Joe was on the high school's distinguished debate club for four years. Many of its members went on to important careers in government, law, politics, and higher education. He was also a National Honor Society member and a Glee Club choralist for four years. He does remember Sister Helen Theresa hinting that with his singing ability he would do well in the back row and on the more difficult notes, he might consider just moving his mouth.

He was active in school plays, had a lead role in *Oklahoma!*, and was the innkeeper in the Christmas pageant his sophomore year. During pageant practice someone smelled gas, and the troupe abandoned school. Joe, waiting inside the "inn," never got the word and remained enclosed listening for his cue to come out. When he emerged, he was quite surprised to appear before an empty auditorium.

Joe readily admits he was not a high school athlete. When they played pick-up basketball in the school yard, one of his closest friends had to make sure he wasn't the last one picked. In his senior year, Joe had a brief one-day stint on the school's baseball team. Maybe gratuitously, he was accepted on the team, but he quickly realized his lack of ability and quit, not wanting to hurt their chance of winning. Ironically, the team did not win a single game that year!

To this day, Joe and one of his best friends joke about their lack of dancing ability as they recount the Friday night dances held in the annex building. During high school Joe had several girlfriends but none of a serious nature.

He was always a hard worker. For several summers, in his younger years, Joe worked part-time at McDonald's. Beginning as a senior in high school and all through college, Joe was at the job he loved, working at *The Transcript* of North Adams, part-time at first, but later full-time. Joe worked his way through college, interestingly with the help of an annual Petricca Construction scholarship, a company that was a competitor of his dad's business many years ago.

He was accepted at Saint Anselm College in Manchester, New Hampshire. While there, Joe worked as the editor of *The Saint Anselm Crier*. This position eventually led to his full-time summer position at *The Transcript*.

The Transcript was a great experience for Joe. He worked at *Transcript* offices in Adams,

Years later, Father Jerome is now a faculty advisor at *The Saint Anselm Crier*. He joins senior Alex Dooley, current editor of the *Crier*, at the 2020 Democratic debate just before the New Hampshire primary.

North Adams, and Williamstown. His broad experiences and exposure to all facets of journalism provided the bedrock for his future journalistic career. He rotated through various jobs, filling in for absences and vacations, reporting on sports, city hall happenings, births, funerals, and obituaries. At one point, he even worked the social desk. (He acknowledges that describing wedding dresses was at times perplexing for him. What exactly is "peau de soie"?) On the sports side, making sense of the myriad of statistics from the Pownal dog track always took time to sort out.

Graduation day from Saint Anselm in the spring of 1975 remains a vivid memory. He found himself consoling his sad departing classmates as they all headed out into the next chapter in their lives. He was encouraging to each of them, telling his close friends they would be bringing their light into the world and everything would be all right. When he returned to his dorm room to pack, he broke down sobbing, and at that moment he knew someday he would return to St. A's himself as a monk, maybe even a priest and teacher. From that moment on, this thought never left him.

Joe graduated with high honors, then began his fifteen-year peripatetic journey to the priesthood. He says today, "It's obvious how God has designed our life's choices, and how he intends us to go."

THE PATH THROUGH JOURNALISM

For several years, Joe taught English at schools in Vermont and New Hampshire, and in between teaching, he worked as a reporter for *The Transcript*. He also continued his education. In 1978, he received his master's degree in Anglo-Irish studies from University College Dublin and taught several more years before joining *The Transcript* in 1980.

He began working as a reporter and after a few years, "with God's grace," he accomplished his longtime dream, becoming Managing Editor. During the 1980s and 1990s, *The Transcript* had been sold several times, and it gradually morphed from a family-friendly business to corporatized journalism. The work became more demanding and less satisfying. After several years of enforced downsizing, Joe began asking himself if the job was worth all the effort, as he was feeling used and worn down. He wondered if there was something else of a higher calling for him.

Joe worked as the editor for other small newspapers before entering the priesthood. When the North Adams *Transcript* closed in 2014, merging with *The Berkshire Eagle*, Joe wrote a valedictory column. The controversial years of *The Transcript*'s existence are aptly described in Loren Ghiglione's book, *The Buying and Selling of America's Newspapers.*

There is a sad sidelight to Joe's time at *The Transcript*. While an editor, he hired a young, aspiring journalist named Danny Pearl. Danny, a recent Stanford graduate, had sent Joe a letter commenting on an article Joe had written on international reporting. Subsequently, Danny answered a magazine advertisement *The Transcript* had placed seeking a reporter.

Following a phone interview, Danny agreed to pay his own travel expenses and come to North Adams for an interview. Joe picked him up at the local bus station, interviewed Danny, who stayed at a guest house across from Harriman Airport, and hired him. Danny became the North Adams City reporter. He was funny, accurate, determined, bright, well intentioned, quick to catch on, and easy to correct. He became a highly regarded reporter for *The Transcript* and in the early 1990s eventually moved on to work for the *Wall Street Journal*. Joe, as Danny's first editor, remembers, "Danny connected with and wanted to build bridges between people. He had a desire to eventually report on the Middle East."

Although they had not seen each other for several years, Joe was touched when Danny returned to North Adams to attend the first Mass that he celebrated as Father Jerome at St. Francis Church, his hometown parish, after his ordination.

In early 2002, Joe received word of Danny's kidnapping by terrorists in Pakistan. He has not forgotten those dark days. At the time, he quickly became involved in the worldwide effort to rescue Danny, personally sending an email to the kidnappers, saying Danny was not a spy but had great insight into the world, was compassionate, and an asset to all who knew him. Father Joe also contacted the student chaplaincy at Stanford and got in touch with several Muslim/Pakistani student groups who wrote pleas for Danny's release, noting that Allah was all merciful and that Danny was no threat to their people.

In retrospect, their efforts were futile. It is thought that Danny was probably already dead, killed by Al Qaeda within a week of his capture. Subsequently, Father Joe spoke at the public service, "Danny Pearl: A Celebration of Life," held in North Adams in March 2002 and attended his memorial service in California.

In the late 1980s, as Joe was ending his secular editorial career, he was approached by his parish priest and asked to meet him in the sacristy. Joe, an adult but with his Catholic guilt mechanism fully in place, wondered what trouble he might be in. It turned out his pastor was in the process of planning a year-long celebration of St. Francis's 125th Anniversary (1863 to 1988) and wanted Joe to write a book about its history.

Joe, who has always had a strong attachment to his church, agreed and after eighteen months of writing and research, with the help of many parishioners, published *Dew Upon the Mountains*. The pastor provided a beautiful foreword commenting on the book's history, a portion of which reads as follows:

> *We need to journey backwards periodically, alone and sometimes with others, in search of our rootedness in this time and place, to revive our sense of identity and belongings, bonds and relationships, to reconstruct ourselves in some sense—as vague as it might be—of spiritual and temporal continuities. We need to see ourselves as part of something larger than simply ourselves, of time and place.*

MONASTIC NOVITIATE

In 1989, Joe Day embraced his future as Father Jerome Joseph Day, and began his new career. He entered the novitiate, taking simple vows with the Order of Saint Benedict at the Saint Anselm Abbey. For the next several years, Father Jerome would serve in the Office of News and Public Relations for Saint Anselm College and under-took seminary studies at St. John's Seminary in Boston.

During this time, he pronounced his solemn (lifelong) vows of Stability, Obedience, and *Conversatio Morum* (simplicity of life and charity) to the Benedictine Order. He became a deacon, then was ordained a priest in 1995. His vows have special meaning: Stability refers to the importance of community and a commitment to Christ. Obedience is to do the will of God, his superiors, and his conscience. And both are to be done while pledging Fidelity to his monastic life.

While living at the abbey, Father Joe became a professor in the English department and taught communication and literature courses. Initially his students found him stern and demanding. As time passed, however, they found they had to work hard to get an "A" from him, but they could depend on Joe's direct advice for those who were in over their head or who perhaps didn't belong in the course. A number of his students moved on to responsible positions in major news organizations in Washington, New York, and Boston.

From the late 1990s through the early 2000s, Father Jerome received a master's degree in dogmatic theology from St. John's Seminary in Boston, a master's degree in philosophy from Trinity College Dublin, and a PhD in communications from McGill University in Montreal. His dissertation was titled *An Analysis of Irish Famine Texts 1845-2000: The Discursive Uses of Hunger.*

In 2002, at the request of his Abbot, Father Jerome agreed to become the pastor at Saint Raphael Church in Manchester, New Hampshire, a position he still holds. As the parish's only priest, he ministers to seven hundred families and over 3000 parishioners, celebrating, by himself, four Masses on weekends.

Father Jerome lives at the parish rectory and goes "up the hill" daily for meetings at the abbey and to teach at Saint Anselm College. He has served on the Abbot's advisory committee and is now on the board of trustees. Between parish work, responsibilities to the abbey, and teaching, Father Joe is busy. His days off, Thursday morning to Friday night, seldom seem to materialize.

Few know that Father Joe is an avid appreciator of beauty. Living in a beautiful rectory built in 1907, he is always on the lookout for ways to restore it. He is a Craigslist devotee, ever since he found some hand-carved, mahogany columns from an old

Victorian mansion listed in the antiques section. Enlisting a parishioner with carpentry skills, they located the columns with arches in the center of the rectory.

Pinching his pennies, he uses Craigslist and his limited salary to collect communication artifacts that serve as discussion

Father Jerome, far right, and his advanced journalism class have the honor of meeting noted journalist Bob Schieffer, center.

topics for his course on communication history. So far, he has garnered a big-horn gramophone record player with cylinder records, a 1930s radio, moveable type, a 1953 telephone (his birth year), 1947 Philco TV, old newspapers, and a 1490 piece in Latin, from Venice, printed shortly after Gutenberg invented the printing press. He has hopes the collection will one day reside in the college's library.

One "find" that his close friends gently tease about is the magnificent oak doors that were salvaged when the *Transcript* building was razed. The doors disappeared, but one day when Joe was visiting North Adams, he came across them in a collectible shop. After some negotiations, he bought them in 2019 and asked his high school friends to move the massive doors to his front porch. Saved, there they wait even today, to be trimmed and hung in his family home.

At Saint Raphael, Father Jerome has found and nourished a vibrant community in an era where some parishes are contracting. He credits much of the parish's success to the good-heartedness of its parishioners and support from the Saint Anselm community. He himself has been a strong supporter, returning to some of the church's older customs such as the May Crowning of Mary, Benediction of the Blessed Sacrament, Vespers, and Friday evening novenas.

He has been an ardent supporter of "blessing" Masses

celebrated for different professions: a "white" Mass for doctors and nurses; a "red" Mass for lawyers, jurists, and legislators; and more recently, Father introduced a "blue" Mass to celebrate and bless all first responders.

The parish celebrates its Irish and German ancestry with an Octoberfest, a year-end Festival of Nations Flags, and a St. Patrick's Day celebration. One group in the parish organizes a travel program called "Roots/Routes of Faith." The group's travel has taken them to New York, Washington, Québec, and farther away to places like Ireland, Greece, Turkey, Austria, Hungary, and Italy (notably, Rome), exploring many churches, shrines, and monasteries during their travels.

At Father's encouragement, this very active parish promotes an end-of-year variety show called The New Raphael Follies. One act is a men's group called "Best Foot Forward," in which the guys dance and sing in different costumes, from top hats to biker gang apparel. Other forms of engagement include the recently introduced Christmas Bazaar and the Valentine's Day Brunch. (Father jokingly says, *Bring your wife or girlfriend but not both!!*) Parishioners are encouraged to include anyone in the community living alone.

The parish has long supported a food pantry, an altar boy society, and the parish scholarship program. He is a strong advocate for Saint Benedict Academy, serving grades pre-kindergarten through sixth grade and located on the parish's campus. Adult Education courses, too, are strongly supported: scriptural classes in the fall, doctrinal/liturgical classes in the winter, and Catholic history or social teaching in spring.

When tasked with studying a church leader during his novitiate, Father Joe explored the life and writings of Cardinal John Henry Newman, writing papers and speaking at conferences about this renowned and recently canonized saint. One of the cardinal's quotes he most appreciates, and clearly tries to emulate, reads, "To live is to change, and to be perfect is to change often."

Father Jerome continues to remain close to his family, especially his four nieces, his brother-in-law, and his high-school friends. Every fall, a group gathers in Manchester, New Hampshire, to have a weekend with Joe. They all stay at the rectory and talk and relive their St. Joe's high school days. Some Saturdays, they look for a forum where a political candidate may be speaking. To date, they've heard Chris Christie, Carly Fiorina, Joe Biden, and Pete Buttigieg.

Father Joe's transcendent personality has allowed him to be a successful editor, inspiring teacher, and approachable and beloved parish priest. His friends describe him as genuine, unpretentious, non-judgmental, good-natured, and calm with a great sense of humor, and a little self-deprecating.

Father Jerome Joseph Day, OSB, has more than fulfilled the long-ago vision from his own college graduation day in 1975 that he would be returning to that most favored place. After twenty years teaching at Saint Anselm, ministering with a full heart to the parishioners of Saint Raphael, in June 2020 he celebrated his 25th anniversary in the priesthood.

"To know him," said a close friend, "is to love him."

COURTESY JEROME DAY

Father Jerome with one of his nieces, Margaret Mary (Corriveau) Clermont, vacationing in Québec.

MIKE DEEP

Over the past forty-five years, this second-generation son of Lebanese immigrants has successfully operated real estate and insurance businesses and more recently acquired one of the area's few golf courses—Waubeeka Golf Links, the ultimate achievement for an avid golfer.

Mike Deep's story begins in the early 1900s when his parents emigrated separately from Lebanon. Anna Handy, born in Beirut in 1908 to Paul and Alice Handy, arrived in the United States via Ellis Island when she was eleven years old. Shortly after, both her parents died. Anna, the oldest, was accompanied by and responsible for her two brothers, a sister, and the family's scant baggage. The parentless children were sponsored and moved in with relatives in Burlington, Vermont.

In March 1900, Anthony "Tony" M. Deep was born in Blouza, a small Christian village in northern Lebanon, to Michael and Filomena (Coury) Deep. He emigrated with his family in 1912 at the age of twelve. They were attracted to the growing North Adams area by family connections. Mike's grandfather, Michael, established M.H. Deep and Son Variety Store on Ashland Street, and so began the entrepreneurial vein that has run through the family. Michael and Filomena had six children, five girls born in North Adams and one boy, Tony. There is some indication that a seventh child, a son, died in infancy.

Family history indicates that when they immigrated to the United States, the grandfather, Michael, who was working with immigration authorities, misspelled the family's name. Instead of using a loop at the bottom of the last letter for *Deeb* he put it on the top and they became Deep. *Deeb* as a surname has Arabic roots and means *wolf* or *strong*.

145

The six Deep children flourished in America. Mike's aunt Nellie, after a World War II tour of duty in the U. S. WAVES, became the first woman mayoral candidate in North Adams history. Another aunt, Agnes, educated at the New England College of Music and described as having a contralto voice of unusual depth and beauty, conducted a number of recitals in North Adams.

Tony worked for his dad (Mike's grandfather) at Deep Variety and service station until he entered the U.S. Army during World War II, serving in a medical detachment. Upon returning home, his close friend Albert Coury introduced him to Ernie Handy, and eventually he met Ernie's sister Anna. Anna and Tony began dating, and married in November 1945. Albert Coury later became Mike's godfather and the longtime proprietor of the beloved Coury's Drive-In in North Adams.

Three children were born to Tony and Anna. Philomena "Phyllis," the oldest, was physically challenged and passed away in her forties. Mike, the middle child, and his younger sister Ellen still live in North Adams.

For many years, Tony operated his father's business, renamed *Tony M. Deep Variety*, on the corner of Ashland Street and Crowley Avenue until the store was torn down as part of the 1960s urban renewal project. Tony, a tireless worker, managed his store seven days a week from 6:45 a.m to 9:00 p.m. On Sundays, he closed from 1:00 to 4:00 for lunch and to pay bills, then promptly reopened at 4:00 p.m.

The grandparents purchased the house at 209 Ashland Street, and Mike and Ellen lived on the first floor with their parents. The apartment had seven rooms: three bedrooms, a den, a living room, a parlor, a kitchen, and one bathroom. There were two apartments on the second floor: one in front of the house (with four rooms), one in back (with three rooms). Later in life, Mike had the clapboard house clad in grey vinyl for his mom. Mike lives there today.

EARLY LIFE

Michael Anthony Deep (middle name after his father) was born at the North Adams Hospital on July 7, 1949. As a young child, he loved to play at the nearby Mark Hopkins School. He and his friends would play from 1:00 to 3:00 p.m. in the summer and go back at night to play from 7:00 to 9:00 p.m., often playing "pick-up" basketball games: skins versus shirts.

They rode their bikes everywhere. When they were thirsty, they went to Fischlein's for a Coke or to his dad's store, which was only three or four blocks away. The boys often rode up the hill and swam at the Fish Pond. At the early age of five, he was a YMCA member and seemed to always have a basketball in his hand. Mike remembers well his first brand-new bike. He pleaded with his dad for a bright red Schwinn with training wheels that the family couldn't afford. His dad bought it anyway from the BF Goodrich store on Main Street. His sister, Ellen, who was younger, now wanted a bike, and their dad bought her one also.

During the week, the family's life was the store. Mike, his mom, and Ellen enjoyed helping customers, making coffee and sandwiches. It was directly across from the old A & P Supermarket, and Deep's lunch counter was busy at noon serving their employees. When not working, they would read the newspapers, Tony always taking time to study the horse-racing sheets. Tony loved to bet on the horses. His cronies would stop by the store and look over the *New York Daily News* race sheets trying to pick the day's winners. Occasionally, he, Anna, Ellen, and Mike would to go to the racetrack at Green Mountain Park.

They knew everyone's first name who came in the store, recalls Mike. On Sundays, Tony would take time to pay the bills, taking cash from the "till" for the bread man, Modern Dairy, Collins Tobacco, and Ashkar Wholesale. Mike loved working there. His dad had a kind, outgoing personality, and "he was easy to work with. People wanted to see my father . . . even the police might stop by to check on a local Lebanese person, if there was trouble, to see what kind of person he was."

They lived only one block away, so Mike would work right after school at 3:00 p.m. until 8:30 p.m. and on weekends. In his free moments, he would read the *New York Daily News*, the *Springfield Republican*, *The Boston Globe*, and the North Adams *Transcript*, never missing a chance to catch up on sporting news. He admits to being a Yankee fan early in life but has since seen the light and now it's all Red Sox.

His mom, Anna, was vibrant and friendly, although slightly more reserved with customers. She didn't naturally mingle like his father. Most of her time was spent as a homemaker and when necessary she was the family's disciplinarian. Whichever side his parents took in a sibling conflict, the kids' standard refrain would be, *Oh you like him/her better*!

Over fifty years later, Mike still remembers some of the prices of their groceries. Bread was twenty cents a loaf, coffee ten cents a cup—or twelve cents to go. Donuts were ten cents each and a Sunday Special was six donuts for thirty-nine cents. Salami sandwiches were their highest priced sandwich at forty cents each, while ham was thirty-five cents and bologna sandwiches thirty cents. The store carried a variety of grocery items, including milk, cereal, soaps, cigarettes, and eggs bought from the Shapiros.

Usually Anna, Mike's mom, wouldn't work all day in the store. She'd go home and prepare supper for Mike, Ellen, and herself. The kids took their baths, and bedtime was at 8:00 p.m., sometimes stretched to 9:00 p.m. until Tony got home to eat. Sometimes Anna would bring his food to the store. She loved to cook and was good at it. Meals were made from scratch, no recipes, and cooked from feel. She was always able to whip up a meal for surprise guests with whatever she had in the pantry.

Anna specialized in cooking Lebanese dishes. She easily made stuffed grape leaves filled with rice, hamburger, and spices, although the preparation of this meal would embarrass Ellen when her mom went up the street to pick grape leaves off the neighbor's fence. She thought people would think the family was poor and resorting to eating grass.

She also made *Lubia*, a dish comprised of green beans, lamb, and sauce; and *Mujadara*, a meal with caramelized onions, rice, and lentils. It was the family's no-meat Friday meal. Another specialty was her *Macaroon Bil Toum*, pasta dumplings coated with lemon and garlic, accompanied by her handmade Syrian bread.

Sunday meals were special, and they all ate together since Tony closed the store at 1:00 p.m. for a few hours. Anna made *Kibbeh*, which the kids described as "the best food in the world." Using top round meat, she'd pound it together with bulgur, a form of wheat, molded it into large meatballs, added her special spices, and it would be eaten uncooked. A hole poked in the middle was filled with virgin olive oil and scallions. Served with Syrian bread, it was the family's favorite. Mike's sister still makes *Kibbeh* several times a year, and it remains his favorite dish.

Seldom was there time for family vacations. Tony worked every day. In the summer, Anna would take the kids to visit their aunt and uncles in Burlington, Vermont. Ellen, Mike's sister, thought it was the best two weeks of the summer. Tony did like to go to the Saratoga racetrack in New York and bet on the horses. Two or three times in August he would drive to Saratoga, leaving around 11:00 a.m., returning for dinner.

As a youth, Mike attended kindergarten at Mark Hopkins School and then St. Joseph's schools through twelfth grade. Busy working at the store, he did not have time to play sports although he was class president in eighth grade and participated in school plays in high school.

After graduating in 1967, Mike worked for Petricca Construction as a fulltime laborer for several years while playing nighttime softball for four different teams. A sore back had him re-consider his career alternatives, and he began attending Berkshire Community College for one year before being accepted at North Adams State College (now Massachusetts College of Liberal Arts).

While in school, he refereed high school and college basketball games and at the same time ran the St. Francis Basketball League, working with kids from the third to eighth grades. With his love for the game of basketball, he decided to be a coach following gradua-tion. After receiving his history degree in 1973, he applied for a local coaching position and was rejected.

CAREER

At this turning point in his life, he overheard two friends discussing a twelve-week real estate course. He decided to take the course and received his broker's license in 1974. So began The Mike Deep Real Estate Agency with the oft-repeated logo "Your Fiduciary Agent." He accepted even the most difficult listings of distressed houses and continued to "school" himself on the real estate business.

Working out of his parents' house on Ashland Street, it took over a year to sell his first property. The first sale was the Pizza House in Adams, and then he quickly sold seven or eight properties the same month. His first three or four years in the business were spent selling properties and then a friend talked to him about buying income property and Mike began acquiring investment property.

Deep & Associates moved to the Colonial Shopping Center in Williamstown. The business flourished and Mike added several agents, further increasing the level of sales. He was active in the real estate business until 1990, approximately fifteen years.

Shortly after becoming a real estate broker, Mike decided selling home and auto insurance would be a nice complementary business. He attended another twelve-week course, passed the insurance agent test, bought the EA French Agency, and moved his office to 34 Ashland Street, right across from the North Adams Post Office, combining both his real estate and insurance businesses.

The agency, in business for over forty-five years, sells home, auto, life, and business insurance to individuals and local companies. Ellen manages many of the day-to-day activities of the Deep Associates Insurance Agency, Inc. Early on, Mike's mom and dad helped out, Tony providing transportation and Anna handling paperwork.

While establishing his businesses in the 1970s and '80s, Mike served five years as the North Adams Lions Club President and for two years on the city council. Like everything else, he threw himself wholeheartedly into campaigning for city council. He visited almost every household in North Adams, and he was pictured in the *The Transcript* holding up a pair of worn-out shoes, with holes from campaigning so hard.

He also promoted his insurance business by subscribing to a half-hour radio talk show on WMNB on Mondays from 8:00 to 8:30 a.m. for fifty-two weeks. He would interview experts in the insurance business, discussing and answering questions on vehicle and motorcycle coverage, workers compensation, property and casualty issues, homeowners or umbrella coverage. One program even featured the Massachusetts Commissioner of Insurance, who came from Boston for the show.

One of his greatest enjoyments during the years he was growing his business was attending March Madness basketball games. Few people know that for twenty years beginning around the NCAA's introduction to the sixty-four-college format, Mike has attended every Final Four basketball game. He would travel with four or five of his avid basketball friends to the sponsoring arena for the playoffs.

WAUBEEKA GOLF LINKS

In 2014, after forty years as a successful businessman, Mike purchased and became the sole owner of Waubeeka Golf Links in Williamstown. He considers this acquisition one of his most notable and enjoyable achievements.

The course, located at the junction of Routes 7 and 43 in Williamstown, was designed, built, and owned by Rowland Armacost, a well-known architect, golf pro, and superintendent. Opened in 1966, the eighteen-hole championship public golf course is 6500 yards long and occupies 130 of 200 acres in a picturesque woodland and field setting. It has been ranked as the number-one course in Massachusetts by *www.golf.com* for condition and value.

The proud owner gives a tour of his beautifully groomed course.

© Dennis Pregent, 2021

Mike is the fourth owner following Armacost, Ed Stawarz, and Jim Goff from whom he purchased the course. Stawarz was a supermarket magnate and golf aficionado. Jim Goff was a PGA pro who invested millions in the course, completely reworking the back nine, building a driving range along with a short-game practice area and a 12,000-foot putting green.

Interestingly, as a young man, Mike played golf maybe once in high school. He took up the sport in his thirties and became an avid golfer. Frequently playing seven days a week, he was a longtime member of the Taconic, North Adams, and Waubeeka clubs. He jokes that for the past eight seasons since he has owned Waubeeka his playing time is way down and his handicap is way up, rising from six to twenty. He hopes this year to spend more time on the course playing with members.

The golf course is usually open from April 15th through November 15th and that's where you will find Mike. He keeps a demanding daily schedule, starting work at 6:30 a.m. at his insurance office, then off to Waubeeka, arriving by 10 a.m. At the course, he helps plan all events, assists employees, and greets guests. He is usually headed home by 8:00 p.m.

Mike has invested over a million dollars in the course since its purchase, strategically removing over a thousand trees from around the greens that over the past fifty years have grown large enough to shade and damage the greens' condition. Waubeeka has also rebuilt two greens. Mike notes that a USGA sanctioned green can cost close to $50,000 to build. In this same time, the club has also created a pond and improved fairways, drainage, and tees.

When the season opens, he employs over forty full-time and part-time people: golf pros, event planners, greenskeepers, waitresses, and pro shop attendants. The cutting crew starts at 4:30 a.m. to ensure the greens are ready for golfers who begin arriving at 7:00 a.m. Often after work, some of the crew members will remain and enjoy one of their benefits—a free round of golf.

Golf course equipment needs are complex and costly. Separate mowers are required for cutting the greens, approaches, and fairways. There are Triplex and walk-around mowers for greens and rough mowers for fairways. The course has several tractors and countless attachments. One of his employees is a maintenance man who has excellent skills and keeps all the equipment running.

The course is costly to run with ongoing expenditures for replacement mowing equipment, aerator pumps, many flags, and rakes. It's notable that with the continuous cost, the previous owner had not made a profit running the course. Mike

Manning the flag on one of the greens.

finds himself in the same position, although revenue has improved each year that he has owned Waubeeka.

Eighty-five percent of Waubeeka's guests are within an hour's drive of the course. Additionally, people are attracted from New York State and the Boston area, especially for the two-day weekend golf specials. In the past, the course held a Ladies' PGA tournament, and the United States Golf Association (USGA) conducted its open qualifier there in 2018.

Mass Golf sponsored a Public Links Championship in 2019, and for the past two years, the North East Junior Golf Association has had its tournament there. The New England Junior Championship sponsored by *Golfweek*, featuring accomplished high school players, is scheduled to be played at Waubeeka.

Mike likes to mention a few celebrities who have played the course. Lewis Black, the stand-up comedian, when visiting the Williamstown theater, takes a quick jaunt over to Waubeeka. Lewis was overheard to say that he loves playing at Waubeeka. A perennial basketball fan, Mike was also proud to have had Jim Boeheim, Syracuse University's basketball coach, play on the Waubeeka links.

During the recent pandemic, there has been a resurgence in golf interest. Membership at the club has grown from 80 members in 2019 to 140 members currently, and 17,000 rounds of golf were played there in 2020. Supporting the recent increase in outdoor activities, Waubeeka offers many programs for aspiring young golfers and for adults.

The Sunday Summer Kids 1st Tee Program offers a beginner's clinic to children ages 6 to 13. It teaches core values for golf that include sportsmanship and integrity. The course's pro will demonstrate and instruct the kids on stance, swing, and follow through. Then, on to the driving range and putting green, followed by a free hot dog or hamburger as the day ends. Mike notes with satisfaction that "early on, the kids will miss the ball, even fall down swinging, but by the end of the clinic, there is a big change. They are hitting the ball soundly, making good shots, and have smiles on their faces."

In June, the PGA Junior League is a program offered at the course. On Tuesdays and Thursdays, aspiring golfers seven to thirteen years old will play on Waubeeka teams and travel to four other local courses to compete.

The course also offers a summer day camp Tuesday through Thursday. Coached by pros, with a small teaching ratio of four to one, the young golfers learn different techniques on the driving range and greens in the morning, then demonstrate their knowledge with four holes of golf in the afternoon. The course provides snacks, lunch, and ice cream at the end of the day.

For the more accomplished golfers, there is a one-week adult camp in the summer. The course employs Golf Trackman technology for this group. It allows individuals to see an analysis of their golf swing, club head speed, and launch angle, and the technology scrutinizes a golfer's body movements.

ALL FUN AND GAMES

No golf course comes without a few humorous stories, and Mike has a number to pick from. He remembers one time after a bad stroke, a serious golfer got angry and threw his club "like a whirlybird" up into a nearby tree and then tried to get it down by throwing up another club, which also got stuck in the tree. Deciding to avoid any more embarrassment, the calmed-down golfer returned later that night with friends, ladders, and flashlights and retrieved both clubs.

Another guest, against the rules, brought his own liquid

refreshment to the course and, failing to drink in moderation, wandered off the path and drove his golf cart into the middle of a creek. Four nearby guests, with some exertion, helped return it to dry land.

Over the past four years, Mike has devoted considerable planning and efforts to replace Waubeeka's fifty-year-old clubhouse in order to allow for an expanded pro shop and, most importantly, a more accommodating service area that could cater to larger tournaments, weddings, and other events. After numerous Town meetings, the residents approved zoning changes, and Mike hopes to move forward with his renewal plans in the next year or so. Studies indicate, and he is convinced, that Waubeeka will only begin to earn a profit when it can offer expanded types of services.

At seventy-one years old, Mike still enjoys water sports, shooting baskets, and above all working at Waubeeka, occasionally playing a round of golf.

With no hesitation, Mike admits that "these last eight years have been the best of my life." With the help of a great staff and devoted family members, he looks forward to each day. He and his sister Ellen are very close. She and her daughter and son provide Mike the family support that allows him to effectively run his different businesses. Ellen thinks he should "slow down," but that doesn't appear to be anywhere in his plans.

PATTY ERDESKI

This Blue Star mother has three children actively serving, or married to someone serving, in the United States Army. Seeing a need, she founded Boxes of Love, which packs and mails hundreds of care packages to deployed servicemen and women.

With two sons and a son-in-law in the military, Patty eagerly gets involved in projects that support the troops. In 2012, on her birthday, she promoted the Wounded Warriors Program, ultimately raising $1400 to provide funds for counseling and prosthetics for returning injured servicemen and women.

Boxes of Love started when her youngest son Arich, a 2011 Drury High School graduate, joined the Army and deployed to Afghanistan. Patty started sending care packages to Arich. In one of his letters home, he told his mom how he appreciated her mailings but many of his comrades never received any packages. This was Patty's call to action. From its inception on November 8, 2012, through 2020, she has mailed more than 1,600 Boxes of Love to deployed service women and men.

Patty explains, "Initially I was going to stop sending packages when Arich returned home from Afghanistan, but I can't do that because there are still people out there that aren't going to be getting packages. I wanted to do everything I could . . . and feel good knowing I put a smile on someone's face."

EARLY LIFE

Patty first put a smile on her parents' faces on June 10, 1962, when she was born at the North Adams Hospital to Peter and Helen (Hubbard) Cardillo, both longtime North Adams residents. Peter was a 1944 graduate of Drury High School and served in the United States Navy as an aviation machinist for the last part of World War II. After the war, he earned a bachelor's degree in education from Westfield State College and was instrumental in the development of McCann Technical School, serving many years as its principal.

Patty's mother, Helen, graduated just a year after Peter. They were high school sweethearts. They married in 1948 and had three children, Patty being their youngest. Helen served as the secretary of Saint Anthony's Parish Center for many years, and she was a master gardener who also loved reading and singing.

Patty's paternal grandparents were Anthony and Anna (Cicchetti) Cardillo. Anthony was born in 1888 and immigrated to the United States from the Italian province of Foggia in 1904, at the age of sixteen. He married Anna in 1916 and worked for the North Adams Highway Department. Anna was born in 1895 in the province of Avillino before coming as a child to the United States. She was a homemaker, and the couple had five children, including Peter.

Patty's maternal grandparents were Clarence and Elizabeth (Miller) Hubbard, both originally from North Adams. Elizabeth had graduated from a two-year college and the couple, at one point, bought a grocery store in Schenectady, New York. They lost the store in the Great Depression and returned to North Adams to be near family. Clarence worked for years at General Electric in Pittsfield, while Elizabeth was a homemaker raising the couple's four children. Clarence passed away in 1962 and Elizabeth many years later in 1996.

Patty's life began on Lawrence Avenue in North Adams, though her parents relocated the family to Clarksburg in 1964, when North Adams State College took over the street during an expansion effort. She is the youngest of three children, her sister ten years older, and her brother seven years older.

As a youth, Patty and her best friends rode bikes and played Wiffle ball and kickball. The girls would walk to Daub's Pond, about a mile and a half from home, to swim. Though the pond was small, Mrs. Daub charged 25 cents for admission. The girls enjoyed the large raft, Crème Orange Squeeze sodas, and chatting on their blankets. The friends also swam at Mauserts Pond at Clarksburg State Park. In wintertime, the girls were all about building snow forts, sliding, and ice skating. In the summer, Patty's family often vacationed at Cape Cod, staying in a shoreside cottage or in a motel at Rocky Neck Beach in Connecticut.

She attended Drury High School and served as class representative, but most of all she enjoyed her afterschool job at the JJ Newberry candy counter, talking with friends and ensuring the little pieces of joy were paid for by everyone. Just before her graduation in 1980, Patty was hired at the North Adams Regional Hospital as a dietary aide and then promoted to part-time supervisor.

Patty received her Dental Assistant certification from McCann Technical School in 1983. She worked a brief time period for a dentist but decided to continue her career at the hospital.

At one point during her nineteen years at the hospital, she met Mark Erdeski, who was working as a cook while attending college. A coworker asked Patty to work her shift, but she would only agree if Mark was working. Someone relayed that to Mark, and that's when their relationship began. Mark graduated from college in 1981, and the couple was married in 1985. Mark now works as a chemist.

Shortly after their marriage, the young couple bought a house in nearby Readsboro, Vermont, and several years later moved to Stamford where they have resided for the past thirty-two years. Their children were born in 1989, 1991, and 1992. The eldest daughter, Taylor, is married to a career Army infantryman. Patty's next oldest, John, is a captain in Army Intelligence, and her youngest son Arich is a combat engineer. All have served Middle East tours of duty.

From 2000 until her recent retirement in 2019, Patty worked in several school systems, retiring as the kitchen manager within Stamford's elementary school. When possible, she visits her grandchildren in Texas for extended periods of time.

FOUNDING BOXES OF LOVE

Shortly after her son Arich was deployed, Patty received a picture from him with a dirty face. She asked him about it. He had been living in a truck for nine days and had no water to wash up with before someone snapped the picture. She began sending him wipes and now includes them in most of her boxes. After some trial and error in sending packages, she better understood what type of items to include in boxes and began developing a list of favorites for the servicemen and women: baby wipes, handheld-non-perishable foods, granola bars, beef jerky, Slim Jims, flip-top cans of ravioli, word puzzles, magazines, soaps, toothpaste, toothbrushes, shampoos, and feminine products.

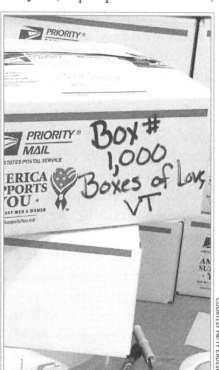

In the beginning, Patty was funding Boxes of Love with her own money. As the list of names and demand grew, she needed to rely on the generosity of others. Several articles appeared in the local newspaper, written by editor Maggy Button in 2012 and 2014. The creation of a Facebook page brought prominence to her efforts. People started donating items and money.

Patty initially mailed packages only to Arich's comrades, but the list of names grew as she became a member of the Fort Bliss, Fort Riley, and Fort

Starting from just one box, now Boxes of Love numbers in the thousands.

Carson parents' groups, as well as the Blue Star Mothers and Parents of Deployed Service Members (PODS). She solicits and is given names, APO addresses, and rotation dates through these groups, friends, referrals, her Facebook site ("Boxes of Love Vermont"), or by word-of-mouth. Names and addresses are often sent to her via private messege, text, or through a phone call. Patty usually has no idea where the APO address is located, just that someone needs a bit of Love.

Sometimes Patty has more names than boxes she can afford to fill and ship. She then prioritizes names and ships packages to those who have been away the longest. Patty and a supporter keep track of deployment and return dates to ensure a box will reach the trooper at the right destination. Some donors started sending her checks. One woman tracked down her house and gave her $200. Others bring items to her home. Patty is often on the road in her yellow and black Jeep picking up donations. She insists this entire endeavor has been a community effort.

Early on, Patty built and placed boxes for donations at sites around town like Zumba in the Berkshires, the post office, Planet Fitness, and Adams Community Bank. In November of each year, Adams Community Bank and its branches still dedicate the month to raising donations for Boxes of Love. Patty has spoken to a Blue Star Mothers group, receiving generous donations from understanding and appreciative mothers.

Donations also come from individuals, school systems, and businesses. Teaching staffs and children of many schools are involved in collecting items or making cards for the servicemen and women. A nearby car dealership conducts fundraisers. American Legion Post 152 will reimburse Patty for her costs, up to a certain amount, for purchases on postage. Children in church catechism classes write notes to be included in the boxes. Local VFWs help.

Donors range from people in nearby Adams all the way to California, where volunteers craft neck scarfs with gel packs that help keep soldiers a little bit cooler in the scorching desert heat. They also make knit caps for soldiers to wear under their helmets during the winter months.

Patty raises money by planting a variety of sunflowers and when the "Sunflowers for Soldiers" are tall and strong enough, she sells them for $1 each. She also found a unique way to send cakes to the troops in quart-size canning jars. After sterilizing the jars, she fills them half full of batter and then bakes at 400 degrees. Cooking the batter fills the jar and then it is sealed and prepared for shipment, packed in Zip-Locs and protected by gobs of loose candy. She always includes a fork and a tub of frosting.

THE LOVE SPREADS

One of Boxes of Love's biggest supporters is Clara, another Blue Star mother, who started having monthly tag sales in her yard, donating the proceeds to Boxes of Love. As the event grew, the local sheriff let her use the department's huge garage for sales and storage. Often weekend sales netted $500 or more.

After moving from the garage, Clara temporarily stored donations in her basement. Recently she found a renovated discount store that the owner, after hearing about Boxes of Love, rents to her for half-price. As of October 2020, Clara was up and running again, selling donated items, often by herself, sometimes aided by her sister, husband, and friends.

Clara takes all product donations; she has no restrictions. If something is unsellable, she brings it home and recycles it. She accepts furniture, toys, clothes, swing sets, shoes, and athletic items. All proceeds go to Boxes of Love. As a wonderful side benefit to this inspirational business, she has also been able to help victims of house fires, the needy, or the homeless with excess clothes.

Clara has a Facebook presence where she keeps her friends up to date on any other Boxes of Love needs. Her friends shop for the items, provide them to Clara, and Clara will deliver donated items and cash proceeds to Patty each month.

Boxes of Love is a year-round operation. When Patty is not traveling to nearby towns picking up donations, she and Mark and their many friends are shopping at stores to make purchases for the boxes. Looking for the "biggest bang for the buck," they frequent discount stores like Walmart, BJ's, and dollar stores. The goal, explains Patty, is to find items "that will feed them, clean them, or entertain them."

The months of September, October, and November are Boxes of Love's busiest months, preparing to ship for the Thanksgiving and Christmas holidays. At this time of the year, the boxes include cards from schoolchildren, gifts wrapped in Christmas paper, and decorations such as stockings, Santa hats, ornaments, or lights to promote a festive spirit far from home.

COURTESY PATTY ERDESKI

Patty, center, and friends show off their labor of love.

Packing efforts ramp up during this period. Her close friends Carol, Paul, Stacey, John, and her spouse Mark will be joined by additional assemblers and packers invited on her Facebook page. Response is always strong. Often there will be up to twenty people gathered to pack boxes, sometimes in the Stamford school gym and more frequently in garages or on porches.

Over time, they have developed an efficient system. One person tapes the bottoms of boxes while other volunteers select from donated items displayed on tables. Others pack the items in the boxes, returning filled boxes to be sealed. Then another creates return address labels, completes custom forms, and brings them to Patty to affix onto each box.

The boxes are loaded into her Jeep, and she delivers them to the North Adams Post Office, where she finds still more community support. She is allowed to drive to the back area, borrow the postal dolly, and offload 20 to 40 boxes in a trip. The boxes are brought inside, and the postal employees will postmark them in their own time, later sending Patty a copy of the customs forms and a receipt.

Boxes of Love uses flat rate boxes (12" x 12" x 6") with postage of $19.60, which is their largest cost item. Some donors write checks directly to the North Adams Post Office to help with the cost of mailing.

Boxes of Love's efforts have not gone unnoticed. Thank you cards from servicemen and women are numerous and continuous. Testimonials populate the website. The Northern Berkshire Community Coalition recognized Boxes of Love with an Award Certificate for Neighborly Acts, and the Williamstown Grange presented Patty with a certificate for outstanding community service. A local actor and comedian even volunteered to take boxes to troops in Germany during his holiday performance.

One special note came from a serviceman in Afghanistan who said, "Your gifts were always welcomed and appreciated by everyone that benefited. One could see the effort and care that was present in the Boxes of Love that you and your crew put into every one of them. Many soldiers' families send care packages on a routine basis, but many others do not. That is, until Boxes of Love arrive. Faces that hadn't smiled in a while light up with joy at the treats, trinkets, and gifts in each package. Long days and nights away from home, family and friends are forgotten for a bit while they rummage through a package and hold up a particular item with a 'Look what I got' or a 'just what I needed' grin on their face. You guys put that there for them. That smile, that grin, that happy thought is priceless. From the bottom of my heart, thank you. I have been doing this since 1983, and seldom have I witnessed such unselfish and thoughtful dedication to giving."

The letter included an Air Force certificate that accompanied a flag flown through the skies of Afghanistan during Operation Freedom Sentinel. Mark, Patty's husband, made a shadow box to hold the flag, letter, and certificate. (The serviceman's name is Duane Johnson, unrelated to the wrestler known as "The Rock," although Patty finds it a nice coincidence.)

Patty is outgoing, fun-loving, with a caring personality, a person whose efforts are contagious and inspire others to help in any noble effort. She herself says, "I want to give each serviceperson something from home they may not have seen in months and let them know they aren't forgotten . . . . I want them to know they aren't just on the news and someone *else*'s child. While they have our backs, we have theirs."

NICHOLAS FLYNN
AND DONATO DAGNOLI

For almost one hundred years, generations of Flynns and Dagnolis have cared for thousands of peoples' loved ones. This family funeral business has been in continuous operation since 1928, serving Northern Berkshire and Southern Vermont.

It all started when Edward Flynn bought Cody's storefront funeral home on Eagle Street in North Adams in 1928. Edward and his wife's uncle Joseph Roach, a former state representative, formed Flynn & Roach, the beginning of three generations of funeral service, and moved the business to Quincy Street in North Adams.

In the 1920s, the funeral business was still mostly horse-drawn affairs where preparations and viewings were done at home with family involvement. Sometimes the deceased was transported to the funeral home, the body prepared, then brought back home for a wake. One of the bigger considerations at that time was ensuring coffins could fit through the doorways or windows for front parlor viewings. In the late 1940s and early 1950s, as the Flynn & Roach business grew, most services began to be performed at the funeral home.

A series of funeral home mergers brought the Flynn & Roach and Dagnoli-Montagna homes together in 1969, forming the Flynn & Dagnoli-Montagna Funeral Home. Additional mergers in the early 2000s included funeral homes in Williamstown and Pittsfield. Flynn & Dagnoli now have three locations: two in North Adams, and one in Pittsfield. Headquartered at 521 West Main Street, the business employs eight full-time and eight part-time employees.

THE FLYNNS

Edward F. Flynn, Nick's paternal grandfather who started the business, was born in 1889, an only child, and raised in Bennington, Vermont. After serving in World War I, he graduated from St. Francis College and attended the School of Anatomy and Embalming in Boston. Margaret Welch-Flynn, Edward's wife, worked full-time as the receptionist of Flynn & Roach. After fifty years as a funeral director, Edward passed away in 1971, shortly after the merger with Dagnoli-Montagna.

Nick's maternal grandparents, William Nagle and Madeline (O'Connor) Nagle, lived in Springfield, Massachusetts, where William worked as a pharmacist. William and Madeline had two children, one of whom was Nick's mother, Florence. Tragedy struck the family when Madeline died young, her daughter Florence left motherless at twelve.

Edward T. P. Flynn, Nick's father, entered the family business in 1951. Born in 1928, he was a 1946 Drury High graduate and served in the U. S. Army Medical Corps in the South Pacific and Korea. After attending Georgetown University and the New England Institute of Anatomy and Embalming for ten months, he joined his father in the business.

Not long after, Edward met Florence Mary Nagle, a 1951 graduate of Our Lady of the Elms College and a second grade teacher at Johnson School. Florence had moved to North Adams to accept a teaching position and was living with her aunt when the young couple was introduced by the aunt's chauffeur, Clarence. They married in 1954 and had six children, including Nick. Florence was deeply involved in her church's Women's and Altar Guilds and served over forty years in its youth education program. Among the many things Nick remembers about his mom was her knack for making excellent cupcakes and for always using Irish-lace doilies under the household lamps.

The young couple seemed an interesting blend of personalities, Florence with a quiet, reserved nature, devoted to her children, and Edward very social and considered a good listener with a kind heart and a sense of humor. Tragically Edward, by that point President of Flynn & Dagnoli, died in a Williamstown auto accident in 1985. Florence passed away in 2008.

GROWING UP

Nicholas Nagle Flynn, one of the current owners of Flynn & Dagnoli, was born at the North Adams Hospital on May 19, 1961, to Edward and Florence Flynn. The family lived in Williamstown, and Nick attended the Williamstown elementary school. As a youth, he frequented the Williamstown Boys Club, where he and his friends enjoyed the arts and crafts programs, archery, and target shooting with BB guns.

Nick attended Mount Greylock High School and was deeply involved in its sports program. In his senior year, he co-captained the cross-country, ice hockey, and baseball teams. Nick graduated from Mount Greylock in 1980.

Often on Saturdays, a busy time at the funeral home, Nick's dad would pick him up after hockey practice and Nick would tag along to help out. Early on, his chores would include cleaning up the home and washing cars. He got his driver's license at sixteen, and the following weekend he was driving the funeral home's limo. All of the Flynn children were expected to work in the family business. They used to joke about getting "family pay," which for them was minimal or didn't exist, although working there did pique Nick's interest in the funeral home business.

Growing up, they were parishioners of St. Patrick's in Williamstown (now Sts. Patrick and Raphael). For vacations, the family would rent a beach cottage for several weeks at Old Saybrook in Connecticut, and Nick's dad would join the family as his growing business permitted. Nick remembers family trips to Montreal, Toronto, and day trips throughout the Berkshires. The family of eight seemed to pack "Dad's big Chevrolet station wagon."

Suppers were always at 6 p.m., usually between viewing hours at the funeral home. Meals were family style: "big portions and big spoons" for six very active kids. Nick's dad wanted to know what everyone was doing before he headed back to work. Nick's mom diligently made spaghetti on Thursdays, fish sticks on Fridays and often hot dogs and beans on Saturdays. Sundays was their big meal, either roast pork, roast beef, or turkey, always served with potatoes and accompanied by homemade pies and cakes.

After high school, Nick attended Bentley College, majoring in management and accounting, and graduated in 1984. In his senior year, he discussed his future with his father, acknowledging he wanted to work for himself and have his own business. His dad suggested Nick remain in Boston after graduation, attend the New England Institute, and join the family business. Nick attended the ten-month school and entered the business in 1986, shortly after his dad's fatal car accident. Today, Nick serves as President of Flynn & Dagnoli.

THE DAGNOLIS

Nick's younger partner and friend Donato (known as Don) Battista Dagnoli was born at the North Adams Hospital on May 25, 1965.

Don's father, Donato Francesco Dagnoli, was born in North Adams in 1931, attended local schools, and graduated from Drury High School in 1948. After graduating from the University of Massachusetts in 1952, he served on active duty as an Air Force officer in the Korean War. After the war he became a reserve officer, served as a liaison with the U.S. Air Force Academy, and retired as a Lieutenant Colonel with twenty-six years of service.

Donato briefly worked for the Sprague Electric Company as a chemist before receiving a mortuary science degree from Hudson Valley Community College and, after acquiring the Montagna Funeral Home in 1968, went into business with his younger brother. One year later, the brothers merged their business with Flynn & Roach, creating the Flynn & Dagnoli-Montagna Funeral Home.

Donato sang in the Saint Anthony choir where he met Marcia Ann Parisien, also born in North Adams, attending local schools and graduating from Drury in 1953. Marcia trained at Henry W. Bishop School of Nursing and received her bachelor's degree from

Boston College School of Nursing. She married Donato in 1964. She helped establish the McCann Nursing program. In addition to enjoying cooking and playing the piano, at one point Marcia chaired the Northern Berkshire Council of Arts and the Garden Club.

Don describes his dad as caring, compassionate, thoughtful, and empathetic, and his mom as outgoing, involved, and devoted to her children.

"My parents did everything for me," Don readily acknowledges. Marcia passed away in 2017 and Donato in 2018.

Don's paternal grandfather, Battista Dagnoli, from whom he received his middle name, was born in 1888 in Limone sul Garda, within the province of Brescia in northeast Italy near the Austrian border. He attended schools in Italy and served in the Guardia di Finanza Corps. Battista immigrated to the U.S. in 1913 and settled in Brattleboro, Vermont. He served in the U.S. Army during World War I, then was a twenty-five-year employee of the Boston & Maine Railroad, working on the Hoosac Tunnel until his retirement in 1954. Battista passed away in 1987.

Don's paternal grandmother, Giacomina, was born in 1904 in the U.S., returned to Italy for a short period before returning to the U.S. While in Italy, she lived in the small lakeside town of Malcesine in the province of Verona, right across the lake from where Battista was born. The couple married in 1929, and in 1952 Giacomina passed away at an early age from cancer.

Don's maternal grandfather, William Parisien, was born in North Adams in 1905. The family moved to Montreal when he was a child, and he attended the Christian Brothers Academy, playing on the school's hockey team. William returned to North Adams as a young man and worked as a Prudential Insurance agent, then worked twenty-seven years in the General Electric tool room until his retirement. An avid golfer, William introduced his grandsons to the game. William passed away in 1980.

Grandmother Helen (Gazzaniga) Parisien was born in North Adams in 1907. She attended local schools, including Drury, and worked for her father at their shop, Gazzaniga's Paint and Wallpaper Store. Shortly after her marriage to William in 1928, the couple purchased land and established the Rainbow Cabins Motor Court on the Mohawk Trail. During World War II, she worked at Sprague in support of the war effort. Very active in her community, she was a member of the North Adams Girl Scout Council and belonged to the Lodge of Sons of Italy, the North Adams Garden Club, the Mohawk Trail Association, and North Adams Republican City Committee, working many years at the polls during elections. Helen passed away in 1995.

GROWING UP

Don lived in North Adams for a short time before the family moved to Orchard Street in Adams, where he, the eldest, and his two brothers grew up. The large, yellow, slate-roofed house built in the early 1900s with its expansive yard was the site for many Wiffle ball and football games. In the nearby woods, the boys played war games, hide-and-seek, and "cowboys and Indians." The chums often walked to Russell Field to play football and street hockey (on the tennis courts).

The most fun was visiting his grandparents' Rainbow Cabins on the Mohawk Trail, where there was a large apple orchard to explore and plenty of places for games. Often his cousins were there to share in the fun. Everyone in the family looked forward to vacationing for two weeks at Watch Hill in Rhode Island. The family rented a cottage for several weeks at this coastal community.

Don attended Commercial Street Elementary School, C. T. Plunkett Middle School, and Adams Memorial for junior high. He graduated from Hoosac Valley Regional High School in 1983. He played on the winning golf team and as a senior was recognized as "All Berkshire." Don also enjoyed playing pick-up basketball, skiing, and swimming.

Evening meals at the Dagnoli house were usually around 5:00 p.m., sandwiched between the standard viewing hours of 2:00 to 4:00 and 7:00 to 9:00. Everyone needed and wanted to be present. Don's mom was a great cook and enjoyed her role. She liked to shop to find just the right cut of meat and the freshest vegetables. Her specialties were stuffed peppers, veal cutlets, and roasts. She also, with a special recipe held only by her mom and sisters, would create an outstanding Italian sauce to accompany her pasta.

Sunday meals were more formal, usually involving roasts, pota-toes, and vegetables with table wine for the adults, although children were allowed sips on occasion. Everyone would enjoy it when Dad brought home sausages from Arnaldo's on State Street.

Meals would usually finish with Marcia's baked-from-scratch apple, blueberry, or cherry pies or occasionally homemade cookies or pudding.

Don attended Williams College, majoring in history. He was on the varsity golf team and proudly remembers winning the NESCAC (New England Small College Athletic Conference) championship in his junior year. Don also enjoyed campus intra-mural sports, especially basketball. Graduating in 1987, he cherished his time at Williams and still today enjoys attending their basket-ball, football, soccer, and lacrosse games. On occasion, he can be seen at away basketball games. Don is a member of the Williams Football and Basketball Booster Clubs with opportunities to attend sports banquets and meet the players.

Growing up, Don also helped his dad in the business, driving limos and hearses, greeting at the door, or serving as a pallbearer. From a young age, Don had thought he might want to work in the business after getting a solid education. He worked there his junior summer of college, and by Christmas he knew for sure. Once Don graduated from Williams College, he attended the New England Institute of Applied Arts and Science for one year in Boston to become a licensed funeral director. Don now serves as Vice President and Treasurer of Flynn & Dagnoli.

THE BUSINESS OF FUNERALS

Nick and Don joined the business full-time in the late 1980s and began learning more of the details handled by their fathers, real-izing they would eventually be partners in running the business. It's interesting how the business model changed over the years. Some of the changes were mundane and others more significant.

Nick noted there had always been a mystique or eeriness around the confidential nature of the funeral business. With the advent of the internet, the spooky, dark-basement aura of a funeral home is now more seen as a supportive community resource. The internet has educated people on the processes of embalming, cremation, and burial, removing the mystery from the entire process. Funeral homes are now seen as a resource that provides help with all the aspects of burial, including grief counseling as well as dealing with financial issues involving life insurance, wills, and veterans benefits.

Nick Flynn, left; and Don Dagnoli, right; at their company's headquarters on West Main Street in North Adams.

Early on, there were no answering machines. A family member at home or someone at the funeral home would need to be responsible to answer the phone at the most unusual hours, never knowing when someone might need help. Children knew when the business phone rang at the house, they needed to quiet down. Eventually, responding to customers transitioned from answering a business phone in the home to using a paging or answering service. These days, response is much less complicated with personal cell phones.

Obituaries have changed, too. In past years when they were listed in the newspaper, they served as a quasi-legal notice. If the deceased owed you money, the family needed to be contacted so you could be paid; conversely, if you owed the deceased money, the family needed to be paid. Almost all obituaries were placed in newspapers, usually crafted with the help of the funeral home and then phoned-in or hand-carried to the local newspaper.

Today, with fewer people reading newspapers and the high cost of placing an obituary in the paper, many people have changed to using either *iBerkshires.com* or the funeral home's website, where they can place photographs, people can offer condolences, and the family has access. It is estimated that at least 40 percent of obituaries are no longer placed in newspapers.

It seems as though life has gotten busier for everyone. Deaths in the past would "stop the family's world" as grievers would gather, sometimes coming from across the country. Now this may interfere with schedules, and so life continues without pause. In the past, wakes and visiting hours used to be two consecutive days from 2:00 to 4:00 p.m. and 7:00 to 9:00 p.m. Now, if there is a viewing, it's one day from 4:00 to 7:00 p.m. or the day of the funeral from 9 to 11 a.m.

The rate of cremations is increasing. In 1988, they represented 5 percent of Flynn & Dagnoli's business. Today, cremations are over 70 percent of their business. This dramatic change is attributable to several reasons. Cremation costs can range from $2500 to $5000, while a traditional funeral costs $10,000 to $15,000.

Also, as the number of churches diminishes and religious rites become less important, there seems to be a lessening of demand for traditional funerals. Another influence may be that the Catholic Church, years ago, lifted its ban on cremations. Families are finding it is much easier to handle their loved one's remains if they are to be transported out-of-state. Flynn & Dagnoli uses a crematorium run by the Pittsfield Cemetery or one in Bennington owned by a funeral home.

While the desire for traditional wakes and church or graveside services has diminished, the essence of service remains the same. Both directors prefer to go to the home of the bereaved, meet those grieving, look at family pictures, and respectfully learn more about the departed person. Often, they will gather vital information, and the family will help them create a draft of the obituary.

These days churches and funeral homes are open to family

participation in the services. Family members will read poetry or scripture, give eulogies, and select music. It's becoming commonplace to have memorial services or life celebrations in residential backyards, and after the services, receptions are held. In many cases, funeral directors double as master of ceremonies.

Technology has had a big effect on the funeral business, from the creation of funeral home websites to how a person's death certificate is processed. In the past, the directors would carry a death certificate to the doctor's office for signature, then carry it to the appropriate city hall for recording and issuance of a death certificate. The director would also transport the person's obituary to local newspapers. All of this is now handled online.

With the advent of technology, crowdfunding has become a vehicle where a family experiencing an unexpected death or young person or family with no insurance or needing assistance with medical payments or children's education, will seek assistance via an internet posting. Flynn & Dagnoli helps by publishing their efforts alongside online obituaries.

The assistance provided is so comprehensive that in addition to pre-planning, it includes significant support to family during their most difficult hour: notifying clergy to arrange services, notifying the cemetery for burial space and scheduling, contacting government agencies for benefits, completing death certificates, crafting obituaries, and providing a list of grief resources, to name just a few of their services.

PANDEMIC-ERA CHANGES

The pandemic of 2020/2021 has had dramatic effects on the grieving process. The loss of life, especially affecting the elderly, has turned the industry upside-down. Older residents in long-term care facilities suffered and died without comfort from even one family member. Church services or rites, often emotionally vital to older, devoted parishioners, might not be held.

For some time, with people rightly fearful of this new unexplained disease, there were no wakes; churches were closed; and the use of funeral homes was very limited. Gravesite goodbyes by a few family members became the norm, with social distancing and masks required. People were unable to grieve with relatives, neighbors, or friends. Drive-by visits came into vogue, where older grievers remained in their cars yet were able to at least visit the cemetery.

Flynn & Dagnoli improvised during the pandemic, handling most communications with family over the phone. They realized the need for ongoing support for pent-up emotions unable to be voiced during the pandemic. A critical service provided by Flynn & Dagnoli has been the livestream services that can be viewed on their website. Either at church or the gravesite, livestreaming the somber events has been very helpful during this time, especially for those who could not travel.

COMMUNITY INVOLVEMENT

Both Don and Nick take an active role in the community. Until recently, Don was the Drury High School varsity golf coach, serving for eleven years. In 2013, his team won the Western Massachusetts Division 2 Championship. He has also been a Rotary member for over thirty years and a member of Unico, another charitable organization. He remains actively involved with Williams College, having served as the class treasurer and agent.

Beginning at the YMCA at an early age, Don acquired a love for basketball and over many years has played in different leagues, on traveling teams, and has sponsored the Flynn & Dagnoli team. He is admittedly a die-hard Celtics fan. When he has time, he plays golf at the Taconic Country Club. He is committed to exercising and enjoys riding his bike, cardio-workouts, strength training, and an occasional yoga class.

Nick has served as chairman of the Development Council and on the Board of Directors for North Adams Regional Hospital, worked on Spring Expos, and been appointed to the board for the former Williamstown Savings Bank. He is occasionally a guest speaker on topics involving end-of-life issues. He has also coached for the North Adams Babe Ruth League.

He is an exercise enthusiast and enjoys working out at the local YMCA, running, kayaking, hiking, and especially golfing. He has coached youth baseball and hockey leagues in North Adams and Williamstown. Nick is an avid fan of James Patterson books.

The Flynn family, Nick, Caroline, Annie, and Daniel, gather alongside a playful moose sculpture at the Mt. Anthony Country Club in Bennington, Vermont.

Don and his girlfriend, Judy, vacation in the wide open spaces of Montana.

THE FLYNN & DAGNOLI WAY

In a single sentence, the Flynn & Dagnoli website describes their devotion to the bereaved: "Our staff is committed to providing the highest level of service to families experiencing the loss of a loved one." When working with someone's deceased family member, they always consider how they would want their own family member to be treated. Throughout the years, over the thousands of funerals they have arranged, they continue to be touched by people's words of appreciation and acts of kindness.

On occasion, moments of unexpected levity occur. One such time was when Nick was introducing a priest at a prayer service, an older gentleman hard of hearing said in "an Irish whisper" to Nick, "I didn't recognize you with your clothes on." Nick, wearing his traditional dark suit, became a bit red-faced, explaining that the man normally saw him in his shorts and tee shirt when working out at the YMCA.

There are also special moments of kindness from the bereaved. Once, while sharing thoughts with a bereaved Irish family, Nick mentioned losing a four-leaf clover given to him by his mom. Several weeks later, the family gave him a four-leaf clover that he now keeps in his wallet.

Sometimes it's the small considerations that mean a lot, like when Nick purchased two rubber grips for a grieving elderly widow who couldn't open her pickle jar. She'd lost her husband who'd previously handled such tasks.

The Berkshire area is fortunate to have these two men who are perfectly suited to their line of work: they are great listeners, compassionate, and very focused on each family's needs. When families open up about their loved one, the conversation itself becomes a tribute to the person's life. Available around the clock, Nick and Don truly will assist in "anything that gives comfort to the family."

DONALD ELIE "BONES" GIRARD

Donnie Girard's life's passion has been leading Notre Dame School's Boy Scouts Troop #38 of Adams, Massachusetts. Eighty-five scouts have attained Eagle rank during Donnie's tenure, which adds up to over a half-century of dedicated leadership.

First of all, it should be noted that Donnie goes by the nickname "Bones," and has for six decades. Many years ago, when he was helping his dad build houses, they needed someone to slip between the concrete cellar forms to tighten some bolts. Donnie was the one selected, and since he was skinny (all bones) and there was another Donald on the crew, his dad conferred the title upon him.

Born on June 21, 1949, Donnie is the second oldest of nine children, five boys and four girls, all born at the W. B. Plunkett Hospital in Adams. His middle name, Elie, was borrowed from his maternal grandfather. Donnie's parents Harold and Isabelle (born Blanche Langlois) were both of French ethnicity. Though Isabelle was born in the United States, Harold was born in 1924 in the Province of Saskatchewan, and his parents immigrated to the U.S. when he was a child.

Harold was a stern and at times unrelenting disciplinarian. He worked most of his life as a welder at General Electric in Pittsfield, while Isabelle managed the home and nine children. Harold also had a second job as a carpenter, building houses. He died in 2011 at eighty-seven years of age. Some believe his occupation as a welder and possible exposure to asbestos may have contributed to his death from cancer.

As an outdoorsman, Harold enjoyed fishing in the Deerfield River and Cheshire Lake. He passed on these interests to the kids and often would drop them off at Cheshire Lake to ice fish. The kids would quickly make a fire for warmth, but also to cook hamburgers brought from home. Their feet seemed to freeze in the green rubber pull-on boots they wore. As soon as Dad arrived and returned them home, they warmed their feet on the potbellied stove.

Isabelle is currently 96 years old and lives in the Pinnacle Park in Adams. Described by her kids as easygoing, gentle, considerate and "saint-like," Isabelle had their five boys and four girls over a sixteen-year span, from 1948 to 1964. Donna is the oldest, followed by Donnie, and Peggy the youngest child. As the kids grew, Isabelle worked part-time as a school bus driver and cafeteria cashier. She was known as "religious," and the family went to Catholic church every week. She still enjoys going with her son Joe to karaoke, appreciates a pinot noir, and remains masterful at cribbage even with limited eyesight.

Donnie's paternal grandfather, who lived in nearby Cheshire, cut and sold wood for a living and also had the odd job of delivering manufactured dentures to dentists for their patients. Donnie remembers driving around with his grandfather to make deliveries. He enjoyed sitting in the front seat of his grandfather's deluxe, four-door, late model black Chevy, feeling the plush front seats against his legs. Interestingly, Donnie's maternal grandfather Elie Langlois was a dentist in Adams, though he died when Isabelle was thirteen.

EARLY LIFE

Initially, the Girard family lived in Cheshire, moving in 1950 to Adams. They lived in brick block apartments near Howland Avenue School. In 1955, the family moved to Dean Street and rented one side of a two-family house with brownish asphalt siding and a slate roof. There were three floors, including an expansive attic and a front porch. The family of eleven shared four bedrooms and a bath, usually two or three people to a room.

In the summer, the boys, seeking fresh air and freedom, would pitch an Army tent in the backyard and sleep outside. It was great fun for them. At night, they would sneak across the street and buy snacks and sodas from the local convenience store.

The Girard kids played a lot outdoors. Baseball took place at Amy Bishop's construction site just down the street where they used rocks for bases, and a foul ball over third base might end up in Mr. Shea's yard. Before a player could climb over his fence, the elderly Mr. Shea might retrieve the ball and keep it, ending that day's game. Eventually the team let his grandson begin playing, and sent him to plead for the return of their errant missiles. A line drive high over second base had the enticing possibility of hitting the Package Store's sign or one of its plate-glass windows. They came close but never made the ultimate hit.

The kids also played on a nearby embankment that provided excellent woods for fort-building, playing Army, and organizing a game of tag. Occasionally the kids ice skated at Russell Field. Inside activities were limited. Some mornings they watched "L'il Rascals" and "Three Stooges" before heading off to school. After school, the boys would often go to the attic and wrestle on old mattresses. Donnie was the one to beat. It was hard evading his smothering headlocks and leg-pins.

Don, as the oldest boy, was in charge of house maintenance. He and the other boys would winterize the house, stretching and stapling plastic sheeting across the windows for extra warmth. He and Donna would coordinate washing the family's laundry across the street at a laundromat. The Girards occupied almost all of the washers and dryers. It was a significant relief for their mom, who only on occasion needed to hang clothes on the backyard clothes-line. One of the siblings said to me, "We knew how hard life was for Mom, so we all pitched in."

Isabelle spent much of her time preparing huge meals. Friday nights was always creamed peas on toast. Lunch was often peanut butter, jelly, and marshmallow sandwiches. Other main meals were spaghetti, burgers, hot dogs and beans, and venison. As the kids grew older, she began cooking two suppers: one served around 5 p.m., then another around 7 p.m. for those working. Isabelle never knew for sure how many people would be eating supper since kids often brought friends home. Likewise, she could never be sure who would come down the stairs the next morning for breakfast.

The list on the refrigerator told the kids what their nightly responsibilities were: for example, clean table, clear dishes, wash dishes. Don and Donna were in charge of the list.

An early entrepreneur, Donnie, with his brothers, using a flashlight after dusk, would catch night crawlers and then add them to the worm bed he had built in the cellar. The best spot to catch crawlers was across the street in the post office's garden beds. The nearby mansion was another good spot. Once gathered, they would put out their sign in front of the house and sell them to local fishermen for a penny apiece. Tragedy struck one day when Donnie accidentally hung an outboard motor near the worm bed. It leaked oil, killing several hundred of his worms! Undaunted, the team replaced the dirt and continued to sell. All profits were given to Mom to help with house expenses.

For the entire summer, the family rented a mobile home at Ann Cottages on Lake Champlain. Harold would drive up on weekends after work, and they all spent much of their time fishing for walleye. Labor Day was the best weekend, because the other nearby families gathered for a giant picnic.

Back at home, Donnie was also in charge of the family's paper route, fifty-plus customers spread all across town. The kids took turns delivering papers. Donnie collected the money, paid *The Transcript*, and gave the proceeds to his mom.

Don attended kindergarten through eighth grade at Notre Dame School in Adams. The siblings' walking path to school took a number of twists and turns, usually following the railroad tracks near the Oasis Bar. With some luck, they would hop a train, grabbing a ladder on one of the cars or jumping on the caboose.

One notable thing about Donnie is that he never wore an overcoat even in the most frigid weather. His friends thought the family couldn't afford a coat, but Don just didn't want one. To his little brothers, he seemed impervious to cold.

In 1963, as a freshman, he commuted by bus to St. Joseph's High School in North Adams. Al, the dedicated bus driver, put Donnie in charge of the kids during their morning and afternoon trips, using his presence to keep the noise and rambunctiousness under control. During the next four years, Don, even as a commuter, was able to play the bugle at all the school's basketball games. He enjoyed being part of the school play *Oklahoma!* and was voted Student Government Representative, attending and running the State House in Boston for a day.

During high school, he worked at a bakery on Myrtle Street and also at Leon Jewelers in Adams, keeping the stores tidy. Many days he worked with his dad building houses or doing general carpentry work. Around 14 years old, he noticed Bud Charbonneau, the proprietor of C.W. Window, working on a roofing project. Donnie saw refuse on the ground and offered to pick it up and keep the site clean. Bud hired him on the spot. In 1970 when Bud retired, Donnie bought his business.

In the summers when not working, Don would escape with friends Tommie, Mike, and Bob and camp for a week at Cheshire Lake, fishing, swimming, and cooking out. In their senior year, someone stole their tent, ending any thought of camping that summer. Don also spent two weeks every summer at Windsor Jambs. He stayed with the boy scouts for the first week and worked the second week in the kitchen supporting the Girl Scouts.

In 1967, Don attended St. Thomas Seminary in Connecticut for two years, receiving an associate's degree in 1969. Concluding he did not desire to become a priest, he matriculated at North Adams State College, graduating in 1972 with a bachelor's degree in education.

Donnie joined the National Guard soon after, serving six years. His military specialty was in Fire Direction Center (FDC) where he helped coordinate mortar fire. He attended Basic Training School at Fort Polk, Louisiana, then a two-month Ground Surveillance Radar School at Fort Huachuca in Arizona. He recalls horseback riding in the Arizona mountains and, in one memorable trip, losing his wallet just after payday. To this day, he presumes it still lies out there in the desert, maybe petrified! On another occasion during evening maneuvers he killed an aggressive rattlesnake. He skinned the rattler, intending to bring it home and show his Scout troop. With few places to store the skin, Donnie hung it in his wall locker, startling an NCO during an inspection!

When Donnie turned twenty-one, he purchased C. W. Window Company for $500. For this price, he received the company's name, its building, and equipment that included some ladders and an old dump truck. The company specialized in installing aluminum siding and windows. He subsequently changed the name to C. W. Construction Co., Inc. and began offering a broader line of services. In 1985, the company purchased the former Howland Avenue School in Adams and performed extensive renovation, preserving the old building from destruction, making it their headquarters.

At different times, all five brothers (including Joe, Billy, Victor, and Gerry) have worked for the business. Two sisters also worked for C. W. Construction, Mary as a secretary and Emily as a laborer. Donna was already a practicing nurse, and Peggy was too young. At one point, Victor and Billy formed a subsidiary that dealt with asbestos removal. Donnie sold the company to his youngest brother Gerry in 2016, and he now works for him.

Donnie married Virginia (Ginny) Corbett in 1975, whose family hailed from Nova Scotia blood and were direct descendants from early Massachusetts settlers. Donnie and Ginny have two children, both married. Kim, with two children, lives in Northampton, MA. Sean, with one child, is a former Eagle Scout who lives in Framingham, MA.

Ginny graduated from North Adams State College in 1973 with a bachelor's degree in education, later receiving her master's degree in education. She has devoted much of her life to helping those with dyslexia. Over the years, she has owned and operated Greylock Language Learning Center, aiding young children all the way up to the elderly. Few people know she suffered from leukemia for several years in the 1980s, at times being deathly ill.

Initially, the young couple lived in a second-floor apartment on Depot Street in Adams but in 1981 moved to their own home on Notch Road where they reside today. Over the years, Donnie has enjoyed fishing at Lake Champlain and deer hunting with his dad in Lanesborough, Massachusetts, occasionally traveling to Maine. At one time, he was an avid stamp collector, but when he was away at Army basic training, his younger brother sold his collection!

Donnie still enjoys riding his 1979 tan and cream Harley Classic 1200. Over the past twenty years, he and Ginnie have used it for their Berkshire rides and one awesome trip to Three Rivers, Canada, just north of Montreal. More recently, he and Ginny attended painting classes and learned to play golf. For a number of years, he taught religious education classes at church and coached youth soccer.

SCOUTS

Don's scouting experience started early. He joined Cub Scouts for three years and then boy scouts in 1960 when he was eleven years old. He looked forward to the Thursday night Scout meetings held in the Notre Dame School's basement cafeteria. The meetings were held from 7:00 to 9:00 p.m. during the months of September until mid-May.

Don became an unofficial Scoutmaster in 1968 at nineteen under the tutelage of Greenie Guertin. He became an Eagle Scout in 1969 and over the years has attended a number of training sessions. He was Troop #38's Scoutmaster until 2018, a career spanning over 50 years.

Leading his troop in the annual Memorial Day Parade in Adams, Donnie sports a fedora.

He still serves as assistant Scoutmaster and treasurer.

With 40 scouts in attendance, meetings followed a familiar pattern: fall-in, dress-right-dress, get into a straight line, roll call, recite the Pledge of Allegiance and the Scout Oath. Then groups of eight scouts would gather into their individual Patrol Groups. Each member would have a chance to be a Patrol Leader, Assistant Patrol Leader, or Scribe. Patrols were often named after animals (foxes, cougars, bears). Groups would learn together and sometimes compete in skill games.

There would be lessons in knot tying, first aid, CPR, orienteering, and map reading. Some of the classes were taught by local EMTs. Lessons also focused on learning information in the Scout handbook, assisting the boys to earn merit badges and advance in rank from Tenderfoot to Star to Life to Eagle.

Games were the last part of the evening's program. Sometimes it would be "Red Rover, Red Rover" or an enthusiastic round of dodgeball. A creative game had the boys lashing sticks together constructing a tower using knots they had learned, drawing a string between two posts lashed to the tower. The final step was positioning a candle on the tower to burn through the string. First patrol to burn through the string won.

Meetings always ended with a "Scoutmaster's Minute," a brief talk on a particular virtue such as trustworthiness, preparedness, or integrity. In closing, the group lined up, the bugler played taps, and they were dismissed, always remembering to put away tables and chairs.

The most anticipated annual event for the scouts was a week-long summer camp that was held for years at Windsor State Forest until it closed and then at Camp Holy Cross in Goshen.

CAMP SCHEDULE

It would always be a busy and full day. Early morning meant reveille, calisthenics, a jump into the nearby pond in all types of weather. Next, breakfast, wash dishes, clean cabins, and personal hygiene.

From 9:00 a.m. until noon, patrols were involved in an activity such as knot tying, first aid, CPR, or survival. After lunch, there were preparations for evening fireside skits, more classes, work on merit badges, and free time. The boys always looked forward to purposely sinking and then righting canoes, and particularly loved to flip over Don's kayak or canoe. Good naturedly, he'd say, "I guess I need to change my pants," upright his canoe, and paddle to shore, absolutely unflustered.

After supper, there were games such as Capture the Flag, volleyball, baseball, horseshoes, badminton, croquet, and bocce.

After dark, each patrol presented good-natured skits,
Taps were played, and then
lights out at 10:00 p.m.

Summer camp usu-
ally involved thirty or more
scouts and fifteen adults.
Don's plan was to count on
feeding fifty people. Meal
preparation began at 6:00
a.m. when the Scout lead-
ers would activate the stove
burners, fueling them with

Donnie displays a wooden table handcrafted by
a devoted Eagle Scout. All the troop members
signed the bottom, and it was presented to
Donnie at the summer camp Court of Honor.

white gas and creating pressure with bicycle pumps. The burner
would be inserted into the stove which resembled a short, silver
refrigerator. Two stoves were placed side-by-side, and a large, flat,
aluminum griddle was placed on top. Food was cooked in deep,
"squarehead" pans.

Meals were substantial and filling, ranging from French toast,
pancakes, eggs, bacon, hash browns, and sausage for breakfast to
subs, luncheon meats, hot dogs, hamburgers, and French fries for
the noon meal. Suppers were usually something like spaghetti and
meatballs, stuffed chicken and mashed potatoes, ham, roasts, shepherd's pie, and vegetables. There would always be some type of
dessert. It was a tradition for one Scout mom to bring nine homemade pies to camp just for one evening meal!

After meals, scouts cleaned their trays or mess kits in two
sixty-gallon barrels of heated water. Donut-styled heating units
with stove-type stacks were attached to each barrel, one for washing
and the other for rinsing.

Desiring to go further afield, the leaders began planning
fundraisers and raffles with the goal of every Scout being able
to participate, no matter their economic situation. Scouts helped
on roofing jobs with the C. W. crew. Whenever a Scout participated, the money would be apportioned to each person's account.
Sometimes it took months and many activities to save enough

money for the trip. Two weeks before one trip, the troop was thousands of dollars short. By the next week, the money had been received. It was always presumed Don and Ginny, who did a lot of the trip planning, had contributed their own money.

For transportation, the leaders and boys retrofitted an old, donated school bus. They painted it the troop's colors, red and black, installed a toilet, and were ready to roll. This gave them the opportunity to take canoe trips to upstate New York, travel to Washington, D.C., visit the National Baseball Hall of Fame in Cooperstown, New York, and take several trips to Disney World in Orlando, Florida. The Disney trip became a challenge when their bus blew a radiator one time, and at a different time, a clutch. Donnie was following the bus in a van when the breakdown occurred. Some leaders and scouts became worried, stranded so far from home in a broken-down bus, looking to Donnie for leadership. Nonplussed, he replied, "I'll let you know when I find a radiator." Within several hours he found one, and with the help of several mechanics accompanying the troop, they installed the radiator and were on their way—epitomizing the Scout motto, "Be Prepared."

One of the kindest acts the troop experienced was when parents of an Eagle Scout, noting how tattered their tents were and appreciative of the troop (and Donnie's contribution) conducted a raffle and with the proceeds bought eight new 8' x 16' wall tents, a number of food coolers, and drinking containers. Surprisingly, they threw in a TV for Donnie and Ginny.

Most of his scouts don't even know Donnie's first name. They just call him "Bones." To celebrate Don's fiftieth year in scouting, one grandfather outfitted a plastic skeleton with a Boy Scout uniform. This "Bones" Scout stands four feet tall, holds a Scout handbook, and is garnished with an outdoor background of leafy foliage. The statue also lights up!

In many ways, Donnie was always ahead of the curve in looking out for his scouts, pushing the Boy Scout organization to do more for the scouts, personally organizing Camporees, always driving for lower participation fees so everyone could participate. Donnie looked out for everyone.

Girls were part of Troop #38 long before the Scouts

organization allowed their participation, including earning merit badges. Two girls unofficially attained the rank of Eagle Scout and inspired others to do the same.

Developmentally challenged children were welcomed into the troop with kindness and patience. Many, even the most challenged, became Eagle Scouts. Often Donnie became speechless when he awarded these scouts their hard-earned awards.

He would often admit boys to the troop before the age of eleven, especially if they needed the support. One of the boys affected said that after his father died, Donnie became a father figure to him and he tried to pattern his life after Don.

Examples abound of Don's kindness and patience. One Scout said, "Bones is absolutely the most patient, understanding, and giving person God ever made. He forgives and forgets so easily. He taught me there was no reason to ever raise my voice, and I've passed this trait on to my kids." During one Disney trip, a child needed an emergency appendectomy. Donnie took him to the hospital, called his parents, and stayed with him while the surgery was performed. The parents could not afford to fly to Florida, so Donnie and Ginny bought them round-trip airline tickets.

Even now at seventy years old, Donnie still works 40 or more hours a week for C. W. Construction, owned by his brother. He is responsible for gathering necessary materials, acting as a construction supervisor, but most often joins the laborers. Just recently he was roofing with his brothers and crew on top of a four-story Victorian house in one-hundred-degree weather.

In the colder weather, as business slows, he and some employees can often be found working on the six apartments he and Ginny own, or one of the nine apartments co-owned with his brother, Gerry.

For many years, Don would grow a large white beard at Christmastime and play Santa Claus for Head Start children. They'd sing songs, read books, and then give out presents.

Over the years, it was Donnie's practice to train employees in all facets of his business. In doing so, it helped a number of them establish their own local enterprises. In turn, they help each other out when one runs short of material or just needs another set of hands. Donnie's lasting legacy will include the hundreds of boy scouts taught and shepherded over the past decades, and the solid employment provided for his family and workers. As one sibling noted, "He's been a good big brother."

GEORGE HADDAD
& ANN HADDAD BARTLETT

Few people know that The Red Carpet Restaurant began as Clifford's Lunch in 1927, almost a century ago. James and Ida (Ziter) Haddad bought the restaurant in 1950, and the Haddads have owned it for the last 70 years. Operating continuously, it became the oldest full-service restaurant in Berkshire County, providing breakfast, lunch, and dinner to its customers.

Initially, the Haddad family lived in North Adams where the patriarch, James, worked as a baker. In the late 1940s, he began leasing and operating the Mohawk restaurant in Adams with his brother. Formerly known as the Barrett House, the restaurant was located on the first floor of the Mohawk Hotel.

In early 1950, James and Ida moved to Adams to operate their recently purchased restaurant, Clifford's Lunch. As a child, James would go with his father Joseph on the trolley to eat at Clifford's shortly after it opened in 1927. Now he owned it. Clifford's was located at 69 Park Street, right beside the former city hall and police station. Ida, who worked in the restaurant, also spent considerable time raising their two children, George and Ann, the future owners.

James, born in 1913 in Worcester, Massachusetts, into a family of ten children, was a first-generation Lebanese-American. His father, Joseph Haddad, had been born in Masser-el-Cheof, a village in the mountains of Lebanon, where the family owned an olive orchard. After emigrating, Joseph moved to North Adams and worked as a mechanic.

The Haddads often gathered in Winston, Connecticut, where a number of Lebanese families shared ownership in a large club.

There were grand summer celebrations with Lebanese food, games, and entertainment including the always popular "Dabke" dance.

Both families had immigrated to the United States for better economic conditions and opportunities. Ida was born in 1914 in North Adams to Sarkis and Kahfe Ziter. The Ziters came from Blouza, Lebanon. Kahfe died during the birth of her fifth child, when Ida was eight years old, and the family of eventually eight children was raised by Rose, Ida's stepmother. When Sarkis remarried, the family moved to Vermont where he worked many years at a quarry in Barre, Vermont. James and Ida were married in 1934 at Saint Monica's Church in Barre, Vermont.

When James purchased Clifford's, it was located in the basement, with a hat shop on the first floor and an apartment on the third

floor. He moved the eatery from its subterranean location to the street level, where there was the additional attraction of a nearby newsstand and taxi service. At that time, he renamed it The Park Street Restaurant.

During another remodel, he moved the outside front stairs inside and replaced its huge pool hall windows with smaller ones. Sometime later, installing a short-lived deep red carpet inspired its final name, The Red Carpet Restaurant.

George and his sister Ann at the front door to the Red Carpet on Park Street, where their family fed generations of Adams customers.

The restaurant was ideally located near the center of town. It served as a handy meeting place for mill workers, families, lawyers, policemen, and hunters. For forty years, a ladies' group of teachers met for breakfast every Friday morning even after their retirement. The restaurant has the capacity to seat eighty-five people, with twelve booths, four tables, and eight counter stools that were usually occupied by longtime, coffee-consuming customers.

The restaurant's menu included a large breakfast offering; pub fare that started at 11:00 a.m. offering hot and cold lunches; and an evening menu that included various appetizers and sides, seafood, steak, chicken, and the favorite Red Carpet Specials. The restaurant also sold beer and wine.

The accessible kitchen is in the back of the restaurant, concealed behind two swinging doors where waitresses come and go. The stainless-steel kitchen, efficiently laid out, has two large grills, a ten-burner stove, two big sinks, a dishwasher, steam table, freezer, prep table, several *bains-marie* (double boilers), and a cooler refrigerator for storing condiments.

When relocating to Adams, James moved his family (Ida, George, and Ann) into a third-floor seven-room apartment at 72 Park Street, across the street from their restaurant. The first floor of the large, brick building had expansive windows and was occupied by Guerin's pool hall.

Ann Haddad Bartlett remembers as a little girl bringing lunch to Mr. Guerin, being sure to stay near the door where her mother could see her from across the street. The hall was dark, foreboding, filled with cigarette smoke, and occupied by serious and scary men.

After several years, the family moved across the street to a seven-room apartment right above the Red Carpet, conveniently just one floor away from their work. For a number of years until his passing, Grandfather Haddad worked in the restaurant and lived with them.

The family attended St. Thomas Catholic Church because it offered the only local English Mass, the language in which they were trying to become better versed. George needed a dispensation from the bishop to marry in the Catholic Church. There was concern about his faith since his dad was a Melkite Catholic and mom a Maronite Catholic.

James, never one to be idle, was a musician, a drummer, and played for the band Hi-Fi. He also became a musical promoter, bringing bands to the North Adams Armory and The Center on

State Street (now the Italian American Club). James and his partner built the teen center.

The family took few vacations, but one of their big summer outings was Labor Day when the restaurant was closed. The family of four often headed to Storytown, Santa's Land, or Fort Ticonderoga, all located in nearby upstate New York.

One time in 1966, when George was in the service, Ann and her mom and dad took an eight-day whirlwind vacation in Dad's Cadillac. They traveled to the Saint-Anne-de-Beaupré shrine in Canada, onto Niagara Falls, then to Ohio where Ann saw her first horse race. Next they drove to St. Louis where she visited the famous Gateway Arch and sailed on a riverboat. On the way home, they visited relatives and the Smithsonian National Air and Space Museum in Washington, D.C.

James and Ida retired, and their two children, George Haddad and Ann Haddad Bartlett, took over the operation in 1980, comanaging the restaurant with the help of their dedicated spouses and families over the next forty years, until its eventual closure on December 31, 2019.

EARLY LIFE

George was born March 25, 1944, at the North Adams Hospital and attended Sarah Haskins Grammar School in North Adams and then Liberty Street School in Adams. In the summer of 1962, George enlisted in the U.S. Naval Reserves, completed basic training at the Great Lakes Naval Training Center in Illinois, and was assigned to a destroyer escort vessel. After weeks on a choppy sea, he decided to switch services. In 1963, nine days after graduation, he joined the Army.

George attended another Basic Training camp at Fort Dix and then went to school at the Redstone Arsenal in Huntsville, Alabama, to become a Pershing missile computer repairman. After school, he remained stationed in Huntsville until released from the service in 1966.

Returning home, he began working for his dad at the restaurant and attended Berkshire Community College for two years, majoring in business.

Several times while working in the restaurant, he noticed a cute local girl and saw her again at the Corner Lunch owned by her family. He asked his cousin Rachel to introduce them, and in short order he and Jacqueline (Jackie) Roulier were married in 1969.

Jackie had been born on October 27, 1949, in the North Adams Hospital. Her parents were Rene and Phyllis Roulier, both of French ethnicity. George and Jackie went on to have five girls and one boy: Colleen, Terry, Tonia, Jamie, Amber, and Jordan. They have six grandchildren who live in nearby New York or in Massachusetts.

Ann Bartlett is George Haddad's sister and co-owner of the Red Carpet Restaurant. She was born on September 10, 1949, at Saint Luke's Hospital in Pittsfield. Like George, she started at Liberty Street School, with middle school at C. T. Plunkett, then finishing at Adams Memorial High School.

Ann and George used to play in the alleys around the restaurant, right next to the police station. When Ann got angry at George, she would stop in and see the front desk sergeant and ask him to talk with George. Dutifully, the sergeant would go outside and call George into the station.

Ann started working in the restaurant at a young age. At four or five, she would stand on a stool and wash dishes. When seven or eight years old, she would go downstairs before school and help set up for breakfast. At noon, she would come home and help serve the lunch crowd.

In first grade, Ann's dad taught her how to make change and write checks. Ann has always been a "front end" person, one who waited on people. Her mom taught Ann the restaurant social skills of talking to and waiting on people. There was always a good dose of humility mixed in with the instructions.

As she was very shy at first, her dad began her waitressing by waiting on one customer. It was Mr. Simmons who owned the nearby furniture store and seemed a very scary old man. That experience went well, so she moved on to Mr. Reid, another longtime older customer. It wasn't long before young Ann was waiting on anyone who walked through the door.

Ann and John Bartlett's relationship began at the Red Carpet. John used to stop in for breakfast after working third shift and at one point asked Ann for a date. Dates led to engagement, and they were married in 1969, the same year as George and Jackie. John, slightly older, worked at General Electric for many years, went to culinary school at Berkshire Community College, and joined the family business.

Ann earned a bachelor's degree in elementary education at North Adams State College in 1971 and began substitute teaching. Desiring to be a full-time restauranteur, she entered the business in 1974.

Usually, the families ate their evening meals in a booth at the restaurant. Thursday was a special night when Grandmother Haddad would make the evening meal for both Ann and George's families. The fare included such Lebanese dishes as cabbage rolls, grape leaves, stuffed squash (*Kousa*), and a lamb dish with a green bean–like stew favored by their father. Grandma also made boiled dinners and pot roasts. It was a close time for the families.

As the restaurant's menu expanded, the two couples started to assume different responsibilities. Often Ann and George would open the restaurant together at 5:00 a.m. to prepare for the day, closing after lunch, around 2:00 p.m. When they expanded their hours in 1992 from 2:00 p.m. to 8:00 p.m. Ann would take the afternoons until closing. Busy days were Thursday through Sunday, with Sunday breakfast especially busy.

Ann and George, who rarely had an opportunity to sit, enjoy a booth by the front door.

Their individual specialties shifted according to their talents: Jackie, initially a grill-cook, suggested they make their own soup and took on that responsibility. She also enjoyed making the restaurant's pies, a job her father-in-law held before his retirement. She specialized in making chocolate and coconut crème, pumpkin, lemon meringue, pecan, apple, and the very popular Tollhouse pie. Jackie also made the restaurant's brown and white gravies.

George often did the cooking, specializing in meatloaf, specialty sauces, chop suey, roasted meats, cooked corn beef, and huge pots of potatoes.

John did the prep work and some cooking, but mainly prep in the early morning for the day, such as preparing pancake batter and chopping onions, peppers, tomatoes, ham, roast beef, and fish.

Ann helped with prepping and cooking and also served as the business's bookkeeper, handling payables, receivables, and payroll.

They all worked together and often interchanged hours or jobs, whatever was necessary to run the business. How else could they coordinate cooking three cases of bacon and forty-five to sixty dozen eggs each week?

Most of the couples' nine children, and some grandchildren, have worked in the business, washing dishes, waitressing, and other clean-up tasks.

THE CUSTOMERS

In talking with George and Ann, both have different memories that enrich them. Ann has specific customer memories, like the time she dropped a hot plate of food in a customer's lap and went to grab and wipe off his lap, then thought better of it. There's the retired mailman who always ordered ham, toast, and coffee. One day when he added pancakes, Ann came from the kitchen to make sure it was him. A lawyer who had moved to Florida returned, and Ann knew right away because of his order for black coffee and an English muffin.

One former customer played a game with Ann and would not eat his meal until she took one of his fries. He was a faithful Wednesday and Friday customer. One week he missed his two days, so Ann called his sister-in-law, who said he was out of town and had some heart issues. When he returned, Ann told him not to leave town without telling her. The customer dutifully called Ann every time before leaving town. He passed away three years ago.

George remembers a retired electrician, a regular customer for sixty-five years, always claiming his special place at the counter every morning. After coming for so long, he has gotten close to both George and Ann's families. He comes to their Christmas party and picnics with the family.

George, though busy at the restaurant, also owned the Sahara Bar (formerly Shorty's Café) on Spring Street. From the early 1970s until almost 2000 he worked both jobs. For twenty-nine years, his day began with opening the Red Carpet at 5:00 a.m., then the Sahara at 8:00 a.m. He returned to the restaurant at 11:00 a.m., back to Sahara from 2:00 to 6:00 p.m., and worked there after dinner, sometimes until close at 2 a.m.

The Sahara had a full liquor license and served snacks. It employed three or four part-time bartenders and featured bands four nights a week, Thursday to Sunday, with big names like Twisted Sister. The bar also used DJs, promoted belly dancers and Karaoke, and offered big-screen TV, a novelty at the time.

Always the entrepreneur, at one point George converted the building's first-floor dance hall into ten single-room rentals, each with a private bath. The three-story, white-stuccoed building also had several apartments on the second floor. Sold in 2000, the bar is now named WOJO's.

In addition to the restaurant and bar, George served from 1985 to 2002 as a Town selectman. He found the job satisfying, if time consuming, and enjoyed being part of a number of the town's accomplishments: successfully relocating the town offices to the Plunkett mansion, moving the police department into the former town hall building, and running one of the first state-sponsored elderly van programs.

Still active, he serves as the town's assistant assessor and recently helped start the Fallen Heroes Banner program, recognizing Adams residents killed in various wars.

The Red Carpet is now up for sale. The Haddads were

considering making apartments out of it, but decided not to. Their daughter currently lives upstairs.

The Red Carpet had supported many charities and sponsored a girls' softball league and the fire department. In the forty years George and Ann co-owned the restaurant, they closed only four or five weeks total, mainly for their children's out-of-town weddings. This landmark, this local institution, opened November 15, 1950, and officially closed on December 31, 2019. George and Ann will miss their customers, and George and Jackie will miss opening their back door and walking one hundred feet through their backyard to get to work.

Everyone will miss the Park Street institution that served tens of thousands of meals to thousands of satisfied customers for almost seven decades.

ALAN DOYLE "TINY" HORBAL

It's easy talking to a genealogist, especially about family. Historical information both significant and not so significant pour out of a conversation. Local facts and lineages and obscure information are on the tip of the tongue for Alan Horbal. He's been helping others discover family ties for over forty years. I first met Alan years ago, while trying to find information on my great-great-grandfather who served in the Union Army, and within a matter of days he had provided me with copies of maps where veterans were interred. He offers free genealogy classes throughout the Berkshires and has a vast knowledge of area history. Alan created the Kempville Flag Program, which displays 300 flags throughout the neighborhood.

Alan was born on August 21, 1944, at the old North Adams Hospital. It was an unsettled time. When his mom left home for the delivery, they lived on Church Street, but they returned home to a house on Chestnut Street. Several years later, they moved to 458 East Main Street, where he resides today. The home, built in the mid-late 1800s, was owned and renovated many times until it was sold to Alan's parents in 1946. It's a two-family home with the upstairs rented out.

In the early 1980s, maintenance workers unearthed a nineteenth century cistern under the home, one of the few remaining water collection systems in the city from a time when no sewer or waterworks existed. Always the innovator, Alan decided to convert the cistern to a large hot tub.

Alan's father, Peter Alex Horbal, was born in Derby, Connecticut, to immigrant parents. Peter had four sons, deferring him from military service in World War II. For most of his life, he worked as an accountant for Armour & Co. in their Hartford, Connecticut, and North Adams locations. He was president of the

Sprague Electric Company's Credit Union before he passed away in 1973.

Doris Veronica (Doyle) Horbal was Alan's mother, born of third-generation immigrants who lived in Bristol, Connecticut. She worked as a telephone operator at Armour, where she met Peter. They eventually moved to North Adams in 1933. Doris had four sons, born in 1934, 1938, 1942, and 1944. Alan was the youngest, and she often called him her baby. Doris was a homemaker for about fifteen years before working at Sprague in the capacitor department. She lived with Alan until she was ninety-four and passed away in March 2001.

Alan's DNA reveals he is 50 percent Ukrainian and a smaller mixture of Irish and Scottish lineage. Most of the Horbals that immigrated to the United States came from a number of small towns in Galicia, which in the 1800s was part of the Austro-Hungarian Empire about seven miles from the Czechoslovakian border.

Alan's paternal grandfather Alexander (Alexi) Horbal was well educated, spoke seven languages and had emigrated from Bartne, Galicia, in 1895. In Derby, Connecticut, he worked as a steamship ticket agent, grocer, and bar owner. His wife, Theodosia Felenceak, immigrated to the United States in 1898 and the couple had three daughters and three sons. She did not work outside of the home and had very limited literacy. In 1914, under suspicious circumstances, Alexi died from drowning. The family believed he was murdered. Theodosia lived until 1936.

Alan's maternal grandfather, James Edward Doyle, a second-generation American, worked in Bristol, Connecticut, as a plumber, eventually becoming a lieutenant in the city's fire department. He passed in 1936. Alan's maternal grandmother was Mary Ellen McKinney.

EARLY LIFE

Attending Houghton Elementary school for ten years, pre-k through eighth grade, Alan belonged to Houghton's Cub Scout Pack and Boy Scout Troop #35. Like many other young boys, he delivered newspapers, shoveled snow, and mowed lawns for pocket money. On occasion, older neighbors would ask him to wash their kitchen ceilings and walls to remove dark shadows from coal burning stoves. Alan found kerosene worked best for this chore.

Starting Drury High School in 1958, Alan joined the football team and was involved in a number of school plays. He took work where he could find it. He worked every day after school for the Rite Way Company, distributing the North Adams *Transcript* to area stores and paperboy pickup areas and held restaurant jobs cooking and washing dishes at The Springs, The Texan, and at Elwal Pines.

He and his high school friends frequently went "over the line" to neighboring Hoosick Falls, New York, where youths could drink under eighteen. At a local bar, he won a five-quart drinking contest, a prideful accomplishment for the young teen.

After high school, Alan worked at Sprague as a mail boy, briefly attended McCann Technical School, and worked at the Veterans Hospital in Leeds, Massachusetts, for three years as an orderly. In the 1960s, he returned to Sprague for six years as a splitting machine operator, in the control lab, and finally as a draftsman.

Still searching for what he wanted to do, he worked part-time as a Park and Provisional Policeman. For a brief period, he was the Dog Officer for the City of North Adams and then drifted back to his avocation of cooking, this time for the Carmelite Fathers in Williamstown.

For almost forty years Alan has nurtured a broad cooking career. In the early eighties, he managed the New England Telephone cafeteria in Pittsfield and opened his own catering business, *Alan the Great Catering Service*. When the Pittsfield cafeteria closed, he worked as McCann Technical School's head cook for seven years, and while there earned certifications in Culinary Arts and Special Education. He was an active member in the Berkshire Chefs Association. He received a bachelor's degree in education from Westfield State in 1986, commuting from North Adams.

Alan, who was devoted to his mother, Doris, and was given her maiden name for his middle name, cared for her at their home until she was in her mid-nineties. When I first asked him if he was married, he said, always the joker, "I've had a few honeymoons but never married. I enjoy being free to do what I want to."

Alan had another part-time business as a tax accountant for small local companies and individuals. During the early 2000s, his cooking career was diverted after he experienced some health issues. He began working for AARP as a volunteer, completing tax returns. He updates his skills each January, and then works several days a week through May preparing about 70 returns a year. His client contacts are now remote, with information scanned and returned electronically.

A TALENT FOR SEEKING OUT HISTORY

In the background of Alan's life, he has always had a keen interest in his heritage and had a passion for history, genealogy, and research. He's devoted his spare time to genealogy, an interest that began in 1978 trying to answer questions about family lineage.

Pre-internet, he spent considerable time in Connecticut where his parents lived, talking with city clerks and searching library records, then traveling several times to small villages in Poland looking for relatives. He discovered many relatives on those visits.

In 2000, and for the next twelve years until it closed, Alan worked at the Silvio O. Conte National Archives and Records Center in Pittsfield, aiding families in finding records of ancestors. When people kept returning to Alan for help, his boss came to appreciate his research skills. Early on, searches were more daunting, involving index cards, microfiche, and old files. Alan said his greatest thrill was to see "the light go on" when people uncovered information on their families.

In addition to his genealogy, Alan has a strong vein of patriotism and is an ardent community supporter. In 2002, he established Kempville Flags, Inc., and with his small social security pension and some donations from a few friends, he purchases flags from local hardware stores and finds McCann Technical School volunteers to weld the necessary flag holder brackets.

Alan then enlists some friends, and they begin mounting the brackets and flags on telephone poles in his neighborhood, Ward II. Every year since 2002, more than 300 flags fly for seven months, from Patriots Day in April until Columbus Day in October.

During the wintertime, Alan stores the flags in his cellar and spends considerable time refurbishing brackets and replacing the flags themselves which after seven months in the wind and rain are often worn out. It takes him hours to replace the cloth flags and then he stores them in 55-gallon drums until spring. The American Legion, the Fire Station, or the Elks club usually volunteer to burn the worn-out flags.

Alan checks over his stock: This barrel of flags is all ready to go.

Alan wants no acknowledgment for his efforts. He says he "just enjoys flying the flag. It's a beautiful thing when I leave my house with a flag on my front lawn and then drive toward the Fish Pond to see the flags on all the poles—it represents my country."

Alan has always had a desire for community involvement, from serving as an officer in the Masonic Lodge to being a consistent blood donor and volunteer Board member for the LaFesta League. With his background, he helped to organize food vendors. He is an ardent SteepleCats supporter and bought shirts for the K group that calls out pitcher's strikes and hangs K's from a nearby clothesline to indicate how many strike-outs the pitcher has made so far. Alan was honored for his neighborly acts in 2006 by the Northern Berkshire Community Coalition.

In the early 2000s, as Alan's health declined and restricted some physical activities, he ramped up his genealogy outreach. He helped catalogue and cross-reference class photos from all the elementary schools in North Adams and began seeking pictures from all past and present grammar schools.

For a number of years, as an adjunct professor, he's offered a genealogical Winter Study course to Williams College students. The students are instructed on how to use government records and various databases to trace their family's lineage. As a civic contribution, the groups digitized a database of births for the Massachusetts towns of Clarksburg, Williamstown, and Cheshire as well as Pownal, Vermont.

As a city resident of North Adams, he began offering one-hour *Introduction to Genealogy* presentations at the Visitors Museum in Western Gateway Heritage State Park. As a member of the North Adams Historical Society, he has held genealogy classes and researched and digitized a history of the streets in North Adams.

One of Alan's biggest efforts was to create databases for the locations of Berkshire County's interred veterans, providing the information to North Adams and Pittsfield Libraries as well as to inquiring veterans and friends.

As the unofficial archivist for the Northern Berkshire Court, Alan has digitized naturalization papers from 1884 to 1906 for the towns of Adams and North Adams. With minimal personal income, he applies for grants for his public service work and has received three to date.

For years, with the help of friends, he has offered four-week workshops at the Berkshire Athenaeum in Pittsfield. Due to the classes' popularity, he offers the two-hour classes twice a week. He titles the class "Western Massachusetts Roots Event," which helps participants find information about their ancestors using 1790 through 1940 census data. The

© DENNIS PREGENT, 2021

Alan sits at the heart of his workcenter, ready for his next project.

very popular classes are sponsored by the Athenaeum's Local History Department.

In 2019, during National Library Week, the Berkshire Athenaeum presented Alan its Volunteer of the Year award, stating, "For years, Alan has been sharing his passion for deep knowledge of genealogy with the Athenaeum community and throughout the state."

The supervisor of the Local History & Genealogy Department for the Athenaeum is a fond advocate of Alan, describing him as "funny, down-to-earth, happy-go-lucky, knowledgeable, engaging with patrons, and really makes a connection with them and their search for personal history. He is a very popular instructor and always willing to help and share his knowledge."

In tribute to Alan, the library established an Alan Horbal Collection, which includes records from Northern Berkshire on naturalization; veteran cemetery maps showing interment from the Civil War to World War II; nearby Pownal, Vermont, birth records (1754-1851); Adams birth records (1763-1843); and Southview cemetery information located in North Adams. The records are available to all patrons.

Currently, Alan, with other volunteers, offers seven pro bono seminars a year on genealogy. The five-week courses have approximately twelve students and have been taught in a number of western Massachusetts towns. Classes have even extended to Vermont and New York State. The only requirement is a willingness to learn, an email address, and computer literacy.

Often the classes start with fresh baked goods. "If someone brings in baked goods, they get extra points," he says. His other frequent rejoinder? "By the time we are done, you will be able to do family research at home in your bunny slippers and pajamas."

His small band of volunteers helps with instruction, computer glitches, and syllabus distribution. The class uses Alan's family background for their research format, and instruction includes an introduction to the use of the U.S. annual census, draft registrations, and ship papers/Ellis Island searches. He also refers to Ancestry.com and FamilySearch.org as well as the Steven Morse search engine for Ellis Island information.

In North Adams, Alan has helped the Historical Society with an archival record project preserving birth, marriage, and death records and is readily available to help anyone with family history searches. When he served on the North Adams Historical Commission, his knowledge helped update information on the Kempville section and record the historical street names for the city.

Today Alan's life revolves around AARP tax work, his flag program, and genealogy. He also chairs the Western Mass Roots' Board of Directors. Much of his work involves helping others with their genealogies, and he prides himself on being able to aid those having a difficult time or, as he describes it, having "hit a brick wall."

Alan strongly believes genealogy instruction needs to be in person and "Zoom just won't work." Since classes have been suspended due to the COVID-19 pandemic, he has spent his time responding to emails and phone calls, helping students or anyone with genealogy research projects. On occasion, if someone wants to pay him, he proposes they donate to one of the Western Roots recommended charities at the rate of $25 an hour for his research time.

Looking back, he says, "My life's accomplishment has been helping people and taking care of my mother until she was ninety-four years old. I have a great deal of knowledge on genealogy which I have learned from the school of hard knocks. This knowledge is free to anyone for the asking."

GUS JAMMALO

I found Gus to be a walking history book of barbering over the last half century. His Union Street shop is a well-known local institution, and he's an expert on many things. Anyone desiring to know about coin collection, the art of taxidermy, or what goes into a close, old-fashioned shave will be wise to stop by for a chat.

Gus Jammalo began barbering in 1956, when haircuts cost one dollar and shaves were seventy-five cents. In sixty-five years, he figures he's given about 120,000 haircuts. Today he continues to cut hair four days a week at his Union Street barber shop in North Adams.

Born Augustine Jammalo on March 22, 1934, at the North Adams Hospital, Gus was the much-welcomed first-born son of Salvatore and his wife Frances, who lived on Magnolia Terrace off River Street in a small apartment.

Gus's dad, Salvatore Jammalo, was born at home in North Adams in 1904. Salvatore had little education, leaving school in the sixth grade to work in the local wool mills. One of his mill jobs was lifting heavy wool blankets to dry, and in another mill, he worked for fifty cents an hour taking bolts of cloth off looms and moving them to the warehouse. Later in his youth, he mowed lawns at Williams College.

Frances Disanti, Gus's mother, was also born in the early nineteen-hundreds at home. She had an unusual birth. Her mother delivered Frances on the family's front porch with the help of neighbors. Frances worked at the Biscuit Company for fifteen years and then was a stay-at-home mom. She and Salvatore had two children, Gus and Ann Marie.

Vincenzo and Catherine (Siciliano) Disanti were Gus's maternal grandparents. Vincenzo immigrated from Salerno, Italy, in the late 1800s and in 1903 married Catherine, who was born in North Adams. Vincenzo was a mill laborer at Arnold Print Works for many years.

Gus's paternal grandfather was Agostino Iemmallo, born in the Calabria region of Southern Italy. He married Maria Cerullo, from the same region, in 1881. Agostino immigrated to the U.S. with his brother-in-law, arriving in New York in 1895. Family lore says he was sponsored by a North Adams Italian family, then landed in New York with thirty-seven cents in his pocket. After a four-year separation, their wives and children emigrated from Italy in 1899. Agostino and Maria went on to have nine children.

"Gus" was named Augustine after his grandfather, Agostino. His parents decided to slightly "Americanize" his name. Initially nicknamed Gussy by his mom, as he grew into adolescence it became, fortuitously, Gus. Years ago, when Gus was renewing his passport, he realized his driver's license name did not match his birth certificate (recorded as *Jamello*). After some research, it was determined through misspellings and misunderstandings that his ancestors' actual name had morphed over the years from *Iemmallo* to *Jammallo*, and finally today to *Jammalo*.

Shortly after his birth, his parents purchased their first house on North Street for four thousand dollars. This is where Gus would grow up. It was a large, grey-clapboard, two-story house with six rooms. Downstairs featured a kitchen in the back, a living room, and dining room with an upright piano. Upstairs were three bedrooms and a flight of stairs leading to a cavernous attic.

The house was heated with coal, which required monthly deliveries and the ongoing task of shoveling coal from the bin to the furnace. This became one of Gus's first household chores. The house had a spacious yard with a greenhouse and an old barn. Gus and his dad planted and tended a large garden besides raising chickens, rabbits, and pigeons.

The family routinely ate their evening meals at 5:00 p.m., right after his dad got home from the mill. Prayers and blessing always preceded the meal. Usually, Salvatore would have a bottle of wine with his supper, and their meals often involved chicken raised in their backyard, but simpler fare too like hamburgers, hot dogs, and spaghetti and meatballs. Hot oatmeal was everyone's breakfast staple.

The family attended the original St. Anthony's Church on Holden Street. The original church was located in the back parking lot of the present Big Y supermarket near River Street. The family always went to church on Sundays. Everyone wore their best clothes: suits and ties for the men and dresses for the women and shined shoes for everyone. Easter Mass was a special occasion and always warranted new clothes for the entire family.

Gus attended nearby Johnson Elementary School. Not the most enthusiastic of students, he clearly remembers when teachers would whack your open palms or knuckles for minor infractions. Major violations got you locked in the closet. Curious as a child, Gus reminisces about how at the age of five he pulled the tablecloth off his family's dining room table, bringing the entire Thanksgiving meal crashing to the floor.

Tragedy struck the family when Gus's mom died from Bright's disease at forty-two years old. Gus was fifteen and his sister Ann Marie only three years old. His mom's death had a big effect on Gus, and the death combined with disliking school resulted in him dropping out of Drury High School in his freshman year. He jokingly says his best subject "was looking out the window daydreaming," although he did like art and math. Spelling was his worst subject and continues to challenge him today.

Five years after his mom's death, Gus's father Salvatore married Margaret, a cheery widow. She was a nice lady, but Gus, now on his own, didn't take well to his mom being replaced. Gus did, however, remain close to his father his entire life.

Gus's first job was washing dishes at the Williams Inn for thirty-five cents an hour. He bicycled the seven miles to and from work for three years. He quit the Inn to work at Greylock Mills for the princely sum of $1 an hour as a shuttle boy. Gus tended seventy-five shuttles and made sure their bobbins of yarn were replaced when they ran out. Running from machine to machine with no breaks was a fast-paced job. Weavers working on piecework would holler for him when their bobbins started to run out of yarn. Gus often worked two shifts, starting at 7:00 a.m. and getting off at 11:00 p.m.

MILITARY TRAINING

In 1952, at the age of eighteen, Gus joined the Army and attended Basic Training, Tank Commander School, and Jump School at Fort Campbell, Kentucky. Weighing only 115 pounds at the time and afraid of heights, he nonetheless requested to attend a three-week Jump School in order to get his "wings." He'd observed that local girls seemed to be attracted to paratroopers. He still vividly remembers the unit's rigorous five-mile runs and twenty-mile forced marches.

The day came for his first jump from a C-119 Cargo plane. As he hooked up his parachute cable and peered out the window at 3,000 feet, he wondered, "What have I done?" Once the plane's interior green light came on, signaling they were over the drop zone, Gus jumped out and found his fear vanished. He loved the exhilaration of falling through the sky. Over the span of thirteen jumps, he had one close call, colliding with the top of a parachute directly beneath, but at the last minute he wobbled to the side and freed himself from the other chute.

Gus was temporarily assigned to Camp Stewart in Georgia for ninety days of armor training. His squad slept in a nine-man tent very close to the Okefenokee Swamp and dealt with giant-size, voracious red ants and numerous rattlesnakes. Disaster struck one afternoon when the soldier sitting next to Gus fell over with a bullet hole in his neck. Blood was splattered everywhere and efforts to save him were useless. The wound was mortal and he died on the spot. Later, it was determined that a stray bullet from a nearby rifle range was the tragic source.

Back at Fort Campbell, Gus passed the high school GED test and was honorably discharged. With $500 in his pocket, and wanting to see a little of the world, he took a sequence of buses and trains to visit his uncle in California. After a brief visit (and almost out of money), he decided to return to North Adams. The meandering 3,000-mile bus trip that took two weeks was a hot, uncomfortable fortnight of thick cigarette smoke, no air conditioning, and no onboard restrooms.

A CAREER APPEARS

In 1955, after arriving home, a friend convinced him to attend barber school. At the time, Massachusetts schools required a high school diploma to attend barber school, so with help from the GI Bill he was accepted at a more accommodating school in Connecticut. The six-month school was challenging. Gus and several other apprentices shared a small room at a boarding house with a community bathroom. They slept on cots and secretly cooked their dinners on a hot plate at night, only occasionally getting caught by the severe landlady.

The apprentices were taught haircutting and shaving skills plus massaging and giving facials. The students used an antiquated massager that vibrated, and sparks flew out of it. Though visually scary, it reportedly was not dangerous. For facials, the students applied cream to a customer's face and hot pads from steamers to relax their pores.

The students practiced their craft on homeless men, offering haircuts and shaves for only ten cents. After practicing with straight razors by shaving a balloon without breaking it, Gus had his first customer. He was a rough, unsavory character who told Gus that he had a knife in his pocket and if Gus cut him, he would cut Gus. The shave saw no blood shed.

Not long after graduating in 1956, Gus and a partner began their business on River Street, renting a building for $50/month. They had two barber chairs and offered haircuts, shaves, facials, and massages. Their work attire was a short-sleeve white shirt, tie, and black pants with a white, buttoned barber's smock. Chair cloths, which covered customers, were white with fine black stripes.

The partners were open six days a week, Monday through Saturday, from 9 a.m. to 5 p.m. All customers were men, and the shop was a great place to socialize and have a smoke. In the mid-1950s, customers smoked cigarettes and cigars; spittoons had recently been removed for hygiene reasons.

As they were located on River Street, many of their customers were workers from Arnold Print Works and, later on, from the Sprague Electric Company. In the 1950s, it was customary for men to get weekly haircuts, a superb model for a recurring revenue enterprise. Gus and his partner charged $1.00 for a haircut and seventy-five cents for a shave. Frequently, customers would get a shave on Saturday before Sunday services. Some local executives stopped in every day for a shave.

In the 1950s, North Adams had over fifty barber shops and most were unionized. Gus's was not. He was confronted by union representatives that wanted him to join the union and raise his haircut prices from $1.00 to $2.00. Independent as always, he refused to join or raise prices, even after a subtle threat of picketing. He remains non-union to this day.

A rare moment with Gus sitting in his own chair. Though prices haven't stayed at $1, today's cut is still a good deal.

Gus says that over the years, shaving customers disappeared. The process required sterilized hot towels; razors with a leather strop for sharpening; and a honing stone to put a fine edge on a razor. In the time it took the barber to shave a person, he could give several haircuts. This time savings, combined with the advent of double edge razors which made home shaving easier caused many barbers to phase out their shaving service. Later, initial cautions around the AIDS epidemic also affected the decision to phase out shaving.

Gus remembers a local funeral home offering him $50 to cut a deceased person's hair. It was tempting, since everyday haircuts were only $1, but he felt uncomfortable and declined. In the 1950s, it was the custom and probably still is for barbers to avoid shaving drunks and people with head lice or impetigo as they were hazards of the trade.

Early on, the barbers also offered scalp massages, especially to bald men whose skin was tight. Seventy years ago, their barber-school training taught the location of scalp veins and how massaging might delay male baldness. It would be difficult to prove whether or not it worked, but it probably felt nice.

DEVELOPING HOBBIES

One summer, before Gus entered the Army, a college student gave Gus's dad a large, mounted blackbird as a gift. The bird's glass eyes and proud appearance was enough to kick-start Gus's twenty-year hobby of taxidermy. He was self-taught, reading books purchased from Northwestern School of Taxidermy in Nebraska. For twelve months, he paid $1 a month for a book and read each one of the series from cover-to-cover.

It was initially difficult work and, though his skill as a barber certainly helped this hobby, he often found himself with cut hands when skinning animals. He mounted pheasants, partridges, and one time received $30 for mounting a deer head. His most difficult and rewarding mount was a porcupine.

Innovatively, he created a special plastic mold to mount fish and was successful with pickerel, trout, bass, and once even a three-foot sand shark. Removing the shark's tough skin, he recalls, was exceedingly difficult. His most detailed mount, which he displays in his barber shop, is of two chipmunks, one sitting in a barber's chair while the other cuts his hair.

As a young man on Thursday nights, when the stores were open late and paychecks had been cashed, he and his friend would look for girls on Main Street near the Mohawk Theater and Anes Soda Fountain. One night they started a conversation with two cuties, had sodas, and then met later at a dance. His friend was with a girl named Marion but that wasn't working out, so they switched partners and found a mutual attraction. Gus and Marion began dating.

They were married in 1960. Gus was twenty-six years old.

Once, when Gus first met Marion, she asked to borrow his prized Nash Rambler automobile but was gone quite a bit longer than expected. They joke now that she "stole the car" even before they began seriously dating. After their marriage, the couple decided to live in North Adams in a small apartment on Meadow Street. One day, the landlord decided to raise the rent from $55 a month to $60 a month (heat included). Upset by the increase, the couple began looking for land to build a house and found a site in nearby Clarksburg. They built their three-bedroom ranch with a one-car garage and moved in a year later. Marion still remembers their mortgage payment to the penny: $70.76 a month. They have lived there since the mid-sixties.

In 1965, Gus and his partner purchased a building on Eagle Street for $12,000. They renovated it, created a two-barber-chair shop, and upgraded the five attached apartments, providing another source of income for the barbers.

Then, in 1978, when the nearby town of Readsboro, Vermont, lost its barber, Gus took on a second job. He rented a shop for $18 a month and cut hair on Thursday nights for the next thirteen years. Business was good, with many customers coming from the local paper and shoe factories. He remembers wondering why his older customers paid with money that smelled moldy, until someone told him they didn't believe in banks and hid their money in their cellars.

During this time period, Gus and Marion had two sons. Mom and the family settled into a routine. Suppers were around 6 p.m. They always ate together, except for the nights Gus cut hair in Vermont. Marion, a homemaker while the kids were growing up, was a good cook and liked to experiment with her cooking. Spaghetti and homemade sauce and meatballs were common fare. As with most families, Sundays were big meals involving meat and potatoes.

Marion was more the disciplinarian than Gus. She kept the boys in line and had them follow the rules. Gus's personality was more easygoing, and he was often busy working six days a week and some nights. As the boys got older, Marion worked at a stationery store, and later she retired from the Hoosac Bank.

Their family vacations were at Lake Winnipesaukee in New Hampshire or Cape Cod with their cousins. Sometimes, in the summers, Marion and Gus would host her sister's children, and the next summer the cousins would switch houses. The boys loved these family exchanges.

Devout Catholics, the family attended Saturday night Mass at Saint Anthony of Padua Church. When traveling, they always found a church for Sunday's services.

During this time, Gus started collecting coins. It all started when a customer who worked at nearby J.C. Penney's brought him a two-and-a-half-dollar gold coin, wondering what it was worth. They researched it, decided it was valuable, and Gus bought it, later selling it to a coin dealer in Pittsfield for $50. His visit to the Pittsfield coin dealer started a long-term relationship and an affinity for coin collecting. Never one to sit still, Gus put a sign in the front window of his barber shop—WE BUY COINS—and founded the Eagle Coin Company. Gus started attending shows across the country in New York, Texas, Florida, and California, setting up a table, showcasing his coins, and often buying and selling with other dealers.

He decided to focus on gold pieces, silver dollars, half dollars, and Indian pennies. Always cautious at the close of the shows, he developed the habit of mailing home his considerable proceeds. Gus has been in the coin business for over fifty years.

Another hobby began on a visit to the Norman Rockwell Museum in Stockbridge, Massachusetts. Gus was inspired to try painting. So, he began (with

Gus painted the Hoosac Tunnel onto a saw blade from the Readsboro Chair Factory, which closed years ago. The truck delivered it for $20 from Vermont to the barbershop, and now it's a work of art.

no lessons) capturing portraits of people. He noticed that Norman Rockwell used individual photos and projected them on a canvas in order to paint his subjects. Employing the same method, Gus projects the person's picture and sketches it out on a canvas with pencil. He then sprays lacquer on the sketch to seal in the lead from the pencil.

One of his first efforts was with a barber shop customer. Gus took his photo and worked on the painting for many days. When the customer saw the picture, he was overwhelmed and started crying. Gus gave him the picture. He admits portraits are difficult and take a lot of hours and hard work.

One of his memorable and largest paintings was from a picture of Frank Sinatra. Gus had seen him perform a number of times and loved his singing. The portrait had Sinatra in a black tuxedo with a bow tie, holding a microphone. Once he was finished, a friend gave him Sinatra's home address, and Gus mailed the portrait to him, enclosing a nice letter. Months later, Gus received a thank-you note from Frank's personal secretary, which is now framed in his barber shop.

His studio or hide-away is a small, cluttered space in his cellar. He paints in the winter months and prefers oil-based paint. Over the years, he has created over 400 canvases and sold about 300 of them. His subjects have varied from painted portraits to outdoor settings, people fishing, airplanes, boats, horses, and chickens. Most sought after are usually his paintings of nearby Mount Greylock, the highest peak in Massachusetts. Intuitively, his outdoor pieces are painted from the background to the foreground. In other words, the mountain gets painted first before the fields.

Gus has also painted a five-foot-tall portrait of President John Kennedy and a large Statue of Liberty. At one point, Gus painted a picture of Johnson Elementary school, which he attended as a youth. He always loved the brick building and its surrounding paths. He loaned the picture to North Adams Mayor Barrett, who displayed it in his office. The mayor had taught at Johnson earlier in his career and liked looking at the picture. Gus reclaimed it and, when the mayor visited his barber shop, he presented it to him as a gift.

The owner of the Olympic Restaurant in Williamstown graciously displays Gus's paintings and refuses to accept any commissions. Gus acknowledges the kindness with a half-gallon of Vermont maple syrup.

At one point, in the 1970s, as long hair grew to be more popular, Gus's barbering business dropped off, and he found himself temporarily closing both shops in North Adams and Readsboro. Other than nursing home or hospital courtesy cuts, he was out of the haircutting business. He stored his barber chairs in a barn.

Not one to remain idle, he converted Eagle Barber Shop into Eagle Variety store. The store was very successful, although it required long hours—from 6:30 a.m. to 11:00 p.m. seven days a week. Then, when short and frequent haircuts returned to popularity, Gus sold the business and returned to the job he loved.

He opened today's shop on Union Street in the early 1980s. Even now, sixty-plus years after his first client, haircuts are just $12 for seniors and $14 for other adults. No shaves offered. Gus says barber equipment hasn't changed much. He still uses an Oster razor and vibrating clippers. He no longer wears a smock or a tie and uses disposable, colorful cloth covers for each customer. Gus uses a sterilizer with germicides to clean his equipment daily, dipping his comb, scissors, and razors in liquid.

Currently his clientele is mostly senior citizens, high schoolers, or college students, and mainly men. He does trim hair for four or five ladies and delightfully finds them to be the best tippers. For years, he has given free haircuts to veterans during Veterans Week in November.

At eighty-seven years old, Gus works four days a week, Monday through Thursday from 8:00 a.m. to 4:00 p.m. Due to the COVID-19 pandemic, only two people are allowed in his shop at a time, one in the chair and one waiting.

One thing is certain: even in hard times, hair keeps growing.

After 65 years of barbering, Gus Jamallo retired on August 19, 2021. His final haircut was given to his first customer, Gene Kemp, who at the time of the first haircut was thirteen years old.

JEFF LEVANOS

This third-generation owner of Jack's Hot Dog Stand continues to preserve a century-old local institution. Jack's has weathered a depression, World War II, and economic booms and downturns, providing an enduring cornerstone for downtown North Adams, serving over 2,000,000 hot dogs to happy and devoted customers. They are, after all, "Fit for a King."

This one started differently from most stories. In the early 1900s, two teenagers emigrated separately from Greece to the United States. One of them, Mary Rougele, married George Collett, and they opened the Pioneer Hot Dog Stand on Eagle Street. After several years, George missed Greece and returned home, leaving behind his wife and young son. While in Greece he was killed in a mishap.

The other emigrating teenager, Jaffros "Jack" Levanos, started a competing hot dog business called the Atlanta located on State Street. Mary, now by herself on Eagle Street, asked Jaffros to help her manage the Pioneer Hot Dog Stand. Jaffros closed his store and began working with Mary. Months later, the couple fell in love and married, and in the early nineteen-thirties they changed the store's name to Jack's.

Since Jack joined the business founded by Mary in 1917, the shop has been operated continuously by a Levanos for over one hundred years. Today, Jack's is managed by Mary and Jaffros' grandson, Jeff Levanos.

Mary (Rougele) Levanos was born in Mitilini, the capital of the Greek island of Lesvos, in 1903, then immigrated to the United States with her parents in 1912, settling in North Adams. She helped run Jack's for many years while also tending her two sons. She lived in North Adams for sixty years before passing away in 1972.

Jaffros ("Jack") Levanos was born in 1895, emigrated from a small village just outside of Athens and ran Jack's Hot Dog Stand for most of his life. Jack and Mary semi-retired in 1955 and often stayed at their second home in Miami, Florida. Jaffros passed away in 1980.

Their son, John Levanos, born in North Adams in 1927, attended Drury High School, served in the U.S. Army during World War II, and took over Jack's Hot Dog Stand from his dad, Jaffros, in 1972. John was involved in the business for the next forty-plus years, almost until his passing away in 2016.

A 1930s snapshot of Jaffros and his son, John, in front of the family business.

He met and married Lucille Jordan in 1949. Born in 1930, she was a cheerleader and debate team leader for St. Joseph's High School and lived with her family in Clarksburg. Lucille operated Mia's Specialty Shoppe for women's apparel. Named after their daughter, it was located right across the street from Jack's. She eventually passed the business on to her daughter and joined her husband at Jack's. After being married for sixty-seven years, Lucille passed away in 2018.

Jeff's maternal grandparents were Alexander and Helen (Lefave) Jordan, both immigrants. Alex, born in the late 1800s, worked at the Sprague Electric Company. Helen, a French

Canadian, was a homemaker. They had five children, one of whom is Jeff's mom Lucille. Alex passed away in 1955, Helen in 1975.

THE THIRD GENERATION

Jeff Alexander Levanos, Jack's current owner, was born on April 17, 1958, at the North Adams Hospital. Jeff's middle name came from his maternal grandfather. Jeff's sister, Maria, was born in 1955. They were raised in Clarksburg and attended Clarksburg Elementary School through the eighth grade.

As a youth, he was always outside. The Levanos lived at the base of a mountain, and he and his friends would often hike up to "the hairpin turn" on the Mohawk Trail, sometimes two or three times in the same day. He and his four or five best friends were not allowed to hitchhike, so they found themselves walking everywhere. They loved target shooting with their bb guns and .22 rifles. As they grew older, they modified and rode dirt bikes and go-carts. After his grandfather bought a pool table, the crew spent many wintery days sharpening their eight-ball skills. Sometimes the troop would go to the nearby Sunny-Side Bar to shoot pool. His dad's swimming pool was always another draw for local kids.

Sometimes the family vacationed in Miami where his grandfather had a second home, but there were few family vacations because John was always working at the business. Supper was a tradition and mandatory. Served by Mom at 5:30 p.m., it was a combination of Greek and American food.

Jeff loved her "American" dishes of pork cutlets, pork chops, hamburgers, fish, vegetables, and potatoes. He was a little pickier about the Greek cuisine. His mom made an appetizer called *dolmathakias*, a combination of grape leaves, hamburger, rice, and spices boiled in a kettle with a main course of pickled cabbage, lentils, and rabbit stew. When he was little, the stew reminded him of his pet rabbit. He did like her *keftethes*, meatballs with oregano and other spices, no exotic ingredients for young Jeff.

His dad often led the supper conversation among the four, and it was usually about the business. If someone might have a comment about Mom's cooking, John would say that there were "no choices, you eat what was cooked, this is not a restaurant."

Sundays were special when Jeff's grandparents ate with them. The meals could vary but usually involved pork roast, potatoes, chicken cacciatore, *moussaka* (potato-based dish), or *dolmathakias*.

Maria, Jeff's sister, has fond memories of helping their grandmother gather dandelions from the front yard for tea and picking sour apples for her dad, who loved eating them with salt. Grandma would also bring chocolate and banana cream pies on Sundays, her dad's favorites.

Jeff and his sister describe their dad as hardworking and thrifty, having a good heart, and always looking for a bargain. Standing five-foot-ten, he wasn't shy about asking customers to finish up eating. Jack's only had twelve stools. He'd say, "We can't have any dilly dallying." On occasion, he might nicely take a customer's almost-finished plate and simply say "see ya later."

Lucille had an easygoing personality, and everyone loved her. People enjoyed visiting her store, Mia's, and chatting with her. When necessary, she handled the children's discipline by herself, not bothering to involve her husband. One friend noted that her early life on River Street had not always been easy, and she was always happy with what she had.

The Levanos were devoted to their faith, and the family attended St. George Greek Orthodox Church in Pittsfield. The church, just off of North Street, is still there. The biggest worship service occurred on Easter, when the three-day celebration included Mass on Friday, Saturday, and Sunday. Most looked forward to the social time held in the downstairs hall with abundant desserts and coffee.

KEEPING IT IN THE FAMILY

Jeff started working at Jack's in the eighth grade. His mom would go in to help and take Jeff with her. He began by washing dishes and sweeping the floor.

Extracurricular activities at Drury High were limited for Jeff, since he was required to work daily. School would end at 2:15 p.m., and Jeff started work at 2:30 p.m. He would work until closing at 4:00 p.m. and then clean up. Few people knew, but he often would go to Jack's to wash dishes during Drury's lunch period. He also worked Saturdays; it was a family enterprise and everyone needed to pitch in.

In his junior year, the new Drury campus opened on the outskirts of town. He could no longer slip away at noon, but he still worked after school. He became the prep cook, responsible for slicing vegetables, parboiling potatoes for French fries, and anything else his dad needed done. Jack's at that time was open from 7:00 a.m. until 4:00 p.m.

Jeff graduated from Drury in 1976. He attended the University of Miami and majored in marine biology for two years. Schooling in Miami was a huge transition for the small-town mountain boy. His world opened up to many new activities like scuba diving, surfing, skateboarding, and jokingly, a bit of "drinking." In his second year, when his interest turned toward meteorology, his dad did not approve and was unwilling to assist in any further school expenses. Jeff returned home to attend North Adams State College for a semester.

It was during this time period that his father approached him about someday owning the business, admitting that he was considering retiring. Twenty-one-year-old Jeff signed on, realizing he loved Jack's and was never going to be a big-city kid. It worked out, although his dad did not in fact retire for twenty more years!

Things did not always go smoothly. John had expectations of his employees and could be a demanding boss. The two had a number of disagreements over the years that resulted in Jeff being fired three or four times. During those lulls, he worked at Bounti-Fare (the former Midway) as a dishwasher, returned to Jack's for a bit, then was employed at Arnold Print Works as a color pourer, then back to Jack's. At one point, John realized Jeff was dedicated and hard-working and could earn more money elsewhere, so he rehired him permanently.

In the early eighties, Jeff met and married Mary Lou Ellis. At the time, he had a second job bartending, and Mary Lou worked at a local hotel. One day, when they were exchanging pleasantries, he asked her out on a date. The next day was her birthday, so he sent her roses, and that's how it all began. They have been married for thirty-eight years, have one son, and remained in Clarksburg most of their lives.

Everybody knows where Jack's is located, the same block as the flatiron building on 12 Eagle Street, formerly known as the Decker building and now known as the Levanos building. One of the oldest structures in town, its interior occupies a space no larger than thirty by fifteen feet, although it wasn't always this small. In the 1960s there was an archway to an area that contained several tables and booths. People used to buy a coffee, then occupy the tables for hours. Jeff's dad decided to block off the archway and rent the room to a barber. The building also houses another business and two apartments above the shop.

Long-ago renovations leveled the post–Civil War slanted floor that now sports twelve stools and a counter. Behind the counter are the two small grills and a fountain machine. The walls are a yellowish tan, similar in tone to a hot-dog bun. The counter is only twenty-two feet long, covered in a greenish laminate. The only seating in the bar-like set up are the twelve green-vinyl swivel stools with dark grey powder-coated supports.

© DENNIS PREGENT, 2021

Another happy customer at the famous counter, halfway through his *hamburg* and a shake.

The walls are decorated with pictures of Jeff's father and grandfather plus magazine and newspaper articles about Jack's. The eclectic collage includes different awards the business has received and a colorful Dagwood/Blondie comic strip that says: "Take a left at Jack's Hotdogs."

There is a memorable photo of a longtime employee, Louis Kanelos, who had five children and worked at Jack's for over 42 years.

Louie returned from World War II after serving in the Navy, and worked days at Arnold Print Works and nights at Jack's. Eventually he moved to all days at Jack's. The hardworking former sailor never missed work, and the hot grill was his domain. Jeff worked with Louie for almost twenty years. His work ethic had a great effect on Jeff.

Louie was also a pilot and encouraged Jeff to get his license. Jeff still remembers Louie telling him how he and his shipmates were all tattooed with a pirate's cutlass on their left forearms as a sign of camaraderie.

The menu and hours of operation have changed over time. In the 1940s and 1950s, Jack's was a full-fledged diner with pies, sandwiches, and soups. A breakfast menu was offered that included bacon, eggs, and sausage, but with the advent of fast-food restaurants, this type of fare became uncompetitive. Also, cooking breakfast on the same grill with burgers and hot dogs was too difficult.

The hours have shifted from 7:00 a.m. until 4:00 p.m. to 10:00 a.m. until 7:00 p.m., Monday through Saturday. At one point, the eatery was open on Sundays until 2:00 p.m., but Jeff's parents kept getting called in and never seemed to have a day off.

In the 1960s, his dad introduced pepper steaks and hot/sweet sausages, and more recently Jeff brought in meals that could be cooked quickly such as popcorn chicken, mac and cheese dishes, and jalapeno tater tots.

Jeff started home delivery about twenty years ago, and it represents about 30 percent of his business. For a minimum $20 order, Jack's will deliver food anywhere in North Adams for free. There is a $3 charge for deliveries to Adams and Williamstown. Business right now is mostly take-out and home delivery. Before the pandemic, the restaurant's stools at noon and dinner on Thursdays, Fridays, and Saturdays were always occupied, sometimes with two or three people waiting behind each stool.

When Jeff's grandfather ran Jack's in the 1920s and 1930s, a hot dog was a nickel, or you could get two dogs for seven cents. When his dad ran the business, hot dogs were fifteen cents, then twenty-five cents. Jeff continues the tradition of producing low-cost, high-quality food in volumes.

"Owning the Levanos building helps keep costs down," he says. And today, after more than 100 years in business, a Jack's hot dog only costs $1.45.

DAY-IN, DAY-OUT

Jeff starts work at 7:30 and sets up for the 10:00 a.m. opening. He remains until 1:00, returning at 3:30 to start the second shift. The second shift closes at 7:00 p.m., with cleanup until 8:00 p.m. Jeff has three dedicated first- and second-shift employees.

Food preparation consumes much of everyone's time. Their burgers are shaped individually by hand, adding a personal touch. Jack's uses between eighteen and twenty-five 10-pound boxes of hot dogs each week. With two hundred hot dogs per box, they run through thousands of hot dogs in a week. They cook 200,000 hot dogs a year—and in their 100+ year history, over two million hot dogs have been served!

Jack's is also renowned for its fresh French fries. The business processes 150 pounds of locally purchased potatoes each day. It takes four hours daily to wash, peel, cut, blanch, and fry them by hand. A lot of work goes into processing over 50,000 pounds of potatoes a year. One of Jeff's fondest memories is when he and his mom would drive to a farm in Hadley to pick up pallets of fresh potatoes. Now more pressed for time, he has them delivered.

After all these years, cooking has become second nature for Jeff. He cooks by ear. The two grills have no thermostats and lack precise controls, making it difficult to tell how hot they are. Jeff determines the temperature from the sound of the sizzle as he puts hot dogs, *hamburgs* (as the sign says), chicken, sausage, or pepper steaks on the grill. From the back of the store, if someone else is cooking, when he hears the sizzle he can tell the cook to raise or lower the grill's temperature. On his deep fryers, he adjusts the heat when bubbles aren't just right.

The grills have a story of their own. Jeff relies on two grills; one keeps the food warm, and its temperature never varies. The main grill, only 20" by 14", was purchased used by his grandfather over

100 years ago and does all the cooking. The grill is in constant use from open to close, cooking burgers, hot dogs, and bacon. Jeff says it's a constant act of juggling customer orders, but he can fit 12 double hamburgers on the grill at one time.

Jeff pauses for a photo, anticipating the lunch rush. Everything is in easy reach, from the fryer to the grill.

No self-respecting hot dog stand would be without a hot-dog-eating contest, and over the years Jack's has sponsored a number of them. As far back as World War II, a returning veteran was credited with eating over fifty hot dogs. More currently, individuals, local colleges competing with each other, and politicians challenge professional eaters to raise funds for charity. Records to beat are posted on the nearby milk vending machine. At one time, the contests were open to anyone at any time.

"They just have to let us know they're going for the contest," says Jeff. Then hot dogs are served up, numbers recorded, and monthly prizes awarded.

Many customers have been eating there for generations. Others who have left town always stop by when they are visiting, bringing along wives, children, and friends. Jeff follows his grandfather's tradition: give people a fresh, good meal at a price they can afford.

Jeff says Jack's has never turned away a customer who could not pay, and remembers his grandfather telling him of food credit slips that piled up during the depression. One customer repaid his grandfather with a handmade clock.

Jeff, as a young Jack's employee, remembers his most reliable customer was Ed, who came in every day at the same time and ordered the same thing. One dog with mustard, one double cheeseburger with mustard, and onion and fries. Jeff would always have it ready for him. Another customer, who began coming to Jack's when she was six years old in 1921, returned for decades until she passed away.

Over the years, Jeff has been involved in the community serving as a selectman and on the town's school committee for a number of years. Jack's has supported a bowling league, girls' softball, and a skating organization that teaches girls to ice skate. They've donated to numerous bazaars and readily helped people in need.

Jeff has held a pilot's license for over thirty years, an accomplishment he credits to encouragement from his friend and long-term employee, Louie. He has not flown in a while but did enjoy his joyriding trips to Lake George and Maine, and then there was that forgettable trip to busy Logan Airport in Boston. Motorcycling is his other passion. Currently, he rides a matte-black 2016 Indian motorcycle with a tan leather seat for around-town cruising and enjoys dirt-biking when he gets a chance.

Eating at Jack's Hot Dog Stand is a tradition, and for visitors it is a mandatory stop. It's getting more rare these days to find a small-town restaurant that offers good food at a cheap price. As the sign says, "always remember, the hot dogs taste better when eaten at Jack's!"

EUGENE MICHALENKO

For almost fifty years, Eugene Michalenko has been at the center of preserving and retelling Adams history. Holding a degree in languages and linguistics from Georgetown University with a concentration in Russian, and having studied five languages, he has become a Town Historian.

Often overheard in Adams are the words "just ask Eugene, he'll know the answer." The relevant inquiry could be about local family genealogy, long-gone manufacturing companies, evolution of downtown businesses, immigrant population trends in 1900, or a history of local churches.

Eugene has been involved in or led the Adams Historical Society since its inception in 1972. He and other members devote considerable time to preserving the Town's trove of artifacts stored on the second floor of the library in rooms adjacent to Memorial Hall. The hall, a meeting place for Civil War veterans, was dedicated in 1899 and today remains a beautifully preserved time capsule of the period. Its one-hundred-and-twenty-year-old, straight-back armchairs, the same ones used by Civil War veterans, and its "mortar" pedestal are still used today.

As Eugene would tell you, Adams' location in northwestern Massachusetts at the foot of Mount Greylock on the Hoosic River made it ideal for dissident religious groups to own land and be far away from Boston to live free from persecution. Settled in the late 1700s by Quakers and Baptists,

A closeup of the town's historian.

227

and named after Revolutionary War patriot Samuel Adams, the town grew to 13,000 in 1915 with the help of many immigrant groups. Its current population is approximately 8,000.

Eugene's civic interest is inherited from his mom and dad who were always active in Adams community life and willingly volunteered to assist any and all groups. The family's heritage gives insight into how Eugene took on the role of Town Historian, caring for everyone's heritage.

POLISH COMMUNITY

Eugene, the youngest of five children, was born at the W. B. Plunkett Hospital in Adams. His parents were Ignatius "Iggy" and Mary Michalenko. With the precision of a historian, Eugene has compiled the following information on his ancestors, a broad snapshot of the immigrant experience:

Ignatius, named after Saint Ignatius Loyola, was born in Adams in 1926. He attended local schools and joined the Marines in August 1944 at the age of eighteen. Corporal Michalenko was sent to the Pacific and participated in the mopping-up operations after the Battle of Okinawa. He found himself assigned to burial details. He served with the 7th Marines on occupation duty in northern China in the city of Tientsin (now Tianjin). During this stay, he worked as a baker.

Returning home, he married a Polish girl from North Adams, his girlfriend and wartime pen pal, Mary, on October 11, 1947. Shortly afterwards, Iggy graduated from the Fannie Farmer School of Cooking and worked at several local bakeries until starting the Adams Specialty & Printing Company in 1950.

Over the years, Iggy was a leader or member of dozens of local organizations. He spearheaded citizens groups on issues like Greylock Glen and preserving the Mount Greylock Veterans Memorial. Iggy belonged to the Lions, was active in the Chamber of Commerce, co-chair of the Adams Bicentennial Committee, and worked most of the Susan B. Anthony Days and Summer Fests. He ran for State Representative in 1980 and '82. He was voted

Berkshire County Republican of the Year in 1980. He was a charter member and past commander of the Burnett-Bednarz V.F.W. Post. Iggy passed away in 1997. The couple had five children.

Mary, Eugene's mother, was born in 1924. The family would tease her about being two years older than Iggy. Mary worked from the 1930s to 1950s as a winder and packing condensers at Sprague Electric Company and as an usherette at the Mohawk Theater. In the 1950s, she started working at the family's print shop and supervised home delivery of their publication, *The Shopper's Companion*. She belonged to the Rosary Society, the Polish Women's Alliance, served as Vice President of the V.F.W. Ladies Auxiliary, and cochaired a Northern Berkshire United Way Campaign with Iggy. Mary had a strong sense of responsibility and duty and was very social, enjoying banquets and conventions. She passed away in 2010.

Eugene's paternal grandfather, Jan Michalenko, was born in 1890 in Zamutov, part of the Austro-Hungarian Empire in what is now the Slovak Republic. Though his family name is Ukrainian-based, he spoke fluent Slovak. Jan fought in World War I, beginning in 1914 with the Austrian Army against the Russians, and then fought in Northern Italy until the war ended in 1918. Eugene heard stories that his grandfather talked about his "king," the Emperor Franz Joseph, who died in 1916 at the age of 86.

During Jan's war travels, he met Victoria Betleja on her father's farm in village outside of Strzyzow in southeast Poland. Toward the end of the war, he left his unit to marry her. Her father was in disbelief that Jan wanted to marry his daughter after only meeting her one time. Jan told her dad that he must marry her, or he would be shot as a deserter. He quickly returned to his unit, only to find it had been decimated in mountain fighting.

The young couple immigrated to the United States with one daughter in July 1921. They were attracted to Adams because Victoria had two sisters and a brother there, and over the next twenty-one years they had ten more children. Both worked in the Berkshire Mills for years. Victoria was a weaver. Jan was a carder.

Eugene's maternal grandfather, Peter Kryston, was Polish and born in the Carpathian Mountains. People from that area were often referred to as Gorals, which defined an ethnic group of high-landers from the northern Carpathians. The area was known for producing wood carvers, and Peter made and sold axe handles.

Sponsored by his brother-in-law, Peter arrived in Adams in 1912. Soon after, he went to Ware, Massachusetts, where there was a large concentration of Polish people (Gorals), to find a wife. He married, and the couple eventually made their home in North Adams. He worked at the mills in Greylock, and later in life, on the railroad.

His wife, Eugene's maternal grandmother Josephine, was born in Poland near the flatlands about forty miles outside of Krakow. She immigrated to the United States in 1911. Josephine worked in the local mills and managed the home. His mother always said that she was "born in a chicken coop in the Beaver," a low-rent house on Beaver Street in North Adams. Her parents were not the most responsible adults; alcohol played an issue. In general, life was a struggle for them and their four children.

EUGENE'S EARLY LIFE

The Michalenko family lived in a three-story tenement on Pine Street in Adams bought by Eugene's grandparents in 1941, just before World War II. The grandparents lived on the first floor, his parents on the second floor, and for a while an uncle and aunt on the third floor. This was Iggy and Mary's first apartment, and she was pregnant when he went off to baking school in 1947.

Eugene attended Saint Stanislaus Kostka school from kinder-garten to eighth grade. He attended C. T. Plunkett School for the 9th grade and transferred to the newly built Hoosac Valley High School in 1970 for the remainder of high school, graduating in 1973.

His best subjects in high school were French and Spanish. He was a good writer and became editor of the school newspaper, *The Labyrinth*. He enjoyed hiking with friends and hanging out on Park Street. Eugene continued working after school at his dad's shop. He had begun helping in the eighth grade by collating, binding, sta-pling, and wrapping bundles of printed material. He received his driver's license at sixteen and made deliveries for the business in his dad's Pontiac station wagon.

The family attended Mass every Sunday at Saint Stanislaus, and Eugene served as an altar boy from the fourth through the twelfth grade. On Monday mornings, he was one of the altar boys that served Mass at the nun's convent. Eugene's dad, coming from a family of eleven siblings, had two brothers who were priests and two sisters who became nuns. The sisters joined the Felician order and later belonged to a community located in Danbury, Connecticut. The brothers joined the Marian Fathers in Stockbridge, Massachusetts. The spirituality, intelligence, and fun-loving nature of his uncles and aunts had a great effect on Eugene.

One of his uncles left the Marians and joined the Campus Ministry at Georgetown University Law School. His other uncle, Reverend Seraphim Michalenko, witnessed the first miracle attributed to Maria Faustina Kowalska. It occurred at Faustina's gravesite outside of Krakow, when a woman was cured of a disease that caused severe inflammation. As a postulator, Reverend Michalenko presented to the Catholic church what he witnessed. His testimony contributed to Faustina being canonized as a Saint on April 30, 2000, by Pope John Paul II.

The Michalenko household was busy. The family's business, started in a back bedroom in the 1950s, moved to a garage next door on the corner of Pine and West Pine Streets. As business grew, it expanded three times. Adams Specialty & Printing remains there today.

Mary handled meal preparation. She was insistent that the meal begin at 5:30 p.m. even if the shop was busy. Her daughters helped with preparation, and Eugene set the table.

Meals varied from spaghetti and Italian white bread to entrees of hot dogs, pork chops, or thick Polish hamburgers, a mixture of half meat and half bread. Golumpki (stuffed cabbage) also made the menu. Friday nights was always a non-meat meal such as fish sticks, salmon cakes, fried cabbage/noodles, or cottage cheese and noodles. On special occasions, it might be fish and chips from a local restaurant.

Saturday's lunch was usually Lipton chicken soup with white-bread baloney-and-mustard sandwiches. Sundays after Mass was their big meal, usually a roast or steak with vegetables and mashed potatoes. His dad only liked carrots and corn, although Mary liked all vegetables and made sure to serve them to the kids.

Family vacations varied, from attending the 1964 World's Fair in New York City to beach vacations at Cape Cod, or trips to Canada visiting the Saint-Anne-de-Beaupré shrine and St. Joseph's Oratory. The family often traveled with Dad to advertising conventions held in Miami Beach, Atlantic City, and eastern Massachusetts. They looked forward to the conventions.

As his dad's business grew, it acquired larger presses, and in 1958, Iggy sold advertising and began publishing *The Shopper's Companion*. The *Companion* had a distribution of 14,000 throughout Adams, North Adams, Williamstown, and Cheshire. Eugene remembers spending a lot of time as a youth folding and collating the three sections of the *Companion* prior to distribution. Iggy sold the *Companion* to the North Adams *Transcript* newspaper in 1978.

Eugene started hiking in high school with friends and still hikes today. He enjoys exploring the Cheshire Cobbles (part of the Appalachian Trail), Pine Cobble in Williamstown, and of course Mount Greylock. Every year on his birthday he makes a point to hike up Mount Greylock. He has also hiked Prospect Mountain, Stoney Ledge, and Ragged Mountain (Fox Pines).

It's been said that a person could put their hand on the Quaker meeting house at the base of Mount Greylock located in the Maple Street cemetery and hike to the top of Mount Greylock in one hour. Eugene says, "It's possible. I've never done it . . . but you just need to take the right trails."

After attending the University of Massachusetts for one year, he was accepted at Georgetown University, attended for 12 straight months, and then took the next year off. He spent that year working at his dad's print shop. He graduated in 1978 with a bachelor of science in languages/linguistics with a minor in history.

The summer after graduation, Eugene traveled to the Soviet Union and studied at Leningrad State University (now St. Petersburg State University) for two months, subsequently visiting the cities of Kiev and Moscow, and the Baltic States.

Returning home, Eugene worked at *The Transcript* briefly and then went to work for his dad in the late 1970s. The business had evolved from his dad's early creation of printed brown paper bags for the potato chip business to printing tickets, wedding invitations, letterhead stationary, envelopes, business cards, and horse racing programs for Berkshire Downs racetrack in Hancock. At one time, their major customers were Arnold Print Works, Pfizer, L. L. Brown, and a mail order business on North Summer Street.

As the business grew, its capabilities changed. The company migrated away from a hand press to offset printing. Iggy considered himself to be one of the first printers in the Berkshires to embrace offset printing in the mid-1950s. The change from hand-setting type to using negatives and metal plates for printing greatly improved the business's production.

Eugene, his sister, and a third partner acquired the business in 1989 and began producing newsletters, brochures, business cards, letterheads, posters, box wraps for Jarisch Box Company, and the annual town reports for Adams, Cheshire, Windsor, Hinsdale, Monroe, and Lanesborough.

The recent pandemic has affected the business, although Eugene continues to service customers. He fortunately owns the building and has embraced alternative energy sources, installing solar panels to lower his carbon footprint and his utility costs. Though he spent many hours at the shop, he still found time to devote to his number one passion: local history.

The Town Historian

Eugene has long been involved in the Adams Historical Society, joining right after it was formed in 1972. During his forty-eight-year membership, he has served as director and for the last thirty-five years (1985-2020) as president. There was a period in the early nineties when Eugene was running the Society alone. Now the Society has a solid group of committed officers and board members who normally meet on Tuesday nights.

The Society has a mailing list of over a thousand members.

His predecessor, Oscar Choquette, began publishing newsletters in the 1970s, and almost immediately membership grew. The 8" x 14", double-sided, black-and-white newsletter is published usually six times a year. Each issue focuses on a specific topic in the town's history. Readers are delighted when they see it in their mailbox.

The group spends much of its time taking inventory, cataloguing/computerizing, and preserving the diverse collection of antiquities located on the Adams Library's second floor. They use special boxes with acidic buffers to neutralize acidity and preserve documents, and have specially made bags for pictures. The group isolates and cleans moldy antiques and photographs, in some cases resorting to scanning images for preservation purposes.

While Eugene thinks he knows where everything is, the group is creating a digitized inventory that should make access easier for everyone else.

The Society's collection is quite unique, ranging from thousands of local pictures and postcards to vintage uniforms from the local fire department, military veterans, Girl Scouts and Brownies. There is a collection of women's and men's hats from the early 20th century and apparel from the 1920s and 1930s.

Donations usually come from local families. The society recently received a fife played during the Civil War by a member of the local G.A.R. (Grand Army of the Republic). It was donated by the soldier's great-great-granddaughters. The Society even possesses payroll and financial records from local industries, including L. L. Brown Paper Co., Arnold Print Works, and the Polish Bakery (no recipes though), which illuminate the economy of local family life.

The Society has a complete collection of *The Packet*, newspapers published from 1976 to 1989 with many local stories chronicling Adams life in those decades. There are Thomas Jefferson and Martin Van Buren signed documents as well as an old, well-preserved quilt collection, known only to a few.

Eugene's favorite item is the two thousand or more photographs and a collection of glass slides from the years 1891–1922. Viewed on a Magic Lantern, they show the Adams scenes and nearby Mount Greylock from over a century ago.

MAJOR ACCOMPLISHMENTS

Eugene is deeply involved in the Town and wrote and published a fifty-page booklet titled *In This Valley: A Concise History of Adams, Massachusetts*. He also writes most of the newsletter content. His articles include: *The Quaker Influence, Streets of Adams—Your Heritage, W. B. Plunkett Hospital 1918–1973, First Churches, Working in the Berkshire Mills,* and *Local Businesses and Bravery and Tragedy in Wartime (World War I),* just to mention a few.

© DENNIS PREGENT, 2021

Eugene in his element, in the storage area of the Adams Historical Society, sorting through artifacts and uniforms.

The Society frequently curates historical displays and presentations on the library's first floor. The exhibits have included or involved the Civil War and World War I, the Cloud Burst of 1901, early-twentieth-century Easter hats, and Christmas cards. In a special exhibit, the Society displayed a large Civil War–era flag that flew on the USS *Brooklyn*, a sloop-of-war that was involved in the 1864 blockade of Mobile Bay, Alabama. In that battle, Commodore David Farragut delivered the famous order, "Damn the torpedoes, full speed ahead."

Susan B. Anthony, the famous women's rights activist, was born in Adams in 1820, and Eugene wrote a featured three-part article for *The Berkshire Eagle* and helped plan a bicentennial celebration in her honor. Few people knew she had started a women's rights newspaper called *The Revolution*. Eugene was also involved in successfully nominating her former home to be included in the National Register of Historic Places several decades ago.

The Society cleans and maintains the Quaker Meeting House, which is open on Sundays from July to October. Eugene occasionally conducts cemetery tours in Adams, pointing out notable landmarks and personages.

The Society participates in Adams events, usually displaying a booth exhibit on the history of Adams. Lately the Society has been transcribing early town records with the help of local genealogist Alan Horbal.

Eugene posts regularly on Facebook groups such as "Adams, Mass. A Blast to the Past," "Voices of Adams," and "You Know You're from Adams if . . . ." He posts old photos and answers questions about the town's history. This media effort reaches thousands of people with an interest in local history. Following in his dad's footsteps, Eugene has been an active Lions Club member for over thirty years, chairing its annual fund drive soliciting donations by mail from the generous people of Adams. At one point, Eugene was a member of the Maple Grove Civic Club, serving as its secretary and treasurer, and also serves as a library trustee.

A notable part of Adams history was the occupation of Saint Stanislaus Church after the Bishop of Springfield ordered it closed, in 2008. During part of the 1150-day, 24-hour vigil, Eugene slept in the church one night a week, his print shop provided graphics for press releases, and he created buttons for the protestors to wear. The church was reopened on April 1, Palm Sunday, 2012.

During the vigil, the parish's school was approaching its centennial anniversary. Seeing an opportunity, Eugene began collecting every photograph of the school's graduating classes, identifying each student. Talking with the different people in the vigil, he subsequently published a book with 91 of the 93 graduating class pictures going back to 1919. Eugene said, "It was remarkable how many people remembered names of their former classmates, their spouses and their families." He still donates proceeds from the sales to the school.

Eugene, always available to anyone seeking historical information, is described as a "walking encyclopedia of Adams history." Usually when you see him about town in his tan Toyota Tacoma truck, he is headed to a historical society or a civic group meeting, picking up donations, or meeting someone to look over their documents and pictures, often helping to identify people in the old photos.

Attention to detail, local knowledge, and decades of volunteer work have combined to earn him the title of Town Historian. "Just ask Eugene, he'll know!"

KEVIN MORAN

This Adams native has returned home to lead the newspaper he read as a boy. As Executive Editor, Kevin Moran supervises the Pulitzer Prize–winning Berkshire Eagle, *one of the region's leading newspapers, which has repeatedly won Newspaper of the Year awards and received the JFK Commonwealth Award from the Massachusetts Cultural Council, "for demonstrating the enduring civic value of community journalism."*

It might have been an early indication of his journalistic career when Kevin won the third annual spelling bee at the C. T. Plunkett School. He placed first among a field of 20 sixth graders and went on to participate in the Berkshire County semifinals of the Scripps-Howard National Spelling Bee, although at the time his main interests inclined to snow skiing and eventually fly fishing.

Kevin David Moran was born on November 24, 1970, at North Adams Regional Hospital. His parents were Frederick and Marilyn (Bieniek) Moran. Frederick had been born in Chicopee, Massachusetts, and Marilyn in Adams, at the W. B. Plunkett Memorial Hospital, both in 1942.

The family lived on Forest Park Avenue across from Bob's Hill (made famous by a collection of historic children's books) between Russell Field and the Forest Park Country Club at the foot of Mount Greylock.

When he was five years old, Dad, Mom, and Kevin all bought skis together. Skiing quickly became a popular family pastime. Kevin easily abandoned Saturday morning cartoons to be outside skiing on the sprawling grounds of the nearby Forest Park Country Club. He would leave home early in the morning, return for lunch, and go right back outside until dark, traversing up and skiing down parts of nearby Mount Greylock, a grueling if exhilarating trek.

Early on, he was destined to become an Olympic skier, he just knew it. He skied cross-country for his high-school team, and when not practicing or competing, he would make his way up the Cheshire Harbor Trail, often on Sundays, traveling four miles to reach Mount Greylock's summit.

When Kevin was in the eighth grade, his dad and mom opened *Points North Fishing and Hunting Outfitters*, which specialized in booking fishing trips. As a high school freshman, Kevin was in charge of videotaping the trips, and his love for fishing began. He accompanied his dad on fishing trips throughout New England.

He gradually turned to fly fishing and became a fishing guide for the family business. At a young age, barely able to drive, he was guiding clients on the Deerfield River, a meandering waterway that stretches seventy-six miles from lower Vermont through Massachusetts ending at the Connecticut river. The river's ideal cold-water temperatures, great scenery, and large trout made for happy customers. The river yielded a mixture of rainbow, brook, and brown trout.

LINEAGE

Fred, Kevin's father, taught high school in Worthington and Lenox, then served as principal and administrator for the elementary school in Cheshire, and principal and teacher at Cranville Elementary in Dalton. He first met Marilyn at Westfield State College where they both received bachelor's degrees in education in 1964. Fred also received a master's degree in education from Boston University. Active in community affairs, Fred was a member of the Town's Planning Board, the Lions Club, and one of the leading activists in "Voices not Vices," a group opposed to the 1970s proposal for gambling at nearby Greylock Glen.

Marilyn, Kevin's mother, taught at Hoosac Street Elementary and was an active Adams community member. She was the Chairperson on the Town's Growth Management Committee, the Committee Planning Board, and the Adams Chairperson for the League of Women Voters.

They operated *Points North Fishing and Hunting Outfitters* for years and were the only Orvis fly-fishing dealer in western Massachusetts. The store featured hand-crafted fly rods made by legend Francis "Digger" Degere, with whom Fred had interned.

Kevin's paternal grandparents were Frederick A. Moran and Adele Jegelwicz Moran. Fred, born in 1914, was a grocery market manager in Chicopee, Massachusetts, and Adele, born in 1912, was a housewife. Both were born in the United States. Adele was known to make scrumptious pierogis, golabki, or kielbasa, and no matter how much you ate, she thought you needed more.

It's little known that Kevin's great-grandfather's name was Apolinari Moron. When living in a tenement in Chicopee, he listed his name as "A. Moron" on the mailbox. Realizing the implications, he changed his last name to Moran. Both Apolinari and his wife Anna Laskos emigrated from Poland separately in 1904 and 1905 and met and married in Chicopee in 1913.

Kevin's maternal grandparents were Stanley Bieniek and Jeannette Roberts. Stanley was born in 1917 and served in the military, training in electronics. When he was discharged, he opened Bieniek Electronics, a radio and TV repair store in Adams. Jeannette, born in 1916, was a homemaker and was considered an amazing French cook.

Their five children, one of whom was Kevin's mother, and many grandchildren gathered for holidays in their apartment on Park Street right above the Bieniek Electronics store. It's interesting to note that Jeanette's father, George Wentzel, was born in Vermont in 1899 and Americanized his name to Roberts.

Kevin's lineage is mostly Polish with a smattering of French and German. His ancestors immigrated to the U.S. in the early 1900s. He often jokes, "I'm so Polish I have an Irish name."

EARLY LIFE

As a youth, Kevin attended Commercial Street and Plunkett schools and spent a typical Adams summer playing Little League and hanging out at Russell Field, enjoying pick-up baseball, hide-and-seek, and war games in the nearby woods. Bob's Hill and nearby Peck's Brook were two of their favorite places to play. In the winter, they skated and played hockey at Russell Field.

When Kevin attended Hoosac Valley High School, he was a member of the cross-country ski team, worked on the student newspaper called the *Eye* (derived from the school nickname *Hurricanes*), served on the Student Council, and in his senior year was class vice president. He graduated in 1989.

Kevin often participated in competitive ski events for Hoosac Valley, and recreationally, he frequently traversed trails and backroads for miles on Mount Greylock. Usually, he placed in the top three finishers within his age group. With skiing his foremost sport, college selection decisions were focused with that in mind. After talking with the University of New Hampshire ski coach and getting a spot on the team, the process was over. Kevin skied competitively for two years with the New Hampshire Wildcats.

Kevin would graduate in 1993 with a bachelor's degree in English. During his senior year at UNH, he'd enjoyed the unique experience of participating in the Greenland Ice Sheet Project (GISP) with nine other students. He spent six weeks helping to retrieve cores of material from the earth's depth that would allow scientists to look for climatic and environmental changes. It was memorable for Kevin, especially the part of living in one-person "Scott Tents" on the snow, partially protected from the wind by snow bricks but keeping one eye open for wandering polar bears.

CAREER

His first post-college job was working at a sketchy Chrysler Plymouth dealership that seemed to over-promise and under-deliver on its commitments to customers. While the job was short-lived, it offered a good lesson on what not to do when dealing with people.

A friend who worked with the North Adams *Transcript* set him up with an interview for a job opening as a reporter. He was sure he'd failed the interview when he couldn't answer the question, "Who are the nine Supreme Court Justices?" Surprisingly, he was offered the job of reporting on the Town of Adams. At first, he felt unsure, but by the second week he had found his life's work and has loved journalism ever since.

In one of his earliest interviews as a *Transcript* reporter, he talked to a new business owner, who also happened to be Managing Editor of *The Berkshire Eagle*. When the store owner asked the young reporter what he wanted to do with his career, Kevin replied, "I want to be editor of the *Eagle*."

The man responded, "You need to put some time in first." Kevin finds it amusing that he is now, in fact, in that position.

After brief stints as an editor for the York, Pennsylvania, *Dispatch* and *The Transcript*, Kevin accepted an editor position at the *Brattleboro Reformer* in Vermont. It was a great opportunity, increased his exposure to the newspaper business, and added the responsibility of editing his staff's work.

Best of all he was introduced to Melanie, his future wife. She happened to be in the newsroom working on a community board article when a mutual friend from Pakistan introduced them. By the end of the week, they had their first date.

Kevin was recruited back to *The Berkshire Eagle* in 2005 as the Managing Editor, while continuing to maintain his relationship with Melanie. He was thrilled to return to the Berkshires. In his leadership role, he would determine what content would be used in the daily news, in addition to editing reporters' stories.

Kevin says, "As Managing Editor of the *Eagle*, you are plugged into the county and the county is plugged into you. It is one of the busiest, heart-pounding, exciting, fast-paced jobs you could want; quick decisions have to be made, and what we do matters to the community. We are a public source of information."

Not long after his return to the *Eagle*, Kevin and Melanie were married on September 9, 2008. The nuptials took place on his parents' front lawn during Hurricane Hanna. Kevin remembers the day was damp and humid from the impending hurricane and just as they were saying their vows, the eye of the hurricane passed overhead, the sky opened up and fortuitously the sun came out.

It then proceeded to pour the rest of the day, and shelter was quickly found in the event tent. In tribute to the day, the couple named their youngest daughter Hanna. Kevin and Melanie have two young daughters.

In 2013, he was appointed Executive Editor, managing not only *The Berkshire Eagle* but also the *Bennington Banner*, *Brattleboro Reformer*, and *Manchester Journal*. It was not long after his promotion that the owners decided to close the North Adams *Transcript*. Circulation had continued to dwindle and the company who owned the newspaper decided there was no financial incentive to keep it open. For Kevin, who knew most of the employees, it was a wrenching decision to implement. A number of the staff were retained and now are called the North County Bureau. Some work from home and others travel to the *Eagle* offices in Pittsfield.

Kevin reports to the board of directors and is home-based at the *Eagle*. He travels to the other newspapers to consult with their managing editors, who report to him. During the pandemic, travel has lessened as Zoom meetings provide a safer environment to keep up on the various activities.

Kevin reveals an early peek at tomorrow's headlines.

It's a most challenging time for newspapers. The largest battle is competing for readers with the internet, new technology, computers, and iPhones. Across the United States, overall dependency on print newspapers is declining approximately 12 percent year over year. Newspapers also struggle with the internet over advertisement revenue. Today, 60 percent of all advertisement revenue goes to Facebook and Google, with 40 percent left for everyone else to split up.

In 2016, the *Eagle* and the other newspapers were sold by Digital First Media, a national chain that had owned the *Eagle* for twenty years, to a group of local businessmen, known as Birdland Acquisition LLC. Many applauded the purchase in an era where cost-cutting seemed to be the first priority. Some believe if the purchase had not occurred, the *Eagle* would be "a shell" of what it is today.

At the time of the purchase, Kevin was quoted as saying, "It's like winning the newspaper lottery . . . (the new owners) are committed to making our newspapers the 'town squares for the communities we cover.'"

Under the new group, the business has thrived. The *Eagle* is one of the best community newspapers in the country. For the past several years, circulation has done very well, and digital subscriptions have increased. Circulation is steady at 22,000 readers. It won the New England Newspaper & Press Association Newspaper of the Year Award in 2018, 2019, and 2020.

Also in 2018, the *Manchester Journal* won the Distinguished Weekly Newspaper Award and the Upcountry Distinguished Specialty Newspaper Award. The Vermont Press Association acknowledged the *Bennington Banner* and *Brattleboro Reformer* as Newspapers of General Excellence. Kevin said,

Kevin gives a tour of the print production area to the author.

"It's nice to be recognized by your peers, and we've been knocking it out of the park. And all the newspapers are doing well."

With his twenty-plus years as a newspaper man, he has a broad inventory of interesting stories to share. One of his earliest assignments was covering the trial of a serial killer. Coverage was intense and the details gory. While the jury deliberated the killer's fate, Kevin noticed the defendant's mother nearby and wondered what must she be thinking. He watched her sit down and try to remove some gum from the sole of her shoe. At the same time, she spotted a nickel on the floor and said aloud to herself, "This must be my lucky day." Soon afterward, her son was convicted of murder.

He also remembers Mitt Romney coming to town as part of the gubernatorial race. As a good politician, Mitt wanted to meet with *Transcript* editors, get the pulse of the community, and have his picture taken for the paper. His advance man noticed everyone at the office was tieless and dressing casual. Upon Mitt's arrival, his aide returns from Kmart and brings Mitt a plastic bag. In the parking lot, Mitt removes his sport coat, tie and shirt, pulls a plaid shirt out of the bag, and puts it on over his tee shirt.

Always involved in his craft, Kevin has served as the President of the New England Associated Press News Executives Association and was on its board for five years.

He has been a mentor for foreign journalists via Alfred Friendly Press Partners, providing training in the United States for journalists from countries with underdeveloped media. Kevin has had the opportunity to mentor journalists from Nepal and Pakistan. He said it's a great testimony to "how journalism works in a democracy and can have a large impact on them."

TIME OFF

Kevin is the guitarist in a punk rock band called The Damaged. He has played the guitar since age fourteen and found it to be a great "avenue of expression." The four-member band has been in existence since 1996. His brother Colin is the vocalist; two others round out the well-known, local group. In years past, the band toured the East Coast from Boston to Atlanta.

They once played at the famous CBGB club in New York City, which opened in 1973. Originally the club was intended to feature country, blue grass and blues (CBGB) but became a famous venue for punk rock bands. Many prominent punk bands played there, and The Damaged felt honored to be on its storied stage as a band from the small town of Adams. The group also plays at local halls like the PNA (Polish National Alliance) Club, Saint Stanislaus Hall and at various gymnasiums. Lately they have been sidelined by the pandemic.

When he has time, Kevin continues to fly fish in the Deerfield,

Green, and Hoosic rivers, haunts of his earlier years. He enthusiastically notes how the Hoosic River, which meanders between Adams and North Adams, has brown trout as large as five pounds.

Kevin's skiing traditions are being passed down to his young daughters, and he serves as the assistant ski coach on the Bill Cook Cross Country League, which mentors kids through eighth grade.

Reflecting on life, he says the kindest thing someone ever did for him was "to say yes." His mom and dad always encouraged him and seldom said *no*. People he has encountered throughout life have always been supportive. It's given Kevin the impetus to say *yes* to others. He remembers his first boss saying *yes* by offering him a job at *The Transcript,* and how it opened many doors for him.

Coworkers aptly describe Kevin as family-oriented, hardworking, ethical, and dedicated. Some who worked with him early in his career remember his sense of humor, recounting the story of working with him one hot summer evening with the office air conditioner broken. Jokingly, he ordered the Sports Editor to sit on a roller chair, then pushed him into the kitchen to get a popsicle. He decided not to stop. He rolled the Sports Editor through the office, all the way outside, and right into the back of a parked tractor trailer.

As the Executive Editor of *The Berkshire Eagle*, his workdays can be frenetic, congested as they are with operational issues, questions from managing editors, and keeping updated on the news. In free moments, he reads *The Boston Globe, The New York Times*, follows MassLive local newsmedia, and peruses websites of other papers across the country. As busy as things can get, he says the three luckiest newspaper editors in the country are those privileged to work for *The New York Times, The Washington Post*, and *The Berkshire Eagle*."

Postscript: In late Spring 2021, the Vermont newspapers were sold to Vermont News and Media LLC. The new owners purchased the newspapers to "invest in the local community and will have The Berkshire Eagle *continue to print the three Vermont papers for at least the next five years." Vermont News and Media LLC also stated it will hire all of the current employees at the Vermont publications.*

JOHN "SKEETS" RICHARDS

Known as "Skeets" since he was two years old, John Richards was a longtime science teacher at Drury High School who, over his lifetime, mastered a myriad of hobbies. Most notably, after retirement, though beset by physical ailments and confined to a wheelchair, John became a nationally known artist.

John Richards' family had little interest in art when he was growing up. His dad and mom were focused on putting bread on the table, although Skeets' father did counsel him to "always do the best you can." Skeets' interest in art started, of all places, at the W. B. Plunkett Memorial Hospital in Adams.

When he was twelve years old, he had an appendectomy and was bored during the recovery time. A cousin visited him at the hospital and brought a paint-by-numbers kit containing a large sailing schooner and several ocean scenes. Upon recovery, he returned home and completed the paintings. In a show of support, as parents will do, they hung the paintings on their living room wall.

Time passed quickly with life's distractions. In the late 1970s, Skeets, now thirty years old, became intrigued with charcoal drawings in a book he was reading, so he started sketching with charcoal. Along with millions of other Americans, Skeets couldn't help but love Bill Alexander's PBS-TV show, *The Magic of Oil Painting*. Alexander and his former student Bob Ross, both accomplished artists, were influential with their wet-on-wet painting techniques.

For many years, painting was just another hobby mixed in with so many others. When he had time, John painted in his cellar and then in his spare room. His wife, Barbara, remembers one of his early painting episodes that she called his "blue phase." Skeets moved to their driveway, painting with large seven-inch brushes, "making awful messes." Recalls Barbara, "it seemed like he was flipping paint everywhere." At different points, he was spilling paint on the lawn and decorating the nearby landscape. Skeets wiped his brushes on the pine tree outside their house. Eventually the family nicknamed it the "blue pine."

John became serious about painting in his forties, and though he tried acrylic paints, he found them too difficult to work with as they dried too quickly. He grew to like oil paints because they allow him longer time to work with canvases. Over the years, he has focused on still life, landscape, and seascape paintings.

Several years ago, he and his wife moved to Maine and designed a modular home with a spacious room for his studio and gallery. Today he alternates painting seascape and still life. His gallery is named "Art on the Run."

The couple live in a wooded area, one hundred and fifty yards from the Atlantic Ocean among nesting bald eagles, wild turkeys, and free-ranging animal life that provides much of his inspiration. With his disabilities and confinement to a wheelchair, Skeets says, "painting and playing the banjo have become lifesavers."

Early Life

John Douglas Richards Jr. was born in Adams on February 3, 1947, at the W. B. Plunkett Memorial Hospital. He was named after his father, and Douglas was his mother's maiden name. John Jr. was nicknamed "Scooter" by his father, whose favorite baseball player was shortstop Phil "Scooter" Rizzuto of the Yankees. Years passed, and his friends started calling him "Skeeter," which evolved into "Skeets."

John Sr. was born in 1924 from a French, Irish, and Swedish background. As many young men did at the time, he quit high school in his junior year to join the Army. World War II had started, and John Sr. was determined to serve his country. Even entreaties from his baseball coach, who wanted his star pitcher to complete high school, were to no avail.

John Sr. was assigned to General Patton's army, and following the D-Day invasion, he served throughout Europe. He drove a half-track vehicle for his artillery unit and was honorably dis-charged in 1945. John Sr. returned home and spent his remaining career at Arnold Print Works in Adams, retiring after forty years as the shipping department foreman.

John's mother, Theophilia (Kozak) Richards, was a daughter of Polish immigrants. Born in 1922 in Adams, she and John Sr. were married at the Saint Stanislaus Kostka Church shortly after his three-year overseas tour and the war ended. As part of their wedding tradition, the bride's father stood at the reception hall door passing out shots of whiskey, ensuring all imbibed in the grand festivities.

Theophilia managed the home. After their children entered school, she worked at the Cornish Wire Company in Williamstown, molding leads on electrical cables. Skeets was her oldest child, followed by a younger sister and brother.

Skeets' paternal grandparents were Edward Richards and Annie Douglas. Edward, born in 1892 in the Berkshires, was a handyman employed by the Mount Hope Farm in Williamstown. Annie, also born in the 1890s, was several years younger than Ed. She was a homemaker and from Irish background.

His maternal grandparents were Ludwig and Victoria Kozak, both born in the late 1890s, emigrating separately from small farming villages in Poland in 1910. Both had been chosen by their families to leave Poland as concern heightened about the upcoming War. As youngsters (twelve and fourteen), their parents put them on a boat headed to the United States. Later, as young adults, they met at a large enclave of Polish immigrants in Philadelphia and were married. They were attracted to the Adams area when they heard about textile mill opportunities.

Shortly after arriving, they bought land, an old farmhouse with an apple orchard on East Hoosac Street, and became subsistence farmers. Skeets' grandmother worked in the Berkshire Mills, and his grandfather, when he wasn't farming, worked part-time tending bar.

Skeets' dad was gifted an acre of land from his in-laws and built the family's home. It was a great location, just up the hill from the

Polish church on the outskirts of town. Skeets lived there with his parents and siblings. He attended nearby Hoosac Street Elementary School from kindergarten through sixth grade, then C.T. Plunkett Junior High. His after-school activities revolved around playing pickup baseball in the fields and pitching in Little and Babe Ruth Leagues. Later in life, he played American Legion, high school, and college baseball.

Fishing for trout in the nearby Tophet Brook was a favorite, and he'd often accompany his dad and uncle fishing from a rented rowboat at Windsor Pond. After school, in the fall, he would walk to the top of East Hoosac Street and hunt for partridge and pheasants with his English setter, Queenie.

Skeets attended Adams Memorial High School and played first base in varsity baseball for three years. He tried out for the high school football team, but a serious injury put an immediate stop to that activity. On the quieter side, he enjoyed playing on the school's chess club and taught himself how to play the guitar. He often shot pool with his friends on Saturday and Sunday afternoons at Guerin's on Park Street. For spending money, he mowed lawns and during college worked at Arnold Print Works as a stockman.

One family story still follows Skeets today. On a freezing wintery day, Skeets drove the family car to a nearby variety store to purchase cigarettes. On his way home, he noticed an elderly man seemingly confused hanging on to a telephone pole. Acting as a good Samaritan, Skeets stopped his car to help the man, and realized it was his grandfather trying to make his way home from the Polish hall. Skeets drove him to his house and was upbraided by his grandmother who attributed his condition to Skeets taking him out and getting him drunk.

CAREER AND FAMILY

Skeets first met his wife in high school, but the beginning was not smooth. Barbara Benz, born in Stamford, Connecticut, moved to Adams during her junior year of high school. When Skeets first saw the recently transferred co-ed in the hallway, he immediately said,

"I'm going to marry that girl." Barbara, on the other hand, thought he was a silly high school boy that seemed to follow her everywhere; she wanted nothing to do with him.

Then at one point, she saw him with another girl after a Saturday night movie date and became intrigued with him . . . and so it began. They started spending time together when she wasn't working at the Crest as a soda jerk or studying, and before long they were dating steadily and attended the school's senior prom together. The couple graduated from Adams Memorial High School in 1965, and shortly afterward, Barbara and her family moved to New Hampshire where she attended Notre Dame College.

Skeets attended North Adams State College (now Massa-chusetts College of Liberal Arts), thus kicking off their four-year commuting relationship. Skeets would visit Barbara in New Hampshire on weekends, staying at the family's home. During one of the visits, her father and brother were working on installing a septic system. Early one Saturday morning her dad drafted Skeets to help. He spent all weekend digging out the noxious leach field. Barbara remembers at the time saying to herself, "If he ever comes back to see me, I'll marry him."

Both graduated, and they did marry in 1969. The young couple lived in Adams for several years, and in 1972 they bought a home in Williamstown and lived there for the next forty-seven years, until moving to Maine in 2018. Family vacations were centered around enjoying the local Sand Springs pool. The couple has one daughter who now resides in Maine with their two grandchildren. Barbara, known as Bo, received her nickname from her. Initially called "Bobbi," the name changed to "Bo" after the TV commercial "Bo Knows."

With a bachelor's degree in physics, Skeets taught briefly at Berkshire County Day School in Lenox and then accepted a posi-tion in the science department at Drury High School in 1970. In 1972, he earned a master's degree from North Adams State College in science education and administration.

His first year at Drury High, he taught chemistry. The remain-der of his career he taught psychology for twelve years and senior physics five periods a day for the next thirty-four years. While Skeets was teaching at Drury, Barbara taught special needs children at Adams/Cheshire Regional and Hoosac Valley schools. A chess aficionado, Skeets coached the school's chess team in the 1970s, including through their participation in various tournaments. He is proud that one of his students became an International Chess Master and wrote a number of books, including *Chess for Dummies*.

With his long-ago leg injury aggravated by standing on hard floors all day, Skeets decided to retire in 2004 at the age of 57. He has good memories of his time teaching and takes pride in educating three generations of students, including grandchildren of former students. During that time, he observed North Adams going through wrenching changes with the closing of many businesses. Fortunately, he has been able, likewise, to witness much progress in its ongoing recovery.

A CONSUMER OF HOBBIES

With a zest for life, Skeets has found interest in many different hobbies. In the 1970s, he and Barbara joined the Mount Greylock Archers in Adams and the Catamount Club in Bennington, Vermont, participating in numerous indoor and outdoor shooting competitions. At one point, Skeets became president of the Adams club, comprised of 175 archers.

The archers love competing and using balloons, metal tags, and paper targets to hold public relations fundraisers and shoot-offs with local police agencies. At twenty to forty yards, both police and archers shoot downrange.

Skeets then became interested in model trains and created a city in his basement built on three 4' x 8' sheets of plywood. He landscaped and built tunnels, mountains, and villages to be navigated by his long parade of colorful, eight-inch cars.

In the 1970s, Skeets was introduced to tropical fish by a Navy friend. Before long, not to do anything half-heartedly, he had nine freshwater tanks located in different rooms through their house. The aquariums ranged in size from five to forty gallons. One tank had show-guppies; another large tank housed an aggressive, large, solitary and colorful cichlid with an unfriendly nature named "Jack Dempsey." Skeets fed night crawlers to Jack, who grew to almost nine inches before his demise. Another tank held his Siamese fighting fish (Bettas) with their vibrant colors and flowy fins.

Reluctant to sit still for too long, Skeets began riding an Enduro motorcycle. His 250cc Yamaha with the green tank, grey and chrome body, and knobby tires was frequently seen zipping across the local forest and fields around Mount Greylock and Savoy. He, his brother Dave, and a friend were able to watch the 1972 ISDE (International Six Day Enduro) trials in the Berkshires. This was the first time the trials were held in the United States.

Skeets has spent a lot of time fly fishing. He learned the craft of tying flies and was successful in recreating the nymphs found in nearby riverbeds. His favorite fishing spots for trout were the Green River in Williamstown and the nationally known Deerfield River along the Mohawk Trail. On his forays, he often stopped to show strangers his fly-fishing techniques and assortment of attractive homemade flies. Skeets served several years as a volunteer on the board of directors for Trout Unlimited.

One day after fly fishing in the Green River, on his way home he stopped for a drink at Bernardi's Restaurant in Williamstown. A patron introduced him to darts and thereafter on his way home from fishing he would stop, grab a beer, and play a game of darts.

Before long he had joined two leagues and a five-man travelling team, competing in Lenox, Pittsfield, Great Barrington, and Lee. The group would play with wooden, large barrel, white feathered American darts in competitive, nine-inning (turns) games of baseball darts. The game has a maximum score of 54. Skeets became a good player, usually averaging 44.

A vegetable gardener for most of his life, he learned the art from his grandfather and father. He has always used raised beds for his plantings, sixteen feet long, three feet wide, and one foot tall. Easier for him to work in with his worsening leg condition, the raised beds also drain better, and the soil warms quicker.

He took up golf and began playing five days a week. Always

competitive, he felt challenged to master the local Waubeeka golf course. Skeets played for years until medical complications caused him to give up the sport.

Skeets has also bowled most of his life. From the age of five and onward, he bowled candle pins in several leagues at the old Saint Stanislaus Hall. After marriage, he played ten pins several times a week at Mount Greylock Bowl in North Adams. His first major knee surgery forced him to quit when he was unable to bend his knee.

In the late 1970s, Skeets' interest in music increased, and although he can't read music, he taught himself how to play the five-string banjo. Barbara says, "He practiced hour after hour and sometimes drove us nuts, but he never gave up." At one point, he joined the five-member bluegrass band *Richmond Train*, named after a nearby geological rock formation.

The band, which included bass, mandolin, fiddle, guitar, and banjo, played for seven years around the county at bluegrass festivals and at the Adams Summer Festival. During this time period, Skeets was able to obtain an autographed 78 record, personally signed by Bill Monroe, often called the Father of Bluegrass. Skeets met Monroe at a festival before his passing. The framed record hangs prominently in his studio.

In 2000, Skeets became interested in growing Bonsai plants. Always ready to jump into a hobby wholeheartedly, he studied at a Bonsai nursery, and his collection quickly grew to thirty carefully nurtured trees. He enjoys the artistry of shaping the plants, and the gardening skills necessary to keep them alive. At one point, the plants (really, small trees) were mounted on pedestals, and Skeets gave Bonsai tours in his backyard.

The ritualistic care and trimming, watering, seasonal treatments, and the passage of time has reduced his population to eight Bonsai plants that are dormant in the winter and carefully protected from the Maine weather in his garage.

When asked why he had so many hobbies, Skeets said, "I'm interested in things, how they work. I like doing things myself . . . and when I find something unfamiliar, I want to learn more about it. Being curious has often opened doors to a whole new world."

PAINTING

After Skeets' retirement, nudged by his consuming interest in art and his approaching lack of mobility, he became more serious about his painting. Although admirably self-taught, he was encouraged by his wife, Barbara, one of his toughest critics, to get lessons, and he came to learn many new techniques. The quality of his paintings improved. Skeets agrees with Edgar Degas, the French impressionist, who reportedly said, "Painting is easy when you don't know how, and very difficult when you do."

He began studying under three artists who have become the main influencers in his craft: Andrew Orr, who lives in Vermont and paints landscapes; Christopher Pierce, who paints still life; and Leah Lopez, who is also a master at still life. Skeets has attended workshops with each artist. At one point, he exhibited his paintings with Andrew. All have become friends.

The weekend workshops, held in New Hampshire and Vermont, provided great opportunities for Skeets to paint a variety of subjects. The workshop leaders would answer questions and provide critiques for the painters. Even today, he continues to take online lessons and practice his craft for hours.

During this time, Skeets has come to appreciate the similarities between physics, a subject he taught for many years, and painting. Both have a major focus on the concept of light. Physics has light traveling through space, reaching our eyes and making an impression. Painting makes use of that light and since paints can only capture twenty percent of the intensity of natural light, artists must use light and dark areas to fool one's perception into thinking that painting is a real portrayal of natural light.

Skeets has also become more aware of technical details. When viewing a painting with hills in the distance, does the painting capture changes in color, or as the hills get farther away do they become duller and more bluish? He also looks at how the artist creates depth in paintings. Not applying black or white until the end of a painting is one technique. Once applied, it's difficult to lighten or darken canvasses, although a touch of yellow might help. He has also learned more about soft and hard edges. The closer his subject, the sharper the edges should be, and the farther away they should become more blurred.

Skeets' paintings each take over ten hours to create, usually over a period of two or three days. The length of time is influenced by the time involved in details, such as painting the rigging on a schooner, or shadows of a rocky shoreline. Skeets takes advantage of the morning light and paints between 8:00 a.m. and 1:00 p.m.

Skeets in his studio, putting finishing touches on a seascape.

Due to a series of knee and back issues, Skeets has been confined to a wheelchair for over two years. His knee surgeries and replacements have limited his mobility. He now uses his skills to paint from photographs in his studio. He misses painting from real life, where the colors are more vibrant.

Lack of mobility hasn't affected the demand for his paintings. He has painted over 700 pictures and sold 450 of them. Over 100 paintings were sold in galleries in Lenox and in Wilmington, Vermont, and the rest privately through word-of-mouth or on his website. He has been invited to display his paintings at a number of renowned art centers.

Initially, as a budding artist, he was unsure how to price his paintings. His first painting sold for $600. Now he prices by the size of the painting. A 9" x 12" painting, framed, costs $500; an 18" x 24" canvas, framed, costs $1400. His major paintings cost between $4,000 and $8,000.

Currently, in his gallery, Art on the Run, he has 30 paintings exhibited on the walls. The gallery/studio is located near Acadia National Park and Bar Harbor where he anticipates, after the pandemic, an influx of tourists.

The Richardses moved from Williamstown to Lemoine, Maine, in 2018. The transition went smoothly though they thought moving from their hometown would be difficult. Living in their self-designed, single-floor home has been much easier for Skeets to navigate compared to their split-level home in Williamstown. The couple also loves being near their only child and grandchildren. And the nearby water and woods provides a beautiful, inspiring setting.

Their new neighbors have been very understanding, realizing Skeets is not mobile. They maintain and plow the nearby road. One neighbor delivers fresh eggs once a week. In summertime, neighbors gather in their garage welcomed by the Polish sign "Na zdrowie," a Polish toast that translates to "here's to you!" Their garage has been named Tavern on Moose Run. As colder weather approaches, a neighbor's heated garage, designated Tavern on Moose Run #2, can be used as a backup gathering place.

Rustica, 12" x 16" oil mounted on linen panel

Both Skeets and Barbara acknowledge their personality differences and appreciate how they blend so well together. She is not a joiner, more of an observer, and he is outgoing, affable, and gets along with everyone. By contrast, however, he can be pensive and slow starting, while Bo is always ready to get moving. She accommodates his Polish heritage, making *pierogis* and *golabki*, and long ago introduced him to vegetables.

Today, Bo lovingly supports Skeets, with his physical restrictions of not being able to walk or raise his arms past his nose. With her help, he is able to paint, play guitar and banjo as well as work on his Bonsai plants. Skeets uses a motorized scooter, a Kawasaki Mule (utility trail vehicle), and a wheelchair lift to get around. He is unabashed about complimenting Bo's devotion.

"She's always there for me . . . she even helps me put on my socks."

BRUCE SHEPLEY

Retired Lieutenant Colonel Bruce Shepley served as an Aeromedical Evacuation Nurse in the United States Air Force for twenty years, deploying seven times. He has applied his medical knowledge in his second career of volunteerism to the great benefit of the Berkshire County community.

In 1991 at the age of forty, Bruce Shepley noticed an advertisement for Air Force Reserve nurses and decided to apply for the program. In late 1992, he was commissioned a 1st Lieutenant in the Air Force Reserves. The ceremony took place, his wife Patricia present, at Westover Air Force Base in Chicopee, Massachusetts. Bruce completed his Air Force training in 1993, which included a two-week course called Military Indoctrination for Medical Service Officers (MIMSO) and then attended a five-week class on Flight Nursing at Lackland Air Base in San Antonio, Texas. The specialized course focused on familiarizing students with different aircrafts, onboard emergent procedures, and altitude effects on patients.

After graduation, Bruce was assigned to the 439th Aeronautical Evacuation Squadron at Westover Air Base, where he would complete weekend drills once a month, two weeks of annual summer training, and ongoing skills testing and flight training. At age fifty-two, he would be deployed twice to Germany, and at fifty-eight, he'd find himself on the way to Afghanistan.

A half-century earlier, life in beaucolic North Adams was more slow-paced. Bruce was born on March 5, 1951, at the North Adams Hospital with the assistance of Doctor Harvey Bianco. His parents, Douglas Shepley and Olive (Dale) Shepley, were recent immigrants from England, still bearing distinct accents. Both Douglas and Olive hailed from the greater Manchester area, their towns just four miles apart. They married at Gorton Parish Church in August 1948, then emigrated the following year. The couple was drawn to North Adams by family connections and job opportunities.

Douglas, born in 1923, had served in the British Army as a gunner with the 151st Field Regiment–Field Artillery during World War II in North Africa. Returning from the war, he began a career as a commercial and residential painter. In the 1960s, after moving to the United States and painting for several contractors, he opened his own business, "Doug's Decorators." He specialized in residential painting and was skilled in hanging wallpaper.

Olive, born in 1927, worked as a teenage machinist during the war. After moving to the United States, she briefly worked at the Sprague Electric Company until the children were born. Later in life, she was certified as a Licensed Practical Nurse, often working with private duty patients. Initially, the family lived on West Main Street, then moved to Ashland Street for ten years, and settled in at 432 Church Street where Bruce and his two brothers were raised.

Bruce met his paternal grandfather Joseph Shepley only once, in 1962, when he travelled to England. His grandmother Lilly Bancroft was already deceased. His maternal grandparents, Olive's parents, were John Dale and Florence Wallis, both of whom died in the 1950s. John worked for years at Gorton Locomotive; records indicate his job was a maintenance engineer.

Bruce attended the nearby Mark Hopkins School from kindergarten through the eighth grade, where he sang and played clarinet in the school band. Outside of school, his life centered around friends, playground activities at Mark Hopkins, and bicycling *everywhere*. In the summers, with his bagged lunch, he walked up nearby Bradley Street to Windsor Lake to attend the YMCA's Camp Stayhom. The day camp had wood carving activities, games like steal-the-flag, and swimming. One summer when he was in middle school, he served as a junior camp counselor.

Church played an important part in his family's life. Bruce belonged to his church's First Congregational Boy Scout Troop #88, where his dad was scoutmaster. Also, from age eight to twenty-one, he sang in the youth choir and eventually with his mom in the adult choir. Sundays were family-oriented. Breakfast, then church services and Sunday School, a big meal at home, and then off to visit friends, most often Bruce's godparents.

Bruce was close to his mother, who taught him to appreciate music. He distinctly remembers his mother taking him to Tanglewood in Lenox, Massachusetts, at age ten to listen to the Boston Symphony Orchestra and the impact that performance had upon him. Now retired, he sings with the Ecumenical Congregational Choir in North Adams during their annual performances.

Every summer, the Shepley family and friends caravanned to Old Orchard Beach in Maine for vacation. The group of friends, including his godparents, rented cabins a short walking distance from the ocean, close enough to enjoy the beach and the boardwalk.

On the home front, his mom was in charge. She was the family's disciplinarian and cared for the home while taking care of the three boys. Her meals spoke of her English heritage, composed as they were of meat, potato, whole milk, and butter. Favorites were roast beef, boiled potatoes, and vegetables, a great steak and kidney pie, sometimes tripe, and often a delicious handmade shortbread. Her dessert specialty was fruitcake concocted in a bowl, covered, and aged for months in the refrigerator. She shopped at the local A&P and Fischlein's Market, though the family's milk and eggs were delivered.

Olive got along with everyone. She had a sense of humor, was outgoing, a people person, and had many friends through her involvement in the church and women's clubs. Every Saturday, she and her closest friend would dress up, meet on Main Street and shop up and down each side. Bruce's father was less social, more focused on his business, boy scouts, and church. He was a good provider but somewhat the opposite of Bruce and Olive's outgoing, social personalities.

Douglas ran his decorating business out of their home and was quite busy with interior and exterior painting, often employing two or three men. Douglas painted until he was sixty-five years old, then still took on occasional jobs. Bruce worked for his dad about ten years during and after high school; unsurprisingly, he now "hates painting."

In 1966, Bruce entered Drury High School and admittedly did not take school very seriously. He participated in the ski club, ran track, played JV football for one year, sang in the chorus, and played the clarinet in the school band. After graduating, Bruce found the 1970s to be a period of change and growth. He married in 1971, had a daughter, and even with a high draft lottery number (342) decided to join the Coast Guard. He was medically discharged after four months of service, then worked at Adams Supermarkets, lifeguarded, and painted for his dad.

It was in the late 1970s that Bruce says he found his "direction in life" while working as an orderly at North Adams Regional Hospital. He developed an acute interest in patient care, became an EMT, and was one of the original members of the North Adams ambulance service. He also remarried and became the father of two daughters. He and Pat just recently celebrated their 40th wedding anniversary.

A Career Taking Shape

Bruce's next step in his budding medical career was to attend a one-year course at McCann, becoming certified as an Operating Room Technician. From 1981 through 1985, he worked as a OR technician at Cooley Dickinson Hospital in Northampton, Massachusetts. During this time period, Bruce received his associate degree in nursing from Regent's College in New York.

For the next twenty-five years (1985 to 2010) Bruce worked in the North Adams Regional Hospital OR. Following his father's strong work ethic, he immersed himself in hospital work, volunteering to be on call, working in other departments as needed, and assisting the medical examiner in autopsies. He continued to enhance his skills through various training seminars and was recognized with the Surgical Services Nursing Education Award.

For almost ten years, Bruce participated in nurses' union activities, both as a board member and for several years as the union president. As president, he managed a contentious contract negotiation and found the discussions to be an eye opener when he had the opportunity to see both sides of issues. Eventually, the negotiations were ratified and settled.

When Bruce began as an orderly, he was known as something of a "cut-up." Sometimes senior staff wanted to sanction his humorous acts that they found a little out of place in their serious atmosphere. He enjoyed visiting the various departments and always seemed cheery and never without a joke. Employees would cringe when their birthday came around, because Bruce was likely to broadcast some misinformation over the PA system to the entire hospital. One time he announced that an employee had an infectious disease and should report to the lab.

Patients and staff began to appreciate his levity and efforts to lighten everyone's day. He had a knack for bringing people together throughout the organization. Bruce would often check up on staff who were at home ill but not miss the chance to spread the word far and wide that the person was home chainsmoking in a velour bathrobe.

For a number of years, Bruce and his wife Pat were central in assisting another nurse, who was raising her son by herself. Their kindness was evident to all. Bruce's supervisor described him as entertaining, charismatic, kind, reliable, committed, and infectious. Bruce was commended for working extremely well with children and

Bruce seems happy working on another of his innumerable do-it-yourself projects.

the elderly, and for being hardworking, available to be on-call. He always went the extra mile.

MILITARY SERVICE

During his more than twenty years of service in the Reserves, Bruce deployed seven times. He had four stateside deployments, and he was temporarily attached twice to Aeromedical Evacuation

Squadrons in Germany (2003/2004) and once in Afghanistan (2009).

The overseas deployments always involved aeromedical transportation of patients, either in-theater to Ramstein Air Base in Germany or home to Andrews or Travis Air Force Bases stateside. Patients landing in Germany were transferred to the huge 1000-bed Landstuhl Army Medical Center five miles from the air base. Those flown to the United States often went to Bethesda or Walter Reed Naval Hospitals. Burn victims, when stabilized, were transferred to Brooke Army Medical Center in San Antonio, Texas.

Bruce's Aeromedical Evacuation (AE) team was composed of two nurses and three medical technicians who would support the Critical Care Team's patients (CCT attended the most seriously wounded), as well as tend to their own patients. When evacuating wounded on C-141 cargo jets, there would be 36 litter (stretcher) and 40 ambulatory patients, keeping both teams quite busy during the long flights.

His 2003 deployment to Ramstein was a six-week voluntary rotation, transporting wounded out of Iraq and Afghanistan. They transported all branches of U.S. service members and some nationals (Iraqi and Afghani) soldiers when they could not be treated in-country. His team was quartered at Ramstein. In 2004, he deployed on a 120-day voluntary rotation that included two weeks pre-training and two weeks post-briefing. As a flight nurse, he flew from August through December, in and out of Iraq with the 791st Expeditionary Aeromedical Squadron. He was gone for Thanksgiving and Christmas and was again quartered at Ramstein Air Base.

The team transported many wounded from the Battles of Fallajuh and Mosul. Initially the wounded were transported by mostly helicopters to a "fixed medical facility" capable of performing major surgeries. Once stabilized, the patients would go to Germany's Landstuhl hospital for additional treatment. The battles stressed the entire medical system. Field hospitals in Iraq were packed, aero evacuations were challenged to capacity, and the Landstuhl hospital became overfilled. Two air crews were added to the overburdened five already in place. It was an almost constant shuttle back and forth from Iraq to Germany.

Bruce remembers one particular soldier wounded at the Battle of Fallujah. The soldier had been shot in the leg, fracturing his femur. Bruce and medical crew brought him to Germany. He later saw the patient on his plane's manifest when they were transferring wounded to Andrews AF Base for admittance to Walter Reed hospital. The soldier had been operated on, had a rod in his leg, and was recovering well. When Bruce rotated home, he Googled the man's name and called, talking to his wife and then to the soldier to see how he was feeling. His recovery was progressing, and he was preparing to medically retire from the Army.

In 2009, Bruce, on another 120-day deployment, was stationed at Bagram Air Force Base in Afghanistan and flew on C-130s, cargo planes that would fly into remote bases picking up wounded and returning them to a field hospital. These tactical missions included five or six air crew members plus his medical team. Bruce noted that advances in medical technology and acute care have been able to save some wounded that in past wars would have certainly died. Others who would have died are saved, but are so badly wounded that, as he explained, they are consigned to vegetative lives.

One of his more poignant memories was his first Afghan mission in 2009 when their plane was dispatched to the remote Camp Bastion, at the time a British Army airbase, to pick up two severely injured Marines blown up by an IED. They sustained traumatic amputations, concussive and shrapnel injuries, and burns to greater than 70 percent of their bodies. The Critical Care Air Transport Team (CCATT) composed of a physician, nurse, and respiratory therapist kept them alive while they were transported to the United States. The highly sophisticated care and speed of transfer allowed the Marines to be with their families when they died at Walter Reed Hospital.

These voluntary deployments, under arduous conditions and long hours, fulfilled a powerful sense of duty to the United States. Bruce served in the Reserves from 1992 until officially retiring as a Lieutenant Colonel in March 2013 on his 62nd birthday. Already retired from a twenty-five-year career with North Adams Regional Hospital, he decided to take an active role in local philanthropy.

COMMUNITY SERVICE

After retirement, Bruce's volunteer's heart has kept him engaged in many activities, often making use of his medical expertise. Initially serving as a volunteer Red Cross driver, he began by helping indigent people get to medical appointments. He volunteers for the Food Bank of Western Massachusetts every other week, distributing foodstuffs to the needy in Adams. As a member of the Northern Berkshire Emergency Commission activated in 2020, he meets every Monday morning with the ten-member commission. Their community involvement ranges from securing COVID-19 personal protective equipment (PPE) to finding clothing or shelter for needy citizens, coordinating municipal resources, and grant writing. They often work in conjunction with the Federal Emergency Management Agency (FEMA).

As a member of The Council on Aging, he has served on the advisory board for six years. In 2016, and until quite recently, he worked as a camp nurse for youths attending the 4-H camp in Goshen, Massachusetts. Bruce served for two years on the Adams Board of Health, a job he found personally rewarding, working with the local Code Enforcement Officer on alcohol, tobacco violations, licenses, septic tanks, diseases, home inspections, and citizen questions. When the Code Enforcement Officer hours were reduced, the Board had to do some of the work themselves.

Recently Bruce was asked to serve on the McCann School committee representing Adams. Early in his medical career, he had attended McCann, and more recently served a ten-year role as a substitute school nurse. In addition to serving on the Adams Cemetery Committee, Bruce has served as Town Meeting Member for Precinct #3 for over 20 years. In this three-year elected position, he represents his precinct at the annual town meeting.

Although retired from the North Adams Regional Hospital, now a smaller satellite medical facility operated by Berkshire

Medical Center, he is a member of the Patient Family Advisory Committee (PFAC). The committee's focus is improving patient care and safety. Bruce offers his professional and personal perspective as a health care practitioner and a consumer.

ACTIVE RETIREMENT

In short, Bruce recommends living life to the fullest. On a friend's 60th birthday card he shared the following life advice: "This ain't practice. You don't get a 2nd chance. Rehearsals are for plays, this is life."

Bruce takes in the view from the top of the Weather Observatory tower at Mount Washington.

He and his wife Pat are members of the Thunderbolt Ski Runners group that volunteers time maintaining the Thunderbolt trail by clearing brush and fixing water bars, which are small ditches that divert water from the trail and prevent erosion. The trail is used for skiing and mountain biking, which he enjoys and thus feels he should participate in its maintenance. The group works in conjunction with the Massachusetts Department of Conservation and Recreation (DCR). He also volunteers two weeks a year to cook and clean at the Weather Observatory on Mount Washington in New Hampshire, helping the meteorologists.

For personal enjoyment, Bruce rides a 2009 Gold Wind or his 2006 Harley Davidson Dyna Glide motorcycle and has taken trips to Key West, Nova Scotia, Cape Breton, and Washington, D.C. Of course, he enjoys long New England day trips. He continues to bicycle and hike with family and friends. When not volunteering, he relishes spending time with his three daughters and three grandchildren.

Bruce feels responsible for all that has been given to him and is compelled to "pay back." His philosophy on life and community is simple: "The system works. Get involved, promote good, volunteer, be an *agent* for good. Volunteers [who] are part of successful organizations have good outcomes."

DONALD SOMMER

It starts out a classic tale: Local boy leaves school in his junior year to join the Marines. Returns home, completes graduate degree studies, and serves in the education field for thirty-four years. But the story takes an unexpected turn when this former Marine decides to establish a horse ranch, open a music center, develop local properties, operate a restaurant, and run for local office.

Don's story is an interesting one. He is the first to admit that when he left high school in the eleventh grade and joined the Marines at seventeen, not one part of him expected he would end up having a career in education that would span over three decades of his life.

Donald Robert Sommer was born December 28, 1934, at W.B. Plunkett Memorial Hospital in Adams. His parents were Anton and Olga Cecelia (Wurtzer) Sommer, both immigrants from Austria.

Anton was born in the 1880s, came to America in 1911, married, and had three children with his wife before she died at a young age. Returning to Austria to find another bride, he married Olga Wurtzer in October 1921 at St. Egid Church in the city of Klagenfurt. The couple returned to the U.S. via Ellis Island, and they had seven children, though eventually separating. Donald was their youngest child; he and his eldest sister survive today. Anton, a professional painter and wallpaper hanger, was younger than Olga, yet passed away in 1941 when Don was only seven years old.

Olga, a homemaker, worked at the Sprague Electric Company during World War II and was employed for 16 years as a blanket-fabricator at the former Dewey & Almy Chemical Company in Adams. She lived with her son until passing away in 1993 at the age of ninety-one.

Little is known about Don's paternal grandfather; there is some question as to his grandfather's real identity. His paternal grandmother's name was Maria. His maternal grandmother's coffee shop had been bombed during World War II, and she immigrated to the United States by herself after the war. She resided with her daughter, Don's aunt.

Don grew up on George Street during the war. The family's two-story house had three bedrooms upstairs: four sisters shared one bedroom, Don and another brother in the second (two brothers were in the military), and his parents had the third bedroom. There was no heat upstairs; the coal furnace just serviced the first floor through large black grates. Getting up was a brisk affair, and the kids would scamper downstairs and close a few doors, trying to capture some heat while dressing in the kitchen.

According to local history, when a large number of residents from George Street served in World War II, and some did not return, the community decided to change the street's name to Victory Street. Don enjoyed growing up on Victory Street, although during the war years, local kids would chase and call him a Nazi because of his Austrian heritage. After a time, the harassment ended, and he made friends and got involved in playing games. The kids played "nipsy" using a tapered broomstick to see how far they could hit an eight-inch block popped up into the air. Kick-the-can was another popular game. Often, they played in the woods at the top of Victory Street, building fires, cooking, and eating their blackened potatoes.

The kids loved to dam up portions of the Tophet Brook, creating miniature swimming pools. There were also pickup basketball games at Plunkett gymnasium on Saturday mornings. Don had his first paper route at twelve years old, peddling to thirty-seven Victory Street customers. As time passed, he added more and ended up with 212 customers covering the Spring, Summer, and Lime Street areas. In the winter, sometimes frustratingly, he would put chains on his bicycle to help him reach his customers in the deep snow.

While his mom worked, his older sister, Olga (named after mom), ran the household and meted out discipline. The family ate promptly at 5:00 p.m., and Grandma always joined them. Suppers were usually a combination of meat and potatoes or homemade spaghetti, with Austrian meals like *Gulasch* (goulash) and *spaetzle* dominating the menu. His mother would spoil Don with her "Kaiser pancakes" (*Kaiserschmarrn*).

Sunday dinner was always chicken served at 2:00 p.m. in the dining room. The timing conflicted with Don's desire to attend the one o'clock movie matinee with his friends. His parents were both raised Catholic. The children would attend Mass at Saint Thomas Church with their grandmother. Don remembers Easter being a special occasion, dressing up with new clothes, attending a jam-packed church, and finishing the day with a huge Easter meal.

Don attended Hoosac Street School through sixth grade, then Plunkett for seventh and eighth grades. Always busy, he seldom was in trouble until having to go to court at sixteen for selling illegal fireworks. He attended a high school located on Liberty Street and admits to not being a great student; he was eventually asked to leave in eleventh grade by the principal.

A DEFINITE PURPOSE

Don decided to follow in his brother's footsteps and join the Marines. He attended Parris Island boot camp and served three years. He graduated first in his class from auto mechanics school, was promoted, and then served his tour of duty at Headquarters Marine Corps in Washington, D.C.

He was honorably discharged as a corporal in 1955 and freely admits his time in the Marine Corps "was the most important education I ever had. It taught me discipline, respect, and dedication to duty. I came out a different person, with a definite purpose in life."

After discharge, Donald, who married when he was eighteen, returned to Adams and bought a three-apartment house, which his growing family shared with his mother and in-laws. Don's mom had a connecting passageway to his side of the house and became a large part of the children's lives.

Now realizing the need for an education, he studied at Drury High School and received his General Equivalency Diploma. He was encouraged by Charles McCann to continue his education. He was accepted to Hudson Valley Community College in Troy, New York, and began a two-year commute, living in the third floor of a boarding house Sunday through Friday, returning home on weekends to work.

During this time, Don had a number of different jobs. He worked as an auto mechanic at Buster's Garage on Commercial Street, as a brakeman for B & O Railroad, and as a "car knocker" repairing railroad box cars. Then he worked on a railroad team replacing ties, and at one point he was part of a track crew in the Hoosac Tunnel. When that job ended, he worked in Adams delivering laundry.

Don studied hard at school and received good grades in the sciences. He graduated with distinction from Hudson Valley in 1958. During his time there, he established a fraternity, one of the first in the New York education system, and was also elected president of the student chapter of the American Society of Tool Engineers.

Deciding to continue his education, he enrolled at Oswego College in New York, purchased a mobile home, and moved his family to Oswego. As a budding entrepreneur, Don and several classmates cleared an old apple orchard, dug a well, and parked their trailers there free of charge. On summer breaks, the family returned to Adams with their trailer, and Don worked as a patrolman for the Town, under the Chief of Police who prosecuted him as a teenager for fireworks violations.

Don received his bachelor's degree *cum laude* from Oswego in 1960, returned to Adams, and began working as an Industrial Arts teacher for the Pittsfield, Massachusetts, school department; then as a school guidance counselor for local elementary schools.

Most of Don's early life, he worked two jobs, and family vacations were limited to visiting his sister's home in Connecticut, another sister's animal kennel in Cheshire, or the Catskill Game Farm in upstate New York. He did install an aboveground pool; his kids loved it and were part of the maintenance crew that disassembled it every autumn, cornstarched the liner, and stored it for the winter.

During this time period, Don became interested in Town affairs and was elected to the Adams School Committee. The former high-school dropout found it extremely satisfying to chair the committee, to help improve local education in his hometown.

Chairing the redevelopment committee for seven years was more challenging, with the Redevelopment Authority targeting a ten-acre downtown area. The area was successfully updated, but not without some consternation from a local taxpayer's association. The project moved forward and was eventually cited by federal and state authorities as a model for small-town development.

Don continued his education and received a master's degree in education from North Adams State College in 1963. His next position was Director of Pupil Services for the Adams Cheshire Schools. He served as president of the Massachusetts School Counselors Association. He also enrolled at the University of Massachusetts and received a certificate of advanced graduate studies in 1973.

Don also served as president of the Northern Berkshire Mental Health Association and worked with the board to upgrade and relocate the clinic's office and increase staffing. With a new director, the clinic expanded its outreach to include elderly day care. For his efforts, Don received a citation from the NBMHA for his leadership and inspiration.

Don has also served as a congressional delegate to the White House Conference on Children and was part of a symposium that met with the Army Chief of Staff to discuss the feelings of male youths toward the military.

After several more guidance positions, Don served as Regional Director of Special Education for the next decade, working out of Pittsfield, managing twenty-two school districts and finally, before retiring, as Special Education Director for the Northern Berkshire School Union. Don has the distinction of working for thirty-four years in public schools, twenty-eight as an administrator.

NEW VENTURES

Don and three friends purchased thirty-seven acres of pasture on Algier Street. Some years later, after buying out his friends, Don built a house and a barn on what now is called Sommer Hill. Eventually three of his four children would live on the property.

At the same time, he was hired to manage Greylock Apartments in downtown Adams. He later bought out the original owners and stabilized the finances as the sole owner of the sixty units. Employing office and maintenance managers, he made ongoing capital improvements and worked with tenants, sometimes using his counseling skills to serve as a moderator. He helped struggling families by offering their children jobs on his farm.

© DENNIS PREGENT, 2021

Don with Sierra, one of his favorite Haflingers.

Don has loved horses and Airedale dogs most of his life. In the late 1990s, while at a horse show in Northampton, he saw a pair of beautiful horses pulling a carriage. Finding out they were Haflingers, a breed developed in his native country of Austria, he decided to acquire one. Don flew to Austria, bought his first mare, and had her shipped to America on Lufthansa.

The horse stirred his love and interest in Haflingers. Since his initial trip, and after more purchases, his mares have produced three Haflinger foals. As one of two Americans on the board of directors of the World Haflinger Breeding and Sports Federation, Don returned frequently to Austria, attending auctions and horse classifications. The Federation classifies Haflingers as gold, silver, or blue depending upon individual characteristics; two of Don's mares are classified silver.

Today Don no longer trades or breeds Haflingers. He just enjoys riding and taking care of the four on his farm. In wintertime, he often hooks them up to a sleigh and gives rides to his children and grandchildren.

In addition to his Haflingers, Don has owned Airedale terriers since he was twelve years old. Abby and Duke are his fifteenth and sixteenth terriers. The terriers and horses provide some work and much enjoyment.

Never a person to remain idle, Don noticed a local restaurant in foreclosure, purchased it from the bank, and renamed it the Haflinger Haus. The early-twentieth-century, two-story pillared building, initially owned by a private resident, was converted over the years to a nursing home, and then the restaurant.

The Haflinger Haus is now an inn, with six bedrooms on the second floor, each with a private bath, renting via Airbnb. Don has updated the kitchen, bar area, and heating system. He has decorated Haflinger Haus with a number of antiques, including two vintage carousel horses, wood carvings, and many pictures and paintings of Haflinger horses.

The dining room features Austrian dishes such as *Wiener schnitzel*, Hungarian *goulash* made from his mother's recipe, *spaetzle* with lobster sauce, and *schweinshaxe*. The menu differs in the attached tavern. In the summer, the restaurant also grows its own vegetables out back in the organic garden. Don says customers seem to like the freshness of vegetables coming from the garden directly to the table.

Bought at auction, the Lowenbrau memorabilia will fit right in at the Haflinger Haus.

The Haflinger Haus has been voted the Best Restaurant in Berkshire County for eight years in a row. As Don considers other opportunities, he has put the Haflinger Haus up for sale and hopes to use the proceeds for a different business venture.

Several years ago, Don purchased the old St. Mark's Episcopal Church at 17 Commercial Street, updated it, and then heard about a group of musicians wanting to open a music academy for teenagers and young adults, hoping to give them an opportunity to work with world-class educators, performing musicians, and recording artists. Don saw the opportunity as a perfect use for the Romanesque Revival-style building and leases it to the group for $1 a year.

The building became the Olga C. Sommer Center for Music and Art, named after his mother and sister who both loved music. It hosts the Berkshire Academy for Advanced Musical Studies.

More recently, Don acquired the empty Baptist Church and parsonage next door to the Haflinger Haus, impressed by its beautiful interior. The sanctuary, balcony, and seating areas as well as the acoustics will make the church a better host for the music academy. He is in the process of restoring it while trying to sell St. Mark's.

Don enjoys his four children, eleven grandchildren, and nine great-grandchildren who live locally and occasionally help him at the farm or the Haflinger Haus. His children have had various careers, from owning an electrical repair business or a real estate company, to working in energy conservation or teaching elementary school.

His day starts with a 7:30 a.m. feeding of horses and dogs. Then it's off to his office at Greylock Apartments. He returns home for lunch to feed the animals, and work in his vegetable garden. Afternoons are devoted to reading, and then Don returns to the Haflinger Haus at 5:30 p.m. for supper and mingling with guests.

He feels fortunate to have traveled to all fifty US states, Russia, China, and numerous trips to Austria involving his Haflingers. For relaxation (when it occurs), he joins his children and grandchildren at Dennis Port on Cape Cod where they bought a retreat home several years ago. There, his dogs get to run on the beach. As a strong supporter of animal causes, Don supports Save the Animals, American Society for the Prevention of Cruelty to Animals (ASPCA), and

People for the Ethical Treatment of Animals (PETA).

His overseas trips are always an adventure. His kids speak jokingly of his technical savvy, remembering the time Don left their hotel with the room phone, and when it wouldn't work outside, a local service provider had to explain that it was not broken, it was a cordless phone that only worked in the hotel. Another family tale is the time they were eating at a nice restaurant in Budapest when, unbeknownst to him, his trousers split open and he strolled through the entire restaurant with his underwear on display.

Don's personality has been described as confident, outgoing, charming, generous, and driven. He is always processing new ideas, is a multitasker, and doesn't like failing at any endeavor. He loves being with his grandchildren and has long been an avid supporter of the Town of Adams, a member of numerous Town boards, as well as the American Legion Commander a number of times.

It's clear that Don doesn't stop for long. Between taking care of his farm, feeding his pets, owning a restaurant, and refurbishing a church, he is as busy as ever.

Jane Swift

As a young girl growing up, Jane Swift was encouraged by political conversations around the family dinner table. At age twenty-five, she became the youngest woman ever elected to the Massachusetts State Senate. Jane was then elected the youngest female Lieutenant Governor of Massachusetts, at the age of thirty-six. Notably, she was the first person serving as Governor to give birth during her tenure, delivering twin daughters a month after entering office. That one may be hard to match.

Jane Swift's political interest was nurtured early on by her father's longtime involvement in local senatorial and mayoral campaigns. He was involved in both Jack Fitzpatrick's and Peter Webber's successful Berkshire-area state senate races. It was said that candidates running for political office in the Berkshires from the 1970s through the 1990s often sought Mr. Swift's advice or assistance. He frequently took his children to campaign events, including Jane, who shared his deep sense of purpose and civic responsibility.

In fact, Jane's second job after college was working in Boston at the Massachusetts State Legislature for Peter Webber as a legislative aide and a liaison with Berkshire towns. Not long after, Jane's father was essential to her campaign strategy and operations when she became elected to the Massachusetts Senate.

EARLY LIFE

Jane Maria Swift was born on February 24, 1965, at the North Adams Hospital. Her parents, both North Adams natives, were John Maynard "Jack" Swift Sr. and Jean Mary (Kent) Swift.

Jack Swift Sr. was born at home in 1941, the oldest of soon

to be six children. He worked most of his life at Ashley Swift & Sons plumbing and also worked as an independent engineering consultant. He loved baseball and coached Little League for twenty years, enjoyed family camping, and was an avid golfer. He served as president of the North Adams Housing Authority and the North Adams Chapter of Habitat of Humanity. Of Irish and English heritage, his son describes him as "a true family man, loyal, a 'Jimmy Stewart' type. He was smart, diligent, had a predilection for engineering, successfully ran a family business, and loved North Adams." The Berkshires lost a great advocate when Jack passed away in 2019.

Jane's mom, Jean, was born in 1940 at home and was an only child. Jean was of Italian and English heritage, taught in Adams, North Adams, and Pittsfield schools, and was a homemaker for a number of years. In the early 1960s, Jean was required to leave her teaching post due to pregnancy, but she returned to her profession later in life.

She and Jack were married in 1963 and had four children: Jane, her sister, and two brothers. Jane's older brother jokes that he and Jane were "Irish Twins," born just thirteen months apart. The family lived all of Jane's life on Olds Street, which parallels Route 2 behind the former Price Chopper supermarket.

Described by family as happy-go-lucky, loving, religious, and very sweet, Jean cherished being a volunteer for the Girl Scouts, working with little kids on arts and crafts. Later in life, she played softball with girls a lot younger than she was and could still hit the ball a mile.

Jane's paternal grandfather, Ashley Swift, was born in 1916 in Plymouth, Massachusetts. Ashley had roots in Ireland, and his lineage could be traced to the *Mayflower*. He played varsity baseball in high school and semi-professional baseball in the Plymouth area. In the 1930s, he moved to North Adams, worked for his uncle Ashley Wood, and then bought his business in 1948 and named it Ashley Swift Plumbing. Over the years, the name was changed to Ashley Swift & Sons. He enjoyed a friendly cribbage game and playing golf. Ashley passed away in 1987, leaving the business to his sons.

Vivian (Scrivens) Swift was born in North Adams in 1917, the eldest of six children. After attending North Adams schools, she worked at the Sprague Electric Company for a short time and then helped her husband establish Ashley Swift & Sons. A number of family members were involved in the business, including Vivian's sisters who helped in the office. Vivian was also a homemaker and a member of Incarnation Church's Ladies Guild. A skilled golfer, she once won the North Adams Country Club's Women's Championship. Vivian died at home in 2010.

Jane's maternal grandfather, Leslie Kent, was born in Lee, Massachusetts, in 1911 and came to North Adams as a young boy, where he attended local schools. He also worked with the Civilian Conservation Corps at Camp Monroe. He was employed as a supervisor at Sprague from 1934 to 1976. Leslie was an outdoorsman. He enjoyed fishing and hunting and even taught Jane archery, which helped her earn a Girl Scout merit badge. He passed away in 2005.

Alma Bartholdi Kent, Jane's maternal grandmother, was born in 1913. She and her mother, Maria, and brother emigrated in 1922 from the Province of Trentino-Arco in northern Italy. Refugees from World War I, the family was eventually joined by her father, Pietro. Alma married Leslie in 1937 at Saint Anthony of Padua church. She worked briefly at General Electric in Pittsfield and then for forty-eight years, from 1931 to 1979, at Sprague. Alma was a member of the Rosary Society, the Sprague Quarter Century Club, and an active volunteer at the local Salvation Army. She passed away in 2001.

Jane and her siblings enjoyed a wonderful relationship with their grandparents. They often played behind Ashley and Vivian's house on Massachusetts Avenue. The long path behind their house led to the Appalachian Trail, where the kids had the freedom to roam, hike, pick blueberries, and catch snakes. On Saturday nights, they would sleep over at Leslie and Alma's house, roaming nearby fields and watching planes take off and land from Harriman Airport.

The Swift family home on Olds Street was a modest, three-bedroom house with a bath and a half, a large double lot, and nearby fields to play in. When the family's fourth child was born, an addition was added. Jane's mom has now lived there for over fifty years.

The close-knit neighborhood teemed with playmates who played Wiffle ball, kickball, kick-the-can, and baseball on the Swifts' side lawn. With upward of twenty playmates, base paths were worn into the lawn. Jane, though slightly younger than her brother and his friends, was right in the midst of the kids playing and competing, foreshadowing her fearless political acumen.

In the wintertime, the kids sledded on Brayton Hill right next to the YMCA, or skated and played "boot hockey" in the frozen swampy area on Demond Ave between Mass Avenue and Route 2. Their playground area also included a bus parking lot and the nearby train tracks. Although at the time girls' sports were very limited, this mixed group of friends reveled in their own games.

Jane attended Greylock School through the fifth grade, then Conte Middle School, the former Drury High School, through eighth. During this time, she took gymnastics and dance lessons at the new YMCA that her mom had lobbied to build. She became a good gymnast, according to friends, always brave, bold, and ready to take chances.

She was also active in the Girl Scout troop her mother led, attending summer camps in Goshen and the Muriel Flagg Camp in Williamstown. At thirteen, Jane won the opportunity to go on a two-week Girl Scouts Wider Opportunity in Wyoming, where she rode a horse for the first time.

Family vacations included camping at South Pond and in upstate New York. The family slept in an eight-person tent and used a small stove with two burners to cook hot dogs, hamburgers, and occasional fresh-caught brook trout. Camping was $14 per night, and passes and boat rides enabled the children to explore many areas. When the kids got older, Disney World in Orlando became their preferred, if pricier, destination. The family also went to Plymouth for one week in the summer where her grandfather's family owned a cottage near McCage's Pond.

Every Sunday, the entire family attended church at Our Lady of Incarnation Church in Blackinton. At the time, altar servers were boys, although Jane was able to wrangle a position with her slightly amenable priest. She served for eight years and then became a lector until leaving for college. After church on Sundays, the family often ate at her grandparents, the Kents. There was a light lunch, then grandmother's Italian repertoire for dinner: pasta dishes, special sauce, meatballs, and freshly grated parmesan cheese. Jane can still remember the taste of her grandmother's sauce and compares all others against it.

During the week, the family of six had dinner every night at 6:00 p.m. after dad got home from work. Their kitchen table was a picnic table covered with a tablecloth, comfortable for the large family. Table talk was usually focused on politics, current events, and sports. Jane's mom made goulash, hamburgers, chicken, pasta dishes, fish on Fridays, and a treat would be Freihofer's cookies for dessert, although Jane says they disappeared quickly with four children.

Competition is natural in large families: Jane remembers that when artichokes were served, her mother and grandmother would tell the children the "hearts" weren't really that good, so the kids avoided them, and mom and grandmother ate them. Jane didn't realize until she was a junior in college that the hearts were considered the most delectable part of the vegetable.

She started working early in life. Her first job was delivering the *Penny Saver* once a week in the Greylock area. Then from the age of ten onward, she did a lot of babysitting. At fourteen, she worked at Charlie's A&W Root Beer Drive-In as the inside girl, putting trays together and running the cash register. She still remembers her mom thinking she was too young, prohibiting her from working as a carhop.

She is close to her older brother, whose friends, at one point, nicknamed Jane "Radar" because she and her girlfriends could always seem to track where John and his friends were hanging out. They even showed up at his fraternity house once.

Always the competitor, Jane still reminds John about winning a foot race with him. Their dad asked if they wanted to race in the side yard, so both took up the challenge. Jane took off her shoes,

John did not; they ran, and she beat him. Still today, she will remind him that she bested her older brother.

Jane was an active member of the Drury High School class of 1983. She played basketball and ran track for four years. She was in the Pep Club, on the school newspaper's staff, a homeroom representative, belonged to the Ring and Prom committees and was in the school's Nu Sigma and Pro Merito honor societies.

After a campus visit and generous financial assistance, she decided to attend Trinity College, a private liberal arts school, the second oldest college in the State of Connecticut. During her college years, Jane held work-study jobs in the dining hall and with the Religion and Philosophy Department, played on the women's rugby team, and was a member of the Kappa Kappa Gamma sorority. She graduated in 1987 with a Bachelor of Arts degree in American studies.

CAREER

After graduation, Jane worked one year for G.F. Fox & Company as a retail manager in Hartford. While participating in the executive management training program, she managed accessories and men's apparel.

Jane Swift, in her office.

A year later, she found the job she most desired: working at the Boston State House for Peter Webber, Berkshire County's Senator, as a legislative aide and a liaison with local towns.

With her dad's advice and supported by Peter Webber, in 1990, at the age of twenty-five, Jane was the youngest woman ever elected to the Massachusetts Senate and quickly became its youngest woman to hold a leadership position, assistant minority leader. She was repeatedly elected and served Berkshire, Hampshire, Franklin, and Hampden counties until 1997. While senator, she secured funding for MASS MoCA in North Adams and helped stabilize funding for dairy farmers.

One of her other major achievements, as part of a group, was writing and negotiating the details of the Education Reform Act of 1993, which was sent to the governor for his signature and created the Massachusetts Comprehensive Assessment System, one the nation's first statewide programs for quantifying academic performance.

While campaigning in 1990, Jane met her husband, Charles Hunt, who attended a town hall meeting in Williamstown to discuss dairy farming issues. In addition to farming, at the time Charles was the interim Athletic Director, baseball, and football coach at Mount Greylock High School. As Jane likes to say, "The rest is history." They commuter dated for a while and were married in 1994. Jane and Chuck have three daughters who are currently attending college. They live on a 25-acre farm in Williamstown, with soaring views of the Berkshires.

In 1996, rather than seek re-election, Jane decided to run for United States Congress in the Massachusetts 1st Congressional District. She lost to a popular two-term incumbent by only four points. She then worked for a short period of time as an executive with the Massachusetts Port Authority and as the state's Consumer Affairs Secretary.

In 1998, Jane, pregnant at the time, campaigned throughout Massachusetts and was elected Lieutenant Governor, serving with Governor Paul Cellucci. Her oldest daughter, Elizabeth, was born just 10 days before the election. During the next two years, Jane was involved in implementation planning for the highly lauded Education Reform Act she'd helped craft.

In greater detail, the act focused on equitable funding for public schools, accountability for student learning, and statewide standards for students, educators, and school districts. The novel assessment system was also expected to help identify individuals and schools needing assistance. Jane also devoted time to improving conditions for foster children and providing tax relief to Massachusetts families.

After serving two years as Lieutenant Governor, Jane became Acting Governor when President Bush appointed Governor

Cellucci as Ambassador to Canada. Her time in office was busy. As she related to me, "I started the gubernatorial job in April 2001, my twin daughters, Lauren and Sarah, were born in May, and the infamous terrorist attack on the United States occurred on September 11."

Those following months in office were consumed by responses and the effects of 9/11. She led a statewide response to prevent further acts of terrorism. She also led a group of forty-five governors urging Congress to create the Department of Homeland Security. She led the movement to abolish private airport security, initiating the birth of the Transportation Security Administration in November 2001.

Jane Swift addressing the fans at Fenway Park.

Jane Swift with Charlie Baker, the current governor of Massachusetts, at a recent Red Sox event.

She established and appointed members to the Carter Commission, which examined airport operations and security and proposed improvements within MassPort. She won high praise for successfully handling a looming budget crisis in the aftermath of the attacks by cutting programs and restricting spending. The *Boston Herald* summarized her response to the crisis, stating, "Acting Governor Jane Swift has had her finest hour during this crisis . . . she has been steady, stable, calming, decisive."

Initially, she considered running for reelection in 2002 but when she considered the needs of her family, the probability of a strong competitor, and the considerable financial requirements to move forward, she decided to seek a career in the private sector. She was succeeded in office by Governor, now Senator, Mitt Romney.

After leaving office, Jane quickly became involved in her signature interests: education advancement, women's issues, and leadership. Over the years she has worked with a series of innovative educational companies in executive positions, including president, board member, or partner. Some of the positions she held concurrently with others.

She has received six honorary doctorates, served as a fellow at the Harvard University's John F. Kennedy School of Government, been a distinguished lecturer in Leadership Studies at Williams College, and served as a visiting professor at Boston College Law School to name just a few of the forums where she promotes women's issues on leadership and education. At one point in our conversations, Jane joked that her mother might have been prouder of her teaching at Williams College than of her being Governor of Massachusetts.

Some of Jane's significant contributions include working with Sally Ride, the first American woman in space, as a director of the company she co-founded, Sally Ride Science, which provides engaging science, math, and engineering content specifically targeted to girls in middle school. When Sally passed away in 2012, Jane designed the communication plan surrounding her early demise at the age of sixty-one.

For a number of years Jane worked as the Chief Executive Officer for Middlebury Interactive Languages in a partnership with Middlebury College to deliver online language instruction to primary, secondary, and home schoolers. Working with a "fantastic team," the courses improved quality learning situations for children in every socioeconomic setting. It was a great preparation for students to learn world languages and unique cultural situations.

Few people may be aware that Jane volunteers on the School of Leadership, Afghanistan (SOLA) as an advisory board member, helping the group with insights on education. She connected with some Afghani students at a local school, invited them and their parents and sponsors to Thanksgiving dinner, and became interested and engaged in helping them.

Currently, Jane is the president and executive director for a non-profit technology company called LearnLaunch Institute. The company works with innovators, public policy leaders, and education practitioners integrating educational technologies within school systems from kindergarten through twelfth grade. Jane describes it as "the best, most challenging, and rewarding work of my career."

Once, when Jane was a guest speaker at her college sorority, she advised students to "stop focusing on what you don't have and start focusing on what you have been given." She also said, "I realized how much I have been given and how much of an obligation I have to give back."

Jane's style when she was a child has been described as bold, courageous, competitive, not intimidated by older children, and needing to prove herself. Even while young, she was always busy, on time, enjoyed helping others, and had a big heart. Every single one of these early qualities has continued through life and translated well in her role as a groundbreaking leader. As an education reformer, she will inspire future generations to equal success.

PAM WEATHERBEE

Pam, a Berkshire County preservationist, has spent her entire life supporting conservation causes with her time and financial support. She continues an enduring legacy of giving back to the community, started many years ago by her grandparents, parents, and uncle.

It's easy to see how Pam's inclination for preservation and philanthropy was derived. Her parents established the Greylock Foundation in 1960 to donate money to a variety of cultural and artistic institutions. Upon her father's death, a significant part of their art collection was donated to Williams College Museum of Art and the Whitney Museum of American Art in New York City.

I first spoke with Pam in February 2021 by telephone. Initially, she had some reservations about sharing her life history but was assured by a friend that I was genuinely interested. After several conversations with Pam and another with her daughter, Adria, the following story unfolded.

Pam Bloedel was born on January 11, 1931, at the North Adams Hospital. Her parents were Lawrence Hotchkiss Bloedel and Eleanor Clare (Palmedo) Bloedel. The Bloedel side had German ancestry, although descended via French Huguenots who left France during the religious struggles circa 1700, and claimed lands in Germany.

Lawrence had been born in the state of Washington in 1902 and came to the Berkshires as a Williams College freshman in 1919. While at Williams he met Eleanor Clare Palmedo at one of the weekend house parties accompanied by her brother, another Williams student. After graduating in 1923, he and Eleanor were married and for a time lived in Bellingham, Washington, before returning to Williamstown in 1926. From 1929 until 1942, he served as Head Cataloguer at Williams College Library. In 1937, he received a master's degree in library science from Columbia University.

Lawrence enlisted in the Army during World War II. Serving as a technical 4th grade, he landed with invasion forces on the North African coast near Casablanca, supporting the battles of Tunisia and Sicily with an ordnance group that repaired artillery. Returning home, he began a lifelong interest in designing and building contemporary furniture and collecting Modern American art. He was an active supporter of the arts and music in Berkshire County. Works from his extensive collection have been exhibited worldwide. Lawrence received an honorary degree, Doctor of Humane Letters, from the College in 1967. He passed away in 1976.

Eleanor Clare Palmedo was born in Brooklyn in 1901, attended schools in White Plains, New York, and graduated from Miss Wheeler's school in Providence, Rhode Island. She married Lawrence Bloedel in 1924. In addition to becoming the mother of Pam and Prentice, she was very active in the community. Eleanor was one of the founders of the Williamstown Women's Exchange and served for many years with the Visiting Nurses Association. She had four terms as president of the Williamstown League of Women Voters and was a longtime member of the Lenox Garden Club. She received an honorary degree from North Adams State College in 1976 for her many civic contributions. Prior to World War II, she was active in the Cap & Bells Productions at Williams College Theater and was highly reviewed for her leading performance in a summer production of "Candida."

Eleanor passed away in 1984. She bequeathed her property and buildings, known as the Field Farm, to The Trustees of Reservations. The couple had built and owned two distinctive houses, both in midcentury modern style, situated on more than 300 acres of land that is now open to the public. The gardens and wonderful views of Mount Greylock captivate thousands of people each year.

The property and its scenery also support live concerts, photography workshops, guided nature walks, and drawing classes. Architect and design tours explore the 1950s and 1960s buildings that house a mid-twentieth century art collection of sculptures, paintings, and drawings.

Pam's paternal grandparents, Julius Harold Bloedel and Mina Louise Prentice Bloedel, natives of Wisconsin, went west to Bellingham, Washington, in the 1890s and founded a forestry company. At one time, after a merger, his company MacMillan Bloedel (MacBlo) became one of the largest timber holders, loggers, and sawmill operators in the Pacific Northwest, eventually purchased by the Weyerhaeuser Company in 1999. Julius donated land to establish a park in Bellingham, Washington, and Bloedel Hall at the University of Washington in Seattle is named in his honor.

One of Julius and Mina's children, Pam's uncle Prentice Bloedel, an executive with the forest company, was also renowned for his philanthropy. A longtime botany aficionado, he donated funds to build the Bloedel Conservatory of Queen Elizabeth Park atop Little Mountain in Vancouver. The site supports a floral conservatory, a forest museum, and a planetarium. The Vancouver icon is visited by hundreds of thousands of people each year.

In nearby Washington State, Prentice contributed significantly to the Children's Hospital and personally funded the Virginia Bloedel Hearing Research Center. The former home and gardens he and Virginia shared, located on 150 acres on Bainbridge Island, are open to the public and now known as the Bloedel Reserve.

Pam's maternal grandparents, Ulrich Palmedo (1862–1909), and Emma Sondern Palmedo (1867–1945) were both from New York. Emma was born in Brooklyn and Ulrich worked as a stockbroker in New York City. It is believed the Palmedos immigrated to the United States from Germany in the mid-nineteenth century.

EARLY LIFE

Pam and her older brother grew up on Bulkley Street in Williamstown, attending the new Pine Cobble School through eighth grade. At an early age, already interested in art, she exhibited a large design of a house on a hilltop captured in bright, flat tones at the Lawrence Art Museum at Williams College. She created the design when she was seven years old.

Pam then attended the coeducational, preparatory boarding school Milton Academy for high school. She thought the teachers were excellent but found the curriculum narrow, focused on literature and languages with little math and no sciences, areas of interest to her. She really enjoyed the art program and separately was very good at archery. Although boys and girls were not allowed to mix, except when working on school plays, Pam requested and was allowed to participate in the boy-only photography club. Sunday walks with a headmistress described as "an old dragon" were a poor substitute for wandering her fields in Williamstown. There were Saturday occasions when Pam and a friend would covertly go to town for a movie.

After graduation, she was accepted at Radcliffe, the women's liberal arts college closely associated with and eventually merging with Harvard in 1999. She was quite happy there, with a diversity of friends, things to do, and the city of Cambridge close by. As a member and Vice President of the Radcliffe Choral Society, Pam sang at a number of prestigious concerts, including Symphony Hall in Boston, Times Hall in New York City, and at the American University in Washington, D. C. She was also a member of the Dabblers Art club at college. Pam graduated in 1952 with a bachelor of arts degree, majoring in biology.

After graduation, she worked for the Museum of Comparative Zoology at Harvard, then at Woods Hole Oceanographic Institute. Pam graduated from the Boston Museum School of Fine Arts in 1957, honored by the school for her outstanding work, and briefly worked at D. C. Heath & Company, a Boston publisher, as a book designer. In the same year, she married another of the school's graduates, Robert Weatherbee from Portland, Maine. Robert was a Marine Corps veteran and a technical illustrator for NASA. He also taught art at Tufts University in Medford.

The couple lived in Boston, where their one daughter Adria was born. Adria, who now lives in Williamstown, said Pam got her name from a vintage embroidered sampler from the Weatherbee side of the family. The source of that name would have been her great-great-aunt. Robert passed away at an early age in the late 1970s.

GOING HOME AGAIN

Pam returned to Williamstown to be near her parents and raise Adria. The family was located "right down the road" from her grandparents, the Bloedels. Pam quickly became involved in local preservation and conservation efforts. As a member of the Williamstown Conservation Commission for over twenty-five years, she was involved with the commission in administering wetlands laws, researching natural history, and many conservation efforts.

At the same time, as a young mother, she directed a nature group for kids at the Margaret Lindley Park, involving her young charges in hiking, butterfly walks, and art projects that included creating mushroom prints. She worked diligently, transferring her interest in nature to the kids. Although Adria was young for some of the programs, she remembers always being by her mom's side. Later on, Pam became a Girl Scout leader for Adria's troop. The family briefly attended St. John's Episcopal Church in Williamstown where Adria participated in Sunday school.

Pam cooked supper every night and Adria attests to her delicious spaghetti and meat sauce. Cod cakes was another popular meal and her "floating island" dessert with custard and meringue was a great hit. Always on the go, they relied on simple fare; weekend lunches might be hot dogs and ketchup. The Thanksgiving meal was always at their house, and Christmas was celebrated at the Bloedel home with a prime rib meal and all the trimmings.

Family vacations involved camping in Maine and on Cape Cod with friends; travelling to Martha's Vineyard for outings; trips out west to Arizona and Seattle, visiting family, and some treasured stops at National Parks. The family bought a small house at Martha's Vineyard in the 1970s, and it became the desired vacation spot for Pam, Adria, and her two children.

Pam was instrumental in Williamstown conservation issues in the 1970s. She was a key supporter to the beginnings of a recycling program in Williamstown, always determined to get things done that help local preservation efforts. She actively protested against Greylock Glen projects in Adams that would have commercialized a significant part of Mount Greylock. Over a number of years, her efforts along with the efforts of many others, defeated the building of a hotel, condominiums, and a golf course project on the foothills of the mountain. The Town and its residents now control use of the property.

Her Mount Greylock involvement piqued an interest in rare plant species. She knew the tallest mountain in Massachusetts with subarctic weather had plants not seen in the rest of the state. Interest in botany drove her to matriculate with the University of New Hampshire and she received a master's degree in botany in 1989. Her thesis centered on Berkshire County plants and lent credibility to her future studies.

Over the course of eight years from 1986 to 1994, she decided to update a 1922 flora survey focusing on Berkshire County. She did extensive fieldwork, climbing mountains, ridges, and cliffs. Mount Greylock was of special interest because the environment was a lot colder and produces unique plants.

Pam in her kayak at Bog Pond in Savoy.

Her fieldwork included hiking Monument Mountain and Mount Everett, the highest peak in the south Taconic Mountains, along with exploring many open areas and fields. She spent considerable time canoeing and kayaking on the Housatonic River. She completed surveys in the Berkshire County towns of Florida and Savoy, visiting a number of ponds and bogs. In addition to her extensive fieldwork, Pam read accounts from other botanists and became an expert on local topography.

She says, with a slight hesitation, that most of her studies were conducted on public lands including wildlife management areas, although she may have "wandered off" them at times.

The fieldwork had her collecting specimens of each plant, numbering and recording the location of the plant. At home she verified their identity, put each one between sheets of paper, piled them up, placed all of them in a plant press, strapped tightly, and allowed them days to dry. Then the plant was glued on special paper, labelled, and became part of a collection, preserved for years.

"The work of collecting and pressing was hard, but I enjoyed doing it," says Pam. "It's rare to find a new species, but I was always on the lookout for native plants not noticed before." She also noted there was little interest in alien flora, plants obviously introduced into this environment from other countries.

Pam published her extensive findings into a beautifully crafted, one-hundred-forty-page book titled *Flora of Berkshire County Massachusetts*. This comprehensive, scientific booklet covers everything from factors that influence vegetation such as the land's topography, climate, and weather to the specific habitats the flora will occupy. In the center section, Pam has cataloged all the plants, specifically noting they were grown without cultivation in Berkshire County. This section is anchored by colored pictures of some of the area's most interesting plants.

Described in news articles as a naturalist interested in geology, ornithology, and botany, she was often engaged to lead large groups or give presentations, acting as an educator and interpreter, to explore and explain the natural flora atop Mount Greylock Reservation.

DEVOTION TO THE ENVIRONMENT

Over the years, Pam has worked as a botanical consultant completing an ecological plan for the Massachusetts Audubon Society and its sanctuary in Lenox. She has also consulted with firms involved in building highways, on the lookout for rare species of plants. She completed a number of comprehensive surveys for companies on plants, habitats, use of land, rare species, and recommendation for protections.

Pam was a longtime member of the Williamstown Conservation Commission and recognized by the Massachusetts Association of Commissions for her "significant personal contribution efforts for over two decades." As a member of the Williamstown Commission, she helped the town acquire land by gift or purchase for the purpose of conservation or recreation. She has long advocated for wetland protections. As one news article noted, "She personally acquired several wetlands in Williamstown to preserve them and has donated, with conservation restrictions, much of her own property."

Several years ago, she donated land near her house to the Rural Lands Foundation, and she also donated a plot of land near Mason Hill to The Trustees of Reservations. She continues to be a strong supporter of both organizations.

COURTESY PAM WEATHERBEE

Pam, out and about, on another nature trail in Plainfield, Massachusetts.

Working with the state botanist in conjunction with the Massachusetts Natural Heritage Program, Pam located and identified state endangered species of plants in Berkshire County. She herself was credited with rediscovering five species believed to have been destroyed and discovering two new plant species.

Pam serves as a member of The Trustees of Reservations, an organization that manages donated properties, including her own parents' buildings and lands. Committee members may also recommend other acquisitions to the Trustees. She belongs to a local committee that creates programs and events such as wildflower and butterfly walks and bird counts to attract people to Field Farm. Usually in the Spring, you will find Pam leading a two-hour walking tour for The Trustees.

Trained as an artist at the Boston Museum of Fine Arts, Pam is accomplished at watercolor paintings and etchings of landscapes, flowers, and still life. She also became interested in ceramics and studied under several local experts. Her stoneware became notable for its decorations that combine her interest in natural history, particularly plants, with the functional forms of pottery. She has participated in local exhibitions, one remembered as "Weeds and Tapestries." Always active, she belonged to a painting group in Williamstown and still enjoys flower and vegetable gardening. She was an enthusiastic cross-country skier well into her seventies, traversing the top of Mount Greylock.

Pam has loved cats her whole life. Today she has four: two rescued young feral cats, Bandy and Tippy, and two older ones, Pansy and Chai. At one point she bred Siamese cats and worked with Animal Dreams (part of the Berkshire Humane Society) to trap and save feral cats. Pam donates money to the Society, and her charities usually include Animal Advocacy Groups.

Her daughter relates a story of one vacation at Martha's Vineyard, when an old Siamese cat, "Monster," disappeared while they were having some dilapidated furniture removed to be discarded. Realizing Monster had climbed onto his favorite perch inside the old couch, and had been hauled away, they quickly drove to the dump and retrieved the bewhiskered, bewildered Monster.

Pam is determined, independent, and eloquent, especially when it comes to her conservation and preservation issues. As her daughter Adria says, "If she believes in something, she is going to do it." Pam and her white Subaru can often be seen headed to her next meeting or cause of action. Her strength of character and devotion to the environment are evident in all she has accomplished. In each birdsong or cycle of bloom, the Berkshires are so much the better for it.

LINDA WILK, SSJ

Now in her seventies, Linda Wilk made the awe-inspiring decision a decade ago to work and live as a missionary in West Africa. After serving forty-two years as an American elementary school teacher, she decided to relinquish civilization's niceties and live a Spartan existence in a poverty-stricken and at times calamitous country. This is the kind of thing Linda does joyfully.

Linda Wilk joined the Sisters of St. Joseph in 1965, an order founded in France more than 350 years ago, established in the United States in 1836. Their initial ministry in Springfield focused on education. The group founded and staffed sixty schools and helped establish the College of Our Lady of the Elms, often called Elms College, located in Chicopee, Massachusetts.

Not long ago, I had lunch with Linda and her fellow missionary, Ruth. They are gratified to be able to work in a desolate, troubled area supporting widows and children. Linda was a classmate of mine many years ago, and I'm amazed by what she does for others.

Linda's remarkable life began February 14, 1948, at the W. B. Plunkett Memorial Hospital in Adams, Massachusetts. Her parents were Theodore Joseph Wilk and Clara (Guerin) Wilk. Theodore, born in Adams on December 12, 1909, worked as a foreman and assistant superintendent at the former Budd Paper Co. for thirty-two years, retiring at the age of fifty-seven for medical reasons. He also worked briefly at Berkshire Fine Spinning Associates. Upon his retirement, he enjoyed silk-screening and operating a small printing press. Theodore passed away in 1992.

Clara was born in North Adams on New Year's Day in 1911. As the family likes to say, she was a 1-1-11 baby. Clara worked at

Berkshire Fine Spinning Associates, became a stay-at-home mom when Linda was born, and returned to work at the Sprague Electric Company in North Adams when Linda entered fourth grade. She was an active member of the Ladies of St. Anne at her church and enjoyed crocheting and crafts. Clara was known for her baked beans and delicious apple pie, and though Canadian, she enjoyed cooking scrumptious Polish food. She passed away in 2004.

Theodore and Clara were married at Adams' Notre Dame Church on September 21, 1931. They had three children: the oldest, a boy, born in 1932 but since deceased; a middle son; and Linda, the youngest, born sixteen years after her oldest brother.

Linda's paternal grandparents were Justyn Wilk and Aniela Kosierowska. Justyn co-owned a bar and grill in Adams on Summer Street, and Aniela was a homemaker. Justyn immigrated to the U.S. at the turn of the century, married, and had three children. After his first wife died, he married Aniela, also a Polish immigrant, and they had seven children, of whom Linda's father was the oldest. Both Justyn and Aniela died in the late 1930s before Linda was born.

Linda's maternal grandparents were Arsene and Vitaline (Breault) Guerin. Both had emigrated from the Three Rivers area of Canada. Arsene was a boiler operator at the Berkshire Mills and Vitaline a homemaker. They passed away in the early 1960s, just six months apart.

As a youth, Linda lived on Siara Street in Adams, near Tophet Brook. She and her friends rode bikes, played hide and seek, waded in the brook making little dams, and chased small fish. Some days, much to her mom's consternation, she remembers getting three or four pairs of shoes wet. Through the eighth grade, she attended nearby Notre Dame Elementary School, a short walk from home. In wintertime, her dad used to drop Linda off at Russell Field on Friday nights and weekends to ice skate with friends.

Linda enjoyed being with her father, an avid fisherman. They spent many hours at Cheshire Lake fishing for bass, perch, and pike. She still laughingly remembers being on her dad's crew for the maiden voyage of his homemade rowboat. Her brother hit a sandbar in the middle of the lake and asked a fearful Linda to get out of the boat, in the middle of the lake, and push them off the sandbar. Of course, she did it, getting wet up to her waist.

EDUCATION AND THE NOVITIATE

When asked, Linda says she knew most of her life that she would become a sister. By the age of twelve she was certain, admiring the nuns at Notre Dame and then being taught by strong women role models in the Sisters of St. Joseph.

She attended St. Joseph's High School from 1961, graduating in 1965. Her close friends were fellow classmates Paulette, Carol, Karen, Judy, and Claire. In high school, Linda bowled and often fished with Carol and Paulette. She was active with the Notre Dame Girl Scouts, looking forward to Wednesday night meetings and summer campouts at Windsor Jambs. She was senior class treasurer, and she enjoyed the very satisfying job of being a candy striper at the North Adams Hospital for several years, showing an early affinity for healthcare.

After high school, Linda entered a five-year formation program with the Sisters of St. Joseph and lived at the Mont Marie Motherhouse in Holyoke, Massachusetts, with fifty-seven other postulants. As a postulant for six months, Linda wore black mid-calf skirts, a black shirt, and black veil. In the following two years during her studies as a novice, she wore a black habit with a white veil.

Spiritual formation began in earnest her first year. The training was complemented by courses of study brought to the Mont by teachers from the nearby college, Our Lady of Elms. Her second year at the Mont was devoted almost entirely to canonical studies, in which the novices received a thorough theological, philosophical, and history-based education surrounding Church precepts. Linda's dad lightheartedly referred to this year as her "boot camp."

In 1968, as a senior novice, Linda chose to make her initial profession of vows of poverty, celibacy, and obedience. She made her final profession of vows in 1978.

During the five years of formation, from 1965 to 1970, the

novices' entire focus was on spiritual formation, their studies, and student teaching. There was little time for extracurricular activities. They did work in the Mont's healthcare center, taking care of elderly, infirm sisters. Family visitations were limited, and only in their last two years of study were occasional home visits allowed.

Upon graduation in 1970, Linda received a bachelor's degree in sociology and education from the Elms, and the Order asked her to select three places she would like to be assigned. Of those three, Linda was sent to Saint Agnes School in Dalton, Massachusetts. In the following years, while teaching, Linda received a master's degree in education from Westfield State College.

Linda lived in a convent with a small group of ten sisters, including the school's principal. She enjoyed community life with the sisters and found the companionship and shared prayer very supportive for a young sister. They had separate bedrooms with minimal furnishings, including a bed, a sink, a desk, and a wardrobe. The women shared a common bathroom.

The sisters maintained a daily schedule that began with morning prayers at 5:30 a.m., proceeded to Mass, and then breakfast. They taught school during the day, then met for evening prayers, ate dinner, and had free time for grading papers or preparing for the next school day. Over the years their attire changed from a full to a modified habit. Eventually in the 1970s, the sisters were allowed to wear "street" clothes.

Over the next forty-two years, Linda taught at Saint Agnes school, working with second graders for eight years and the remainder of her career teaching the fourth and fifth grades.

In the late 1970s, Linda was given permission to live at home in nearby Adams to help her mother attend to her ailing father. She was now teaching during the day and assisting mom at night. She continued to live at home when her dad passed away and became a support during her mother's last days.

While teaching at Saint Agnes, Linda encouraged her fifth-grade class, and eventually the whole school, to participate in Operation Christmas Child as a service project. Operation Christmas Child delivers shoebox-size care packages to needy children in countries all over the world. The school collected and filled hundreds of boxes containing soap, toothpaste, toothbrushes, washcloths, crayons, toys, stuffed animals, shoes, t-shirts, and school supplies. In 2005, Linda was invited by the local organizer to travel to Africa to distribute the boxes. The Sisters of St. Joseph granted her permission, and she was on her way.

This was a first trip of many, and often things didn't go smoothly. In this case, the shoeboxes were held up in Customs and not released until after she returned home. Providentially, on her first trip, she met Ruth, a woman who had established an interdenominational missionary organization called Sheltering Wings some twenty-one years ago. The organization funds projects through the donations of generous benefactors, and its missionaries work with and support the local populations, especially widows and orphans.

Linda vividly remembers visiting an orphanage in West Africa founded by Ruth, and the moment she walked through the gate, her "heart ignited." She had an overwhelming desire to be there. Up to that moment, she'd had no thought of changing her life. She loved teaching in Dalton.

"GOD HAS SENT YOU TO HELP ME"

She returned to Massachusetts and continued to teach while enthusiastically supporting Operation Christmas Tree. Linda helped set up Giving Trees with donation tags in both the school and church. Her class collected bottles and redeemed them, using the money to support two children from the orphanage. A number of times over the next few years she sent Ruth over $7,000 received in donations. Despite these efforts Linda says, "I never felt like I was doing enough."

In 2008, Linda returned to West Africa, traveling with friends and a local team to distribute over 200,000 Operation Christmas Child packages. They would often visit three villages a day.

Linda's defining moment came in 2012, when she traveled with another sister and a fellow teacher. They stayed at an orphanage cleaning, organizing supplies and medicine, playing with and feeding babies. The group visited a small remote clinic, witnessing a number of malnourished mothers and emaciated babies. One mother was close to death; she had been abandoned by the tribe due to sickness and lack of support when her husband had died.

Linda shares a smile with village children.

COURTESY LINDA WILK

Linda and her group transported the deathly ill woman to a hospital, while her baby was taken to an orphanage. During the trip, Linda asked the woman why she was not afraid of having three strange white people transport her. She responded, "I feel God has sent you to help me. I have not eaten in three days." Later, as Linda related the story to friends, she burst into tears, quite naturally comparing the women's plight to the people in her Dalton parish who had enough to eat and readily available healthcare.

Seeing her tears, the friends challenged her enterprising spirit: "What are you going to do about it?" Linda was convinced she needed to spend more time in Africa where the needs were so great. As she deliberated, she asked Ruth, "Am I too old to be a missionary?" Ruth, who is the same age as Linda, said of course not.

In 2012, Linda petitioned the Sisters of St. Joseph for permission to go to Africa and work with Sheltering Wings. There was no hesitation on the part of her Order. The president and leadership team approved her request. In January 2013, Linda attended a one-month formation program in San Antonio and was on her way to Africa in October 2013.

As part of Sheltering Wings, Linda and Ruth have coordinated school sponsorships for over 240 children in ten villages, providing clothing, books, food, and accessories so the poorest of the poor can attend school. Sheltering Wings also sponsors a program that provides food for widows, arranges a milk program for mothers, builds medical clinics that provide the most basic pharmaceuticals, and funds the digging of wells. Water is always a constant source of concern, and food is difficult to grow.

She arrived in a small, landlocked West African country* in 2013, living in and helping the same small village until 2019. (*Geographical specifics aren't given for security reasons.) She vividly remembers her first days, sharing a two-room, tin-roofed concrete-block building with Ruth. One room was designated for grain storage. Initially, there was no electricity, no running water, and only a primitive outside latrine. At one point, they secured solar panels to charge their phones and provide for intermittent light from a single incandescent bulb. Every ten days or so, they went to a larger village to charge their laptops.

The women slept on cots with thin, mice-infested mattresses, and owned two plastic chairs, a bench and table, and single-burner gas hotplate. There were no screens on the metal, louvered windows, and they hand-washed outside in a cubicle-like, cinder-block shower using plastic pails. The idea of baking a cake on the hotplate required some ingenuity on the part of Linda and Ruth. Sometimes, reluctantly, they would eat a large can of sardines, then pack the sardine can with cake batter and immerse it in a large sandy-bottomed pot to successfully cook on their one burner hotplate. The resulting banana or spice cakes were delicious.

Cheerfully, she recalls her first few nights of getting used to mice, with the noise of rats' toenails scratching on the nearby table. The late-night aerial antics of bats had her pulling a sheet over her head. In the morning, they needed to sweep out bat droppings and chase geckos from the room. Initiation to village life was startling for this small-town Adams girl.

After a number of months, conditions improved slightly when Sheltering Wings built a new cinder-block house with screened windows and a cement floor. They received local hand-made beds with foam mattresses—and water, a scarce resource, piped into a kitchen sink from a nearby water tower, closely filtered for safety reasons. Bathroom facilities still do not exist, and the ladies continue to take bucket baths and use an outside latrine. Screened windows have helped eliminate the need for mosquito nets, although the hot, humid climate encourages creatures such as scorpions, mice, bats, lizards, and snakes to try and take up residence in their home-away-from-home.

Lack of refrigeration and a small propane stove keep daily meals modest. Linda and Ruth have a small breakfast, consisting of coffee and bread. Lunches consist of rice, macaroni, or locally grown mangos and pineapples with yogurt. Meat is unavailable, and fruit and vegetables are scarce, needing to be transported from miles away, and usually arrive spoiled. Eggs are available on occasion. A real treat might be flatbread with sauce for a homemade pizza, or a baguette purchased from a local bakery.

When they are in-country, it is time consuming to prepare food every day. With no access to refrigeration, they can keep few leftovers so usually they are shared with neighbors. Linda and Ruth are more sensitive than local people about eating leftovers or food that remains out overnight.

Local residents, truly subsistence farmers, rarely eat three meals a day. In the morning, they may have a porridge made from corn. Later in the day, their main meals consist of a thick gruel, akin to tofu, somewhat tasteless and served with sauce. Linda thought it comparable to "cold mashed potatoes." Warm homemade beer is available at the nearby marketplace.

Both Ruth and Linda noted that even with their busy schedules and the ever-present heat, it's not really an easy place to lose weight. The food is very starchy, comprised mainly of rice and pasta. While they sweat profusely when working, the local villagers remain skinny which they attribute to long hours of fieldwork and only eating two meals a day.

The West African country is largely patriarchal with a significant Muslim population where men are allowed to have multiple wives. Women are vulnerable, largely uneducated, and raised to be wives and mothers. Without the support of a man, they can be subject to starvation and abuse. The country's literacy rate is one of the lowest in the world and 30 percent of its children are malnourished.

Families often settle in compounds where the man has a house and his wives and children live in nearby huts. The compounds can include other relatives and their children. Within these familial settings, groups can reach forty to sixty people.

Everyone farms, and women are expected to grow food for themselves and their children. Main crops include millet, peanuts, sesame, cotton, and corn. Men often grow a specialized crop such as sesame to sell to the government. Other than farming, there are nomadic cattle herders.

Communities have a designated market day, where locals and people from other towns set up booths and sell sauces, cloth, batteries, blankets, and food staples. These are items similarly found in a general store. Colorful cloth is available for purchase and area tailors are ready to sew men's and women's clothing.

Traditionally, women wear long skirts, t-shirts, and head wraps. For colors, it's the brighter the better, such as oranges, reds, greens, and blues. Men wear pants, t-shirts, and button-down shirts that look like tunics. They also enjoy bright colors; pink outfits for men are not uncommon. Donated clothes are often seen promoting U.S. baseball teams' names.

Linda and Ruth, always culturally sensitive to Islamic customs, dress modestly in skirts, blouses, and t-shirts with sleeves, complemented with flip flops or sandals.

Their days pass quickly, rising at 5:30 a.m. for their small breakfast, devotions, and prayers. When not visiting villages, they spend much of their days planning, ordering supplies for distribution, packing them, and working with local partners and pastors to distribute goods. At 6:00 p.m., it's dinnertime followed by washing their dishes in a barrel while it's still light. Then, bucket baths with unheated water, darkness, and bedtime. They handwash their clothes. With the scarcity of water, there is much thought given to what is considered dirty or not.

When visiting a larger town for supplies, they might stay at a guest house and enjoy a real treat, a hot shower. When they return home to the States, a luxury is a cold glass of milk or water, and a juicy hamburger.

THE MISSION

Linda and Ruth travel back and forth between continents one or two times a year. Prior to their departure, they need to maintain inoculations for typhoid, hepatitis, meningitis, and yellow fever; while in-country, they take malaria pills daily.

Their trips occur from August through March, during the dry season, when they help with distribution of supplies to outlying villages. During the interim, they return to the United States to fundraise, speaking to various groups and meeting with benefactors. They focus on raising money for projects and securing donations to subsidize mission expenses such as rent, utilities, food, and transportation.

In October there is another "distribution," often bringing school supplies to children. Children receive books, educational supplies, soap, rice, ten pounds of macaroni, school fees, and uniforms. Widows receive 100 pounds of rice, soap, and on occasion buckets, blankets, tea, sugar, and sardines.

COURTESY LINDA WILK

Linda delivers a new distribution of supplies, including rice, pasta, and soap.

While French is the country's official language, there are 70 indigenous dialects. Neither Linda nor Ruth can speak the dialects, thus they work through an interpreter assigned by the village chief to determine the village's needs. Linda and Ruth speak French, as do most pastors and contractors, and that is helpful.

Since 2000, Sheltering Wings with its missionaries, local help, and benefactors, has been able to build thirty churches, two medical clinics, maternity wards, orphanages, schools, and they have dug over thirty wells. The group also sponsors milk programs for babies at risk.

There are no doctors managing clinics. None are available in the remote areas where Linda and Ruth work. The medical clinics are staffed with local nurses who speak the region's dialects and manage the clinic's six rooms. Three rooms are dedicated to transfusions and the others for private examinations and consultations. Serious medical cases are sent by ambulance to a larger village.

Maternity clinics, open to all women even beyond the village, are staffed around the clock, offer prenatal care, and have labor and delivery rooms. It is not uncommon for a woman to travel as far as 35 kilometers on a motorcycle to have her baby delivered. Women who deliver usually stay overnight. Linda and Ruth bring new mothers baby gifts in tote bags that include onesies, hats, outfits for mother, a blanket, and soap. Some new moms have never received gifts, and they get very excited and often cry. Irene, one of Linda's former classmates, and other friends knit items for the babies.

Working with malnourished babies can be the most heart-wrenching. Sometimes a father, usually worried about transportation or medical cost, will wait too long to agree on referring a baby to a clinic, and the baby will die. These times are difficult on the missionaries, when they know that in the U.S. the babies might have survived with more timely medical help.

Successful interventions often occur when babies can be treated at larger clinics, where mothers are taught how to feed and nourish their babies with fortified and enriched food, often peanut-butter based. Moms may need to be gone a month to six weeks for these lifesaving programs and require a husband's permission, especially if it's harvest time. There is great satisfaction to see babies go from being lethargic to laughing and cooing. Linda gets teary when these little miracles occur.

One time a mother of newborn twins was walking by the clinic with one baby strapped to her back and the other on her front. Linda and Ruth saw that the children were severely malnourished, estimating they weighed less than five pounds at six months old, and decided to intervene. The woman had given birth over the years to ten children, and five had already died. With her husband's permission, she was taken to the clinic in time and now has two healthy six-year-olds.

In another case with twins, one swallowed acid as a child and burnt his throat and esophagus, so he must have a feeding tube that sticks out from his stomach. The mother feeds liquid into the tube and uses a twig as a stopper. While his sister is thriving, this one is very small for his age and nothing further can be done.

Though based in a village, Linda travels short distances to outlying homes or smaller villages to distribute goods or offer assistance. At one time, the mission had an old Mitsubishi truck for transportation. Their tales about the truck, while memorable, seemed to be quite exasperating, like needing to refill the radiator every thirty minutes while on the road or requiring two people to get it started—one inside cranking it and the other outside under the hood vigorously pumping the fuel pump.

Another time, the oil cap fell into the engine block and could not be retrieved. Tires often get punctured on the rough paths and roads. With little experience, they sometimes rely on questionable local mechanical assistance. One self-described mechanic suggested they drill a hole in the radiator cap to let out steam in order to solve an overheating problem. The battered truck was finally replaced several years ago, and the replacement seems to be a great relief.

Sometimes they struggle mightily driving on recommended motorcycle paths, scraping through narrow thorn bush passages only to find out later that there was a nearby wider, more accessible dirt road. Once they had a flat tire far from village in the "middle of nowhere." Very fortunately, some locals were delivering bread and stopped to change their tire.

Once, two local friends who were riding with Linda and Ruth began directing them to negotiate a large drop-off in the road. They indicated it was easily negotiable, although they wanted to get out of the truck and stay a good distance away until the truck was safely over the drop. The women eased the truck over the drop and only then their friends decided to get back on the truck.

At times, traveling in remote areas, down isolated roads, or barely passable trails, security is non-existent and can cause concern for them. In these situations, where terrorists are active, they restrict their travel and rely on local help to complete distributions to the 240 children and 25 widows they support at six different locations.

Consulate warnings and advice from village people have eliminated most night travel for Linda and Ruth and can restrict day travel to just close-by villages. Village security is limited to a few concerned citizens patrolling with shotguns, no match for terrorists with automatic weapons. Any substantial police presence is hours away. Most villages also have only one road in and one road out. They have thought seriously about and have in place evacuation plans should it become necessary.

Difficulties aside, daily work continues as the missionaries collect, aggregate, and distribute to their charges, as well as seek donations for additional village buildings. Small cinder block classrooms or maternity clinics with solar panels can cost $40,000 each to construct. Trying to provide one drinking well for every 500 people is a constant consideration, as well as keeping old wells open and drilling new ones at a cost of $7,000 each.

Just another day.

Many benefactors provide support for distributions to the children and widows at a cost of $35 per month for a child and $20 per month for a widow.

In 2019, Sister Linda and Ruth had to move to a more populated area when the local police chief determined their beloved but isolated village, the first place they called home, was no longer safe.

Both Sister Linda and Ruth are in their seventies yet readily embrace personal sacrifices, undergo intense conditions, and endure long separations from their families to serve the poor. Their commitment to help the needy is ongoing and admirable. Though they enjoy good-naturedly recounting mice nesting in mattresses, endless 100-degree days of heat, and trucks with cranky engines, the "good news" they most like to tell is their love for the people of West Africa.

CHRIS WONDOLOSKI

North Adams has its own murder-mystery series—and its own Agatha Christie in Chris Wondoloski, who took up writing after retiring from teaching. His historic crime mysteries, The Hoosac Tunnel Murders *and* The Textile Mill Murders, *are based in North Adams and feature the spunky heroine Ginger O'Leary.*

It wasn't that unusual for the time; the baby was coming, and she knew her husband was busy and out of reach. They had just moved to North Adams, hadn't met many people, and her obstetrician was in Greenfield, forty miles away. So, Genevieve hopped into the family's 1942 army-surplus Willys Jeep, drove across the mountain to Farren Memorial Hospital, and soon after birthed a son, Christopher Henry Wondoloski. It was October 13, 1950.

Her husband, Stanley Wondoloski, had also been born in Greenfield, in 1912, and had left school early to support the family. He married Genevieve Winiarski in 1933. After working for a granite company, he was employed during the War in a defense job at Pratt & Whitney Company. His position exempted him from military service. Always a sports enthusiast, Stan played league baseball and football for local teams. He was a right fielder for Sauter's Groceries and ran the ball for a Greenfield football team.

On more than one occasion, the football team visited North Adams to play the St. Anthony "Saints." The visits attracted Stan to the area, and in 1946 the couple moved to North Adams. Stan's Greenfield family became more distant than just a mountain range away, and he seldom returned except to visit his mom. Initially, after arriving in North Adams, Stan managed the OK Rubber Welder shop, but in 1950, he bought the shop and changed its name to Stan's Rubber Welders.

The business primarily consisted of recapping tires, so it was busiest in the winter, selling and recapping snow tires, then in springtime helping many of the same customers change over to their summer tires. In order to ensure year-round business, he bought equipment to perform car repairs and installed pumps to sell gas. Chris was always proud of his dad's work ethic in managing his own business. Stan, like most of the generation, smoked and now and then enjoyed a shot of rock and rye (sweet, spiced rye whiskey) followed by an eight-ounce can of beer as a chaser. In 1986, at the age of seventy-three, he was stricken with a heart attack and passed away.

Chris's mom, Genevieve, was born in 1916 in Warren, Rhode Island, and attended school there. Early in life, she worked for several cotton mills, a Sears store, and Farren Memorial Hospital as a nurses's aide, which perhaps explains her grit and focus during that 1950 drive. Genevieve met Stanley at a community dance in Greenfield. Stanley was nineteen years old and Genevieve barely sixteen. How they loved to dance. He nicknamed her "Blondie," and after the briefest of engagements they were married in 1933. After moving to North Adams, Genevieve, active and independent, ran the family household, was active in the Houghton School parents' group, and served as chaplain for the North Adams Women's Emblem Club. For many years, she was also the bookkeeper for her husband's business. Stanley and Genevieve were married over fifty years. She passed away in 2004 at the age of eighty-seven.

Chris was the youngest of their four children, three boys and a girl. Their births spanned a twenty-one-year time period. The closest in age to Chris was his brother Tony, five years older. All his siblings have since passed away. Genevieve, anticipating that Chris would be a girl, had decided to name the baby Mary. Surprised to deliver a boy, she saw it was the day after Columbus Day, so he was named Christopher. His middle name, Henry, came from his godfather, his dad's best friend.

Chris never knew his grandparents; they had all died before he was born. He jokingly describes himself as a "Polish thoroughbred" when reciting their names: Wondoloski, Winiarski, Sucharzewski, and Goloskie. Both of Chris's parents spoke fluent Polish and used their native tongue when needing to discuss things the children shouldn't hear.

Chris's paternal grandfather, Antoni Wondolowski, came to the U.S. in the late 1800s. For some unknown reason, he soon dropped the second "w" in his name, and the rest of the family became Wondoloskis. Antoni had been raised in a small town in northeast Poland bordering Lithuania. He was slight in stature, about five feet eight inches, and weighed 150 pounds, wiry and quite strong from his work as a stonemason in Greenfield. Toni kept a side job for extra money, bootlegging during Prohibition. On weekends, he drove a truck transporting illegal beer from Greenfield to Canada. Caught several times and briefly incarcerated, he eventually gave up this lucrative sideline. Sadly, he died early from cirrhosis.

Mary Sucharzewski, who would be Chris's grandmother, emigrated from Poland in the late 1800s. She met and married Antoni, was a homemaker, and the couple had six children, five sons and one daughter.

Chris's maternal grandparents, the Winiarskis, also emigrated from Poland. His grandmother, Louise Goloskie, married an abusive man named Piogr Winiarski and when Genevieve was very young, Louise left him and decided to remarry. Her next husband, Genevieve's stepfather, was no better, and he abandoned the family when Genevieve was fourteen. Genevieve dropped out of school and survived by working at a Sears Catalog store with older ladies who took her "under their wings," occasionally offering shelter at their homes when she wasn't sleeping at the YMCA.

THE SPORTING LIFE

Chris's early life revolved around sports. At age five, he was roller skating at Broyles Arena in Pittsfield, and at age seven, he was performing there in a pink tuxedo made by his mom. His mother was a skier into her forties. Chris followed her example, and at the age of eight became an avid downhill skier. Whenever he could get a ride, he found himself at Dutch Hill in nearby Heartwellville, Vermont. He skied regularly into his twenties.

Chris attended St. Joseph's from kindergarten through the twelfth grade. He joined the altar boys in fifth grade and stayed through his senior year of high school, becoming the leader that year. He was also a member of the elementary school chorus that enjoyed singing old Irish songs.

An avid baseball fan, like his dad, Chris played in the North Adams Little League as a catcher for the South League and at one time was a member of the Modern Dairy team. Throughout the years, he honed his skills playing with different leagues and on various teams. For several years, he was on the Ashkar Sales baseball team within the Schouler League. It was in the Schouler League that he learned a lesson on self-discipline when he was ejected

COURTESY CHRIS WONDOLOSKI

from the league for throwing a baseball at the taunting opposition. In the summer, he played shortstop for the American Legion.

Chris went on to play varsity baseball for the St. Joseph's "Gaels" for three years as a shortstop, captaining the team in his senior year, starred on St. Joe's varsity basketball team, and played local church league basketball with the St. Francis team. High school was a busy time for him, between sports, singing in the

Chris is suited up for a Legion game, late 1960s.

senior class play, and serving as the sportswriter for the *Scribe*, the school's newspaper. He regularly played the guitar with seven other students in a band called the Christian Minstrels that performed at church folk masses and for the community. After sports and social involvements, there was little time left for studying, although he came within points of making the honor roll.

He characterizes his high school years as good times. He says, "I was a good Catholic boy, involved in the right things, and followed the rules." He found that the nuns could be demanding, although being athletic and a rule-follower, he remained on their good side.

It was at St. Joe's that he met Sharon Mulcahy, on the first day of class in their freshman year. Sharon, whose dad had recently died, had previously attended public elementary school. Chris and Sharon were both assigned to Sister Olivia's homeroom. Chris remembers the moment he saw Sharon—she was throwing away some trash in a wastepaper basket—and from then on and for the rest of his life, he was love-struck.

On the home front, Chris's mom was in charge. She had the time and patience to handle all the children's discipline. After raising his two older brothers and sister, there wasn't much that she hadn't seen or dealt with. A severe look was all the kids needed in order to cease and desist. Genevieve did all the cooking, and supper was always at 5:00 p.m. Everyone was cautioned not to be late. Woe to Stanley if he stopped at a bar for a drink with friends. She spent much of her day preparing the family's evening meal. Common fare was spaghetti and meatballs, ham, or roast beef, described by Chris as "meat and potato meals." There were always leftovers for additional meals. On Saturday, Genevieve made apple and blueberry pies. Chris especially remembers his mom making French toast or flapjacks (crêpes) for his breakfast.

Genevieve was an excellent seamstress and spent considerable time making dress shirts and sports jackets for her sons, and dresses and gowns for herself and her daughter.

Family vacations were infrequent because of the demands of Stanley's business. The family did enjoy local recreation spots, buying season passes for ski areas and state parks.

After high school, Chris attended the University of Massachusetts, playing center field on freshman and sophomore baseball teams. Chris interrupted his studies when he and Sharon were married in 1970. After one semester at North Adams State College, Chris began commuting to UMass, graduating in 1973 with a bachelor of science in zoology and a minor in chemistry.

With the Vietnam War winding down, his draft status and high lottery number ensured he would not be called up.

During his college summers, he was employed as a firefighter with the North Adams Fire Department. He was offered a job after graduation but declined, hoping instead to teach. In 1973, he was hired at Brayton Junior High to teach chemistry to eighth graders. He continued to teach when Brayton and Freeman were merged into Conte Middle School, the old Drury High. He taught at Conte and also coached girls' junior varsity basketball, served as a student council advisor, and oversaw the annual yearbook.

In 1983, Chris moved to the newly constructed Drury High School on the outskirts of town, teaching 10th grade biology and health. Over the years, he helped develop the environmental science, honors biology, and forensic science programs. For two years, he chaired the department of science. In 1983, he received his master's degree in education/administration from Massachusetts College of Liberal Arts.

Airborne coach

Drury assistant coach Chris Wondoloski jumps for joy while Coach Irene Bianchi remains anxious after Dede Taft's free throw put the Blue Devils ahead of Westwood, 42-39, with 20 seconds remaining in Saturday's Division 2 state championship game. Drury held on to win, 42-41, and became the first Berkshire County girls' team to capture a state title. Story Page 20

Coach Wondoloski celebrating the exciting win.

His real pleasure was coaching. Beginning in the mid-1970s through the late 1990s, he devoted much of his spare time to supervising successful sports teams. Shortly after Title IX was enacted, requiring gender equality in school sports, Chris became Drury's JV girls' coach and assistant girls' varsity coach.

The girls varsity team won the State Championship in his second year of coaching, and in 1982, he assumed the head coach role for the varsity girls for the next three years. During those nine years, he had the opportunity to coach hundreds of athletes and became deeply invested in their success.

Chris notes that in the 1970s and early '80s there still existed biases against women's sports: Drury basketballers were minimized as the "Lady Blue Devils," their away-game uniforms had to be entirely powder blue (the players called them pajamas), and some players were given technical fouls for being too aggressive—"for not playing more like a lady." Biases even existed against male coaches of female teams, presuming that if the coaches were any good they would be coaching men. Over years, these prejudices diminished.

He coached the boys' varsity soccer team from 1983 to 1996; in 1984, they won the Southern Division Championship, giving the team more area prominence and launching them into the Northern Berkshire Leagues, a more competitive division. He well remembers being the lowest-seeded team in the Western Massachusetts Quarter Finals Tournament, defeating a much higher-ranked team and how angry the opponents' fans got. After the rock-throwing ended, The Blue Devils needed an escort to leave town.

The athleticism and camaraderie of coaching appealed to the self-described "gym rat," and the extra pay helped compensate for the demanding job. Chris was practicing or playing games with his teams every weekday and on some weekends. When not involved with his teams, Chris coached his six-year-old son in soccer and then for several years in Little League.

Practices would get him home just in time for the family supper at 6:00 p.m. Sharon, who worked as a paralegal for many years, would somehow always have supper on the table when he arrived. Some of the family's favorite meals were chicken with gravy and potatoes and Sharon's delicious lasagna, and her baked zucchini squares and apple pie were always popular.

During their early years of marriage, the couple enjoyed taking short vacations with their close friends, traveling during winter school breaks to New York City, Boston, and one time to Plymouth. Chris and Sharon even joined close friends on their honeymoon to Bermuda.

THE WRITING LIFE

The Wondoloskis lived on Foucher Avenue in the Greylock section of North Adams for twenty years. Their family grew to two children, a boy and a girl (and, eventually, four beloved grandchildren who frequently stop over). After considerable do-it-yourself renovations, including room enlargements and installing a swimming pool, Chris and Sharon decided to buy his parents' home on the Mohawk Trail. Renovations continued as they fixed up their anticipated retirement home. His part-time hobby of carpentry and remodeling was a great help at both houses. With the expanse of front windows, the Mohawk Trail home has breathtaking views of both Mount Greylock and the Petersburg Mountain range.

As his retirement from the school system approached, and his class commitments wound down, Chris started reading voraciously within the genre he and Sharon most loved, murder mysteries. Every night, they would discuss the books, and Chris would offer an opinion on how he could improve upon what he had read.

So Sharon challenged him to write a book.

After some research at the library, on the internet, and via in-person interviews, he decided to focus his writings on the mid-1800s. It was a time of large-scale growth for the North Adams area. There was much to write about: burgeoning immigration, opening of textile and cotton mills, political intrigue, and construction of the Hoosac Tunnel.

It all started late one night when an opening scene popped into his mind featuring his soon-to-be main character, the outspoken and energetic Ginger O'Leary. Chris took out his yellow legal pad, started writing, and when Sharon came downstairs the next morning, he was just finishing up his first chapter. Chris likes to write sitting in his recliner in his living room. He says he does not have a specific time of day to write and added that his inspirations come from different sources.

After his first manuscript was complete, he asked a few friends to read it, and they gave it the greenlight. Sharon, a lifetime avid reader and an English major in college, edited the book, which they named *The Hoosac Tunnel Murders: A Ginger O'Leary Mystery*.

Chris wove a captivating story of intrigue, merging mystery, local history, romance, and the eeriness of clairvoyance to keep his readers enthralled throughout the book. The 19th century setting

At the North Adams public library, Chris displays his first two mystery novels.

provides a well-researched picture of the Berkshires and, in addition to the set-piece murder, introduces little-known details on trials and tribulations involved in building the famous Hoosac Tunnel.

They found early interest with literary agents in Manhattan, but after long discussion, the manuscript was thought to have more of a local interest than a commercial one. Not to be discouraged, in 2015 the couple brought the book to life through CreateSpace, a publishing subsidiary of the Amazon Company, and it is still in print today, available on both Kindle and in paperback.

Sharon, however, had been suffering through multiple chronic health issues, and several months after his retirement, her condition began to require considerable attention. From 2008 on, the couple dealt with debilitating medical concerns. Sharon encouraged his continued writing, but by the time his second novel was ready for editing, as much as she wanted to, she was unable to help. A good friend helped Chris proofread the manuscript and suggested chapter titles. Chris followed up his first novel in 2019 with *The Textile Mill Murders,* using the same well established historical setting and already developed characters to successfully spin another mystery yarn. This book uses North Adams' old mills as a backdrop with colorful characters to delight readers. Both books engage local interest through familiar names, locations, and customs, providing wonderful intrigue while displaying the charm and beauty of the northern Berkshires.

Over the course of those twelve years, Chris was Sharon's main caregiver. In June 2020 she passed, ending a fifty-year love affair. The two books she inspired and encouraged live on, with high praise from reviewers and local readers, and it's looking as if Ginger O'Leary may yet return for a third act.

Today, Chris continues his home renovations, adding a two-car garage with a bonus room about one hundred feet from the house. He is working and researching the next novel, always accompanied by his two rescued black Labradors, Dolly and Molly. The books are enriched by Chris' distinct interest in local history. He belongs to the North Adams Historical Commission, which oversees heritage buildings, reviewing proposals affecting the buildings' structural integrity. Chris also volunteers at the Historical Society and was a member of the city's Tree Commission. Local residents enjoy keeping up with his daily Facebook posts featuring Historical Society newspaper photos and articles.

Close friends admiringly describe Chris's personality as friendly, easy to talk to, and forthcoming. He is humble, articulate, and respected at his former school and in the community—and is handy with a hammer. Many in town admire the devotion he showed to his elderly mom and to Sharon, caring for them over the many years.

His accomplishments are legion: as an educator for over thirty years; as a coach for hundreds of athletes; as an author of two well-regarded mystery books; and as a hometown historian, his contributions have enriched this beautiful corner of the Berkshires.

ABOUT THE AUTHOR

Dennis G. Pregent, author of *The Boys of St. Joe's '65 in the Vietnam War*, was born in the Berkshires. He is the son of Dennis Pregent Sr., an engineer who worked at General Electric in Pittsfield, and Alice Trottier Pregent, who was a registered nurse at the W.B. Plunkett Memorial Hospital in Adams.

Dennis Pregent, visiting Gus Jammalo's barbershop, 2021.

Pregent resided in Adams and North Adams, attending local schools, and joined the Marines in 1965. He served six and a half years and was decorated during his two tours of duty in Vietnam. After being honorably discharged as a staff sergeant, he attended and graduated from North Adams State College in 1975 (currently Massachusetts College of Liberal Arts) and received his MBA from the University of Massachusetts in 1977.

For over thirty-five years, until his retirement, he worked in the human resources field, serving as an international vice-president for the Evenflo/Spalding and ConAgra companies.

He and his wife, Carol, have six children, fifteen grandchildren, and reside in Garner, North Carolina.

PHOTO BY GUS JAMMALO; © DENNIS PREGENT, 2021

Made in the USA
Middletown, DE
06 July 2023

34636463R00189